Women's Rights under International, American, Islamic, and Egyptian Law: An Irresolvable Conflict?

Studies in Intercultural Human Rights

VOLUME 12

This series offers pathbreaking studies in the dynamic field of intercultural human rights. Its primary aim is to publish volumes which offer interdisciplinary analysis of global societal problems, review past legal responses, and develop solutions which maximize access by all to the realization of universal human aspirations. Other original studies in the field of human rights are also considered for inclusion.

The titles published in this series are listed at *brill.com/sihr*

Women's Rights under International, American, Islamic, and Egyptian Law: An Irresolvable Conflict?

A Cross-Cultural Examination of Gender Equality

By

Mohammad Ibrahim

BRILL | NIJHOFF

LEIDEN | BOSTON

The Library of Congress Cataloging-in-Publication Data is available online at https://catalog.loc.gov
LC record available at https://lccn.loc.gov/2025007225

Typeface for the Latin, Greek, and Cyrillic scripts: "Brill". See and download: brill.com/brill-typeface.

ISSN 1876-9861
ISBN 978-90-04-72935-3 (hardback)
ISBN 978-90-04-72950-6 (e-book)
DOI 10.1163/9789004729506

Contents

Foreword

Dr. Ibrahim's book undoubtedly enriches the scholarship related to women's human rights and generally the status of women in Islam. A well-known, but still indeed very much a cutting-edge theme in international law remains the perceived conflict between the international law of human rights, as it relates to women's human rights, in countries where Islamic Law constitutes the basis of the legal system, resulting in a graspable lack of equality between woman and man. In a balanced and well-documented book, displaying a strong command of the issues involved, of the law in the books and the relevant case law in international and domestic jurisdictions and of the literature on the subject, the author presents the reader with a wealth of information to examine the validity of this perceived conflict. It is also refreshing to read the soundly reasoned and the well-substantiated conclusions that side with those who believe that gender discrimination is not necessarily inherent to Islam, but rather on the religious law's interpretation by patriarchal regimes.

Dr. Ibrahim has laid out a daring scope for his book. He sets out to explore three legal arenas: (a) the global system of human rights protection vis-à-vis women's rights; (b) Islamic Law as a major, and largely dominant, developed legal system; (c) two representative domestic jurisdictions: the United States and Egypt. To make the book manageable, he exemplifies the broad area of women's human rights through three major pertinent rights: (a) a right to abortion (or lack thereof); (b) the right to equality in employment; (c) the right and/or duty of women to wear Islamic religious attire, in various jurisdictions under review. To that end, he organizes his work into three major chapters, and each of them comprises four distinct sections, i.e. analyses of the right under discussion as contained in the regimes of international law, U.S. law, Shari'a law and Egyptian law.

In *Chapter 1*, the author deals with the right to abortion under international law, discussing the right presenting pro-choice arguments and pro-life arguments. His analysis of U.S. law contrasts freedom of choice and the right to privacy as well as their limits under the jurisprudence of the Supreme Court. The discussion of Shari'a law focuses on issues related to the prohibition of murder as well as the scope of a right to, and the prohibition of, abortion. Egyptian law is considered under the captions of a "crime of abortion" and respective arguments for exceptions to this prohibition.

In *Chapter 2*, under international law and U.S. law, the author discusses a woman's right to equality in employment, her right to equal treatment before the law, her right to equal employment opportunities, equal payment, and issues related to discriminatory practices. Under Islamic law he considers two opposing views: one restricting a woman's right to employment and the other one supporting a woman's right to work. The same issues are discussed under Egyptian law, focusing also on a special restriction for women upon holding important positions in government.

Chapter 3 deals with a woman's right to wear Islamic clothing. He starts this chapter with the discussion of the perceived duty or free will decision of women under Shari'a law to wear Islamic clothing, to be followed by the law on the books and the law in action in Egypt. Then he discusses this issue from the perspective of the international law of human rights related to the freedom of manifestation of religion, to be followed by U.S. law and its application as it relates to the free exercise clause of the Constitution. The last pages constitute his conclusions.

Right from the start, the author makes clear the intellectual tasks he poses himself through four questions that he poses and sets out to answer in the course of the book, namely:

1) Do international human rights law and American law protect and promote women's rights or not? And are these laws in agreement in approaching such rights or not?
2) Is Islamic Shari'a law in line with international human rights law and American law in tackling women's rights?
3) If the answer to the last question is negative, does Shari'a provide a proper framework of women's rights or not? And could violations of women's rights in Muslim countries be ascribed to Shari'a?
4) Do international human rights law and American law succeed in respecting a woman's choice to wear Islamic clothing in order to perform her religious duties?

Indeed, his book clearly succeeds in performing the task undertaken. His conclusions are much in line with his extensive research and critical analysis of the three rights and practices explored. It is appropriate to discuss in more detail each of the topics discussed by the author.

A Right to Abortion

The discussion of a right to abortion is one that falls into the context of a conflict of individual rights, namely the right of a woman to autonomy and privacy, and the right to life of a human being in international law, and, in this case, the right to life of the unborn. Unquestionably, this is a very difficult topic to dwell upon in international law, for the reason that this body of law does not expressly address this matter. Being a consent-based regime, international law establishes a minimum standard that is acceptable to nation-states. This is the only way that a convention or treaty on human rights might have a chance to have nation-states agree to it and to collect enough instruments of ratification needed for the agreement's entry into force.

The author embarks on an exhausting analysis of the global and regional systems of human rights protections. While he discusses the African System of Human Rights, which would be directly applicable to Egypt, he also examines other regional systems of human rights protection, i.e. the European and the Inter-American systems, to determine any cross-fertilization of the stances of the respective instruments and their monitoring bodies, as well as the similarities of any other practices, including case law regarding the treatment of the rights at issue. The first connection he makes is the consideration of abortion as a necessary measure to protect a woman's right to life if jeopardized by pregnancy. Then he addresses all other situations. The discussion of monitoring bodies' general comments, their concluding observations on specific country reports as well as their views on individual complaints, are an important element of the book, because, most of the time, a proper interpretation of the scope of rights and their limitations, as contained in the various articles of the conventions, may only come to life through such general comments and concluding observations, particularly regarding issues where there is a dearth of case law.

The author articulates with necessary strength the relevancy of each human right under review to support the thesis the author is promulgating. The author discusses cases in detail, making the intellectual point of the reasons why he analyzes these cases, as in the *Open Door* case, or in sub-section (C) *Comparison between Regional Systems*. The author gets to the essence of provisions and cases, respectively for each system and jurisdiction, simultaneously checking and identifying both consistencies in the arguments that the courts or commissions have made, as well as the divergences amongst regions as it relates to the problem—whether they would have to be classified as more pro-life or more pro-choice.

The discussion of U.S. law relating to abortion is thorough and a very good read. In detail, the author traces the history of U.S. Supreme Court jurisprudence regarding abortion, starting with the enunciation of a woman's right to terminate her pregnancy under the federal constitution in Roe v. Wade (1973) and ending with its overruling in Dobbs v. Jackson Women's

Health Org. (2022). The Supreme Court now leaves the issue of abortion to be regulated by the individual states.

Women's Right to Equality in Employment

Employment equality is a right that, *de facto*, has been proven to be amongst the hardest to be implemented and is routinely violated by the private and public sector worldwide. Even in most developed countries it is a common truth that women are hired based on their experience and men are hired on the basis of their potential to succeed. Clearly a discriminatory standard, though *de jure* written nowhere. Also, when it comes to employment, both quantitative (how do women fare vis-à-vis men in numbers of employment and unemployment?) and qualitative (what kind of jobs and at what payment rate do women engage in?) data are important to discuss.

In some countries and regions this problem is even more acute and prevalent. It is an important right to discuss, and a wise choice by the author to look into this right in the context of international law, Shari'a law as well as two domestic jurisdictions: the U.S. and Egypt.

The author finds Egyptian law to be in default of its obligations under Shari'a law, which in the author's view, is much more progressive and very much in line with international law standards and even with the practice of countries such as the United States. This is his stance, though I wonder whether this conclusion would be acceptable in the real world. The devil lies in the details: (a) how does the meaning of "haram jobs" translate into real life? I would say this constitutes discrimination; (b) what would be the meaning and the interpretation of "work [...] compatible with her [woman's] physiological, physical, and spiritual nature as a female"? I would assume that a comprehensive study of these attributes "naturally" attached to the "female" would indeed translate into discrimination; also (c) a guardian's permission and (d) a woman's top priority being her "marital duties"–lead, by default, to discrimination against women in employment. While the written government law might talk about equality, its application, if based in Islam, would hinder women's employment. However, this is my Western review of an insider's stance, and thus I am not completely sure that my view is necessarily the correct one.

Muslim Women's Religious Duty to Wear Islamic Attire (*hijab*)

Women's clothing has been and continues to be a major issue worldwide. In many cultures, there is a certain preset vestiture that binds women, and at times even men. For some it is part of culture, and for others it is part of religion.

For Muslim women certain items of women's clothing are mandated to be worn. The author maintains that verse 31 of chapter 24 of the Qur'an has been the basis for the obligation of women to wear Islamic clothing – though, in his view, also echoing the view of others, the Qur'an has given full power to women to decide what they want to show and what they want to hide under their clothing, maintaining, however, a level of "modesty." Quoting several times an article by Shaira Nanwani, he notes that it is the woman who commonly chooses to wear the *hijab* or the *niqab*. He describes the various items of clothes such as *sitar, burqa, niqab and hijab,* and focuses on the last two, as the ones mostly worn (the *hijab*) and the one perceived as the most oppressive (the *niqab*).

A discussion follows of the opinions of supporters of *hijab* and those of the more conservative *niqab*, promulgated by the Shafi'a's and the Malikia's scholars. From the heading "*Hijab* is the Mandatory Islamic Clothing," to the discussion that follows, the author supports the view that indeed *hijab* is mandatory for a Muslim woman to wear, whereas *niqab* is neither mandated nor banned. The author illustrates the requirement of modesty by an example of two women, one wearing a *hijab* but still revealing and the other not wearing a *hijab* but modestly, not revealing. He finds both in some kind of stratified violation: the former violating the Qur'an and the latter violating its interpretation. While it seems that women are free to choose what to wear, what they can display or not, the basic question remains: who chooses for them: the women themselves? The husband? The father? He clarifies the situations when in some countries the government mandates the wearing of full-face veils in public, and then he gives more support for one side or the other.

However, the author goes to great lengths to convince the reader that actually women are the ones who choose what to wear, one way or another. While this could be partially true, a more representative analysis might have been more desirable. It is commonly thought though, even amongst some Muslim communities, that women do not always have a choice in this regard. The author remedies the problem in his conclusion, where he very clearly expresses his view that whenever a woman is forced into wearing an Islamic dress, whether by family or government, there is a violation of women's human rights and freedoms, and intervention to protect their rights is welcome.

When wearing Islamic clothing is at the will of a woman out of her own consideration of a religious duty, then it is a right to manifest or practice one's religion, within the scope of the right and its corresponding limitations. It must be protected by the law.

I found the discussion of women's Islamic clothing under Egyptian law to be very elaborate, from the constitution to laws to court cases, and it leads into a clearer conclusion that, at least as a matter of law, women are the ones who decide whether they wear a *hijab* or a *niqab*, but it is still mostly a choice amongst the two—there does not seem to be an alternative of choosing to wear none of them. It is still the social environment, in addition to her personal preference, that creates the surrounding conditioning factors for either decision.

The sections related to international law and to U.S. law mirror the line of discussion examined when discussing the right to abortion. I might, however, have to take exception, at least from my perspective, at one conclusion that the author draws, i.e. that the European Court of Human Rights has routinely issued discriminatory judicial decisions as it relates to Muslim women. The court is a judicial body and it only determines the outer limits of a right, by leaving a margin of appreciation to the state. The states implement human rights, and indeed the states have a broad leeway when it comes to the nuanced application of human rights within their territory and under their jurisdiction. The court cannot but take under consideration the margin of appreciation afforded to nation states that are in the best position to assess the magnitude and pace of implementation of women's human rights. Having said that, there are circumstances when the court errs in its analysis, at least as perceived by us – the outsiders to the Court.

Dr. Ibrahim's Comparative Findings on Shari'a Law

Upon the surveying, review and analysis of international law, U.S. law, Shari'a law and Egyptian law related to women's rights to abortion, to equal employment and to wearing Islamic religious attire, the author finds Shari'a law very much in line with what he establishes as an international standard to a perceived right to abortion. He also concludes that Shari'a law is for the most part in conformity with the international standard of equality in employment. He concludes differently for Egyptian law, finding it to lack compliance with both international law and Shari'a law.

Dr. Ibrahim's conclusion would be highly desirable if it were applied across the board of the schools of Islamic law. However, different from, for instance, the Catholic view on human rights, including women's rights, which are universally applicable, the Islamic view on these issues varies amongst schools, interpretations, and doctrines, hence the author's conclusion is, with much hope, more of a statement *de lege ferenda* as it is necessarily *lex lata* across the schools. It is appreciated that the author espouses the more liberal view as it is to be expected from a young scholar of human rights.

Conclusion

I find this book to be the product of extensive research and very good analysis. His chosen topic and the respective subject matter have demanded strict inquiry and thorough investigation of various areas of law and legal systems. Dr. Ibrahim has done an excellent job in this regard: thoughtful, well researched, informative and relevant to law, policy and advocacy, the book represents a tremendous benefit in understanding discrimination as it relates to Muslim women and the Shari'a.

Although the author's respect for Islamic law is obvious throughout the book, it is not carried to extremes nor to a partisan position. On the contrary, it is encouraging to see that he sides with the progressive interpretation of Islam and he maturely and critically analyzes and appraises the interpretation and application of Islam in a domestic jurisdiction, Egypt.

The author has an excellent mastery of the subject-matter supported with exceptional research, and this book will be a noteworthy tool for all those who set themselves in the quest to fully understand the true status of women in the countries where Shari'a prevails, and how these countries fare compared to those based on other legal systems.

Dr. Ibrahim's novel and mature analysis of a very difficult and controversial legal issue represents an admirable contribution to the field.

Prof. Dr. Roza Pati | St. John Paul II Distinguished Professor of Law
Founder & Director | John J. Brunetti Human Trafficking Academy
Director | LL.M./J.S.D. Program in Intercultural Human Rights, St. Thomas University Benjamin L. Crump College of Law

Acknowledgments

This book is an edited and updated version of my J.S.D. dissertation in intercultural human rights at St. Thomas University in Miami, Florida.

First and foremost, I would like to express my deepest appreciation and gratitude to my supervisor, Professor Roza Pati, the Distinguished Professor of Law and the Director of LL.M. and J.S.D. Programs in Intercultural Human Rights at St. Thomas University. Her unwavering support, insightful comments, helpful instructions, and encouragement to excel have been pivotal in my journey to becoming a Doctor of Law and in completing this book.

Professor Pati's patience, assistance, and continuous guidance during the course of my study have been essential to my success. Our valuable discussions and her constant encouragement have been unforgettable and instrumental in enabling me to accomplish this work. Her sincere advice, innovative ideas, detailed feedback, and amazing recommendations have profoundly shaped this book. Her belief in my potential has been truly inspiring. The ability she has shown to challenge and provoke me to think critically and push the boundaries of my understanding has favorably influenced this work. I am deeply grateful for her commitment and invaluable mentorship. Her support has been a cornerstone of my academic progress, and it has been an honor to learn from her.

I would also like to convey my heartfelt appreciation to Professor Siegfried Wiessner, the Founder of St. Thomas University's Graduate Program in Intercultural Human Rights, for his visionary leadership and unwavering dedication to the field of human rights. His insightful guidance and support have been instrumental in shaping my academic pursuits. Additionally, I extend my gratitude to Professor John Makdisi, all the professors, and the entire staff at St. Thomas University, who have been extraordinarily cooperative and helpful in providing support at all times to help me accomplish my objectives.

Finally, I must express my sincerest gratitude to my parents for their unconditional love and support, without which I would not have had so many opportunities. My mother, Dr. Nadia Hassan, deserves special thanks for her unfailing compassion and genuine encouragement throughout my journey. Her steadfast belief in my abilities has been a constant source of motivation and strength.

My father, Mahmoud Bayoumi, having passed away before the completion of this book, was a wonderful and hard-working person who inspired and motivated me to be the best version of myself. His dedication, resilience, perseverance, and tireless endeavors have left an indelible mark on my life. I am deeply grateful for the countless and tremendous sacrifices he made for our family and specifically for me. His kindness, thoughtfulness, and generosity have been guiding lights, and the memories we shared continue to motivate and inspire me.

I am profoundly grateful to my parents for always standing by my side during challenging moments and for encouraging me to achieve my dream of earning a doctorate degree. This book would not have been possible without their constructive support and endless love.

Judge Dr. Mohammad Mahmoud Bayoumi Ibrahim

Introduction

The status of women in Muslim countries, particularly in the Middle East region, has deteriorated, and their rights are being violated. Many feminists argue that Islamic law, as found in the Qur'an and Sunna, is the reason for this deterioration and an obstacle to the implementation of equal rights for men and women.[1] They claim that the Qur'an and Sunna embody a system that is diametrically opposed to international law, and as a result, women are discriminated against in Muslim countries.[2] They compare the status of women in Muslim countries to that of women in the United States and Europe, attributing to Islam the substandard position of women in Muslim countries.

Through a comparative examination of international human rights standards and Islamic Shari'a, this book will investigate whether or not such arguments are valid. In addition, the book will discuss the application of laws in two of the largest secular and religious states, the United States of America and Egypt. The United States was chosen for its prominence on the global stage, while Egypt was chosen due to its status among Muslim countries and the author's Egyptian citizenship. The book will focus on the status of women in both countries. In addition, it will explain whether decisions of the United States Supreme Court and Egyptian high courts are in line with international standards of human rights and Islamic Shari'a, respectively.

The book will shed light on two major women's rights: the right to an abortion and the right to equality in employment. With regard to abortion, it is a controversial subject because of its association with the potential existence of a new human life. The second right was selected to compare the status of female workers under Islamic Shari'a with international human rights standards and American law and to clarify whether or not discrimination against women in Muslim countries can be traced back to fundamental sources of Shari'a. The international and American legal perspectives on these rights will be discussed first, followed by the Islamic Shari'a and its application within the Egyptian legal framework.

Furthermore, the book's approach will be reversed by discussing the Islamic law-mandated religious obligation for Muslim women to wear

1 Joelle Entelis, *International Human Rights: Islam's Friend or Foe? Algeria as an Example of the Compatibility of International Human Rights Regarding Women's Equality and Islamic Law*, 20 Fordham Int'l L.J. 1251, 54–55 (1997).

2 *Id.*

 | DOI:10.1163/9789004729506_002

headscarves. The book will clarify that obligation under Egyptian law, whose major source is Shari'a. The book will also examine whether international human rights law and American law respect such a religious duty and permit a Muslim woman to freely express her religious beliefs. In addition, numerous decisions of the European Court of Human Rights and the United States Supreme Court will be cited in support of the arguments presented.

The book will endeavor to provide precise responses to the following questions:

1) Do international human rights law and American law protect and promote women's rights or not? And are these laws in agreement when approaching such rights or not?
2) Is Islamic Shari'a compatible with international human rights law and American law with regard to the protection of women's rights?
3) If the answer to the last question is negative, does Shari'a provide an appropriate framework for women's rights? And could violations against women's rights in Muslim countries be ascribed to Shari'a?
4) Do international human rights standards and American law respect women's choice to wear headscarves in order to fulfill their religious obligations?

CHAPTER 1

The Right to Abortion

Abortion is a highly contentious and problematic issue due to the extreme dichotomy between a woman's right to choose an abortion and the fetus's right to life. Concerns regarding the commencement of human childhood, the fetus's right to life, a woman's right to autonomy, and/or whether the woman or someone else should determine choices pertaining to a woman's body predominate in abortion discussions.

Pro-choice advocates support a woman's right to choose whether to have an abortion.[1] They consider abortion to be a fundamental human right, and therefore a woman is granted the full right to control her own body and have the procedure.[2] According to their point of view, a woman should be allowed to decide, without government intervention, whether or not she carries the fetus to term and gives birth because this decision "involves changes in a woman's body, her health and her range of life choices."[3]

In contrast, pro-life supporters believe that elective abortion unfairly terminates the life of a defenseless human being.[4] They consider the unborn child to be a member of the human family, and therefore killing him or her for the benefit of others is a grave moral transgression that devalues humanity.[5] They criticize pro-choice advocates for considering a distinctive human being with inherent moral worth as a dispensable instrument.[6]

In the case of urgent reasons for an abortion, the whole issue becomes more complicated.[7] It is reasonable to assume that pro-choice arguments may prevail, at least to some degree, in some exceptional circumstances, such as cases of incest, rape, fetal deformity or a perceived risk to a woman's life or health due to pregnancy.[8]

1 Joan Williams, *Gender Wars: Selfless Women in the Republic of Choice*, 66 N.Y.U. L. REV. 1559 (1991).
2 Lisa Shaw Roy, *Roe and the New Frontier*, 27 Harv. J.L. & Pub. Pol'y 339, 356 (2003).
3 *Id.*
4 Joan Williams, *Symposium: Michael J. Perry's Mortality, Politics, and Laws: Abortion Incommensurability, and Jurisprudence*, 63 Tul. L. Rev. 1651, 1668 (1989).
5 Georgia Warnke, *Law, Hermeneutics, and Public Debate*, 9 Yale J.L. & Human. 395, 402 (1997).
6 Carolyn B. Ramsey, *Restructuring the Debate over Fetal Homicide Laws*, 67 ohio st. L.J. 721, 765 (2006).
7 Gerard v. Bradley, *Life's Dominion: A Review Essay*, 69 Notre Dame L. Rev. 329, 331 (1993).
8 *Id.*

 | DOI:10.1163/9789004729506_003

This chapter of the book will provide a comparative analysis of international law, American law, Islamic Shari'a, and Egyptian law to answer the question of whether a woman has the right to an abortion in all circumstances or whether the fetus is a distinct person with its own right to life. This chapter will also explain whether or not these legal systems compromise the whole matter by permitting abortion under certain restrictions and conditions. In addition, this chapter will illustrate the view of each of these legal systems in order to determine which of these systems is more pro-life or pro-choice.

1 Abortion under International Law

This section will discuss this issue in accordance with two lines of argument. The first defends a woman's freedom of choice. However, the question is whether an abortion is part of a woman's rights or not. According to international law, a woman's rights must be respected, protected, and promoted. Therefore, this argument will review international law that supports a woman's right to an abortion without consideration for the fetus.

Concerning the second argument, this section will examine abortion in accordance with international law from another perspective. It will seek to determine the legal position of the fetus under international law and whether its rights are protected. Is the fetus considered under international law to be a human being who has the right to life? And does this right, if it exists, prevail over a woman's right to an abortion? Additionally, which one of these rights will be acknowledged according to international law? In other words, is there a balance between a woman's right to an abortion and the fetus's right to life under international law?

This section will first illustrate the pro-abortion views. Later, arguments against abortion will be discussed. Since abortion is not explicitly mentioned in any international human rights document, this section will clarify a woman's right to abortion in the context of other rights mentioned in international human rights instruments.

Although Egyptian and American laws are basic parts of the book, the United States has not ratified the American Convention on Human Rights. Therefore, the African Charter on Human and Peoples' Rights is the most specialized regional human rights document pertinent to the subject. However, for the purpose of assessing cross-fertilization of human rights systems, this section will refer to all regional systems of human rights protection where cases are relevant to the discussion. In other words, this section will attempt to distill the core principles underlying these cases across regional systems, draw attention to areas of agreement and disagreement, and assess the relative pro-life and pro-choice orientations of these various jurisdictions.

A *Pro-Choice Arguments*

i Protection of the Right to Life and Life-Threatening Pregnancies

Abortion could be a means of protecting the right to life if a woman's life is jeopardized by pregnancy. Therefore, protection of the right to life could be an argument supporting a woman's right to an abortion.

The International Protection of the Right to Life is as follows:

Article 3 of the Universal Declaration of Human Rights (UDHR) states that every human being has "the right to life, liberty, and security of person."[9]

Article 6 of the International Covenant on Civil and Political Rights (ICCPR) stipulates that "every human being has the inherent right to life" and "[n]o one shall be arbitrarily deprived of his life."[10]

Regarding regional protection, Article 4 of the African Charter on Human and Peoples' Rights (the Banjul Charter) states that "human beings are inviolable. Every human being shall be entitled to respect for his life and the integrity of his person. No one may be arbitrarily deprived of this right."[11]

Although the UDHR is just a declaration and not a binding treaty, its conception of rights has a significant impact on all other international and regional treaties because it largely reflects customary international law.[12] Article 3 of the UDHR identifies the right to life broadly, as it does with other human rights; however, the right to life enshrined in the UDHR does not place enough affirmative obligations upon states.[13] Similar to other human rights instruments, the UDHR does not determine when a human being's life starts and when it comes to an end.[14]

---

9 G.A. Res. 217 (III) A, art. 3, Universal Declaration of Human Rights (Dec. 10, 1948) [hereinafter UDHR].

10 International Covenant on Civil & Political Rights, art. 6, *opened for signature* Mar. 23, 1976, 999 U.N.T.S. 171 (entered into force Dec. 16, 1966) [hereinafter ICCPR].

11 African Charter on Human and Peoples' Rights, art. 6, *opened for signature* June 27, 1981, OAU Doc. CAB/LEG/67/3 rev. 5, 21 I.L.M. 58 (1982), (entered into force Oct. 21, 1986) [hereinafter African Charter].

12 Sarah Helena Lord, *The Nicaraguan Abortion Ban: Killing in Defense of Life*, 87 N.C.L. REV. 537, 595 (2009).

13 *Id.*

14 *Id.*

Concerning the right to life under the ICCPR, the United Nations Human Rights Committee (HRC) states that it is a supreme right against which no derogation is permitted, even in cases of public emergencies threatening the nation.[15] In addition, the Committee states that the scope of the right to life must be interpreted broadly.[16] This includes ensuring legal access to abortion, removing barriers like medical providers' objections, and providing comprehensive reproductive health services.[17] The Committee also indicates that when reporting on the right to life, member states should provide statistics on pregnancy and childbirth-related deaths.[18] Additionally, the HRC requires states to report on any measures that help women prevent unwanted pregnancies.[19] It encourages states to ensure the eradication of "life-threatening clandestine abortions."[20]

ii Protection of the Right to Health If Jeopardized by Pregnancy

In addition to the right to life, a woman's right to an abortion could be supported by her right to health if her health is threatened by pregnancy.

In 1946, the preamble of the World Health Organization's constitution defined health broadly as not only the "absence of disease or infirmity" but also the state of "complete physical, mental and social well-being."[21]

The right to health has been widely regarded as fundamental in international human rights documents. Under Article 25 of the UDHR, "everyone has the right to a standard of living adequate for the health and well-being of himself and of his family, including … medical care and necessary social services."[22] In addition, it emphasizes that motherhood deserves "special care and assistance."[23]

Article 12 of the International Covenant on Economic, Social and Cultural Rights (ICESCR) protects the right to health, requiring member states to

---

15 Human Rights Comm., General Comment 36, para. 2, U.N. Doc. CCPR/C/GC/36 (Sep. 3, 2019).

16 *Id.* para.3.

17 *Id.* para.8.

18 Human Rights Comm., General Comment 28, para. 10, U.N. Doc. CCPR/C/21/Rev.1/Add.10 (Mar. 29, 2000) [hereinafter General Comment 28].

19 *Id.*

20 *Id.*

21 World Health Organization [WHO], Preamble to the Constitution, 2 Official Records of the World Health Organization 100 (1946).

22 UDHR, *supra* note 9, art. 25(1).

23 *Id.* para. 2.

ensure that everyone enjoys "the highest attainable standards of physical and mental health."[24]

Article 12 of the Convention on the Elimination of All Forms of Discrimination against Women (CEDAW) requires states to prevent any discrimination against women in relation to the right to health. In other words, under the Convention, states should provide women, on an equal basis with men, with "access to health care services, including those related to family planning."[25]

Regarding the regional protection of the right to health, Article 16 of the Banjul Charter stipulates that everyone should have "the right to enjoy the best attainable state of physical and mental health. State Parties to the present Charter shall take the necessary measures to protect the health of their people and to ensure that they receive medical attention when they are sick."[26]

From the articles mentioned above, it is clear that the ICESCR and CEDAW declare a woman's right to health without mentioning the word "abortion"[27]; however, the monitoring bodies of both treaties refer to a woman's right to abortion in light of her right to health. In other words, they grant a woman the right to abortion if her health is threatened by pregnancy.[28]

The monitoring body of the ICESCR, the U.N. Committee on Economic, Social and Cultural Rights, issued General Comment 14 to clarify Article 12 of the ICESCR.[29] In this General Comment, the Committee affirms what is meant by the clause "the highest attainable standards of physical and mental health."[30] General Comment 14 is considered the most authoritative

---

24 International Covenant on Economic, Social and Cultural Rights, art. 12, *opened for signature* Dec. 16, 1966, G.A. Res. 2200A, at 49, U.N. GAOR, 21st Sess., Supp. No. 16, U.N. Doc. A/6316 (entered into force Mar. 23, 1976) [hereinafter ICESCR].

25 Convention on the Elimination of All Forms of Discrimination Against Women, art.12, G.A. Res. 34/180, at 193, U.N. GAOR, 34th Sess., Supp. No. 46, U.N. Doc. A/34/46 (Dec. 18, 1979) [hereinafter CEDAW].

26 African Charter, *supra* note 11, art. 16(1).

27 ICESCR, *supra* note 24, art. 12; CEDAW, *supra* note 25, art. 12.

28 The Right to the Highest Attainable Standard of Health, ICESCR General Comment 14, U.N. Committee on Economic, Social and Cultural Rights, 22d Sess., Agenda Item 3, U.N. Doc. E/C.12/2000/4 (2000) [hereinafter General Comment 14]; Comm. on the Elimination of Discrimination Against Women, Rep. of the Comm. on the Elimination of Discrimination Against Women on its Twentieth Session, General Recommendation 24, U.N. Doc. A/54/38/Rev.1 (Aug. 20, 1999) [hereinafter General Rec. 24].

29 General Comment 14, *supra* note 28.

30 *Id.*

statement clarifying the scope of the right to health.[31] It provides a highly condensed explanation and clarification of an individual's right to health under international law.[32]

According to General Comment 14, the right to health is extensive, fundamental and inextricably linked to other human rights.[33] This General Comment expands the definition of the right to include public health, health care and the necessary conditions for everyone to enjoy a healthy life.[34] These necessary conditions include adequate nutrition, potable drinking water, sanitation, a safe workplace, housing, and a healthy environment.[35] Moreover, General Comment 14 ensures that the right to health encompasses "freedoms and entitlements."[36]

The freedoms have their origins in the context of civil and political rights, including the right to "sexual and reproductive freedom," the right to "be free from interference," and the right to be "free from torture, non-consensual medical treatment and experimentation."[37] On the other hand, the entitlements represent the rights to receive methods of health protection and to have equal opportunities with others so that everyone can enjoy the "highest attainable level" of physical and mental health.[38]

General Comment 14 provides a broad interpretation of the right to health and clarifies the obligations imposed on states to protect that right.[39] In addition, it describes the violations that may have a negative impact on the enjoyment of the highest level of health and lays out standards for implementation.[40]

Additionally, General Comment 14 reviews the guidelines for the right to health in the context of specific factors such as availability, acceptability, accessibility, and the quality required by goods, services, and facilities.[41] Concerning the availability, it addresses the existence of essential health resources, such as uncontaminated drinking water and sanitation.[42]

---

31 Lawrence O. Gostin & Lance Gable, *The Rights of Persons with Mental Disabilities: A Global Perspective on the Application of Human Rights Principles to Mental Health*, 63 Md. L. Rev. 20, 603 (2004).
32 *Id.*
33 General Comment 14, *supra* note 28, para. 1.
34 *Id.* para. 11.
35 *Id.*
36 *Id.* para. 8.
37 *Id.*
38 *Id.*
39 *Id.* para. 33.
40 *Id.*
41 *Id.* para. 12.
42 *Id.* para. 12(a).

In addition, it emphasizes the importance of the availability of functional health services including health care professionals and people's access to important medicines at public hospitals and adequate treatment facilities.[43] The term "acceptability" expresses the requirement that health care standards must be satisfactory regardless of the traditions, cultures, and ethics dominating the society.[44] The term "accessibility" refers to the requirement that health services be available to everyone without discrimination or barriers.[45] The General Comment stipulates that health care services must be in accordance with the required and appropriate medical and scientific standards.[46]

In General Comment 14, the Committee clarifies that states have three obligations regarding the right to health.[47] The first is to respect the right to health. In other words, states themselves must not violate the right to health. The second duty is to protect the right to health by taking measures to prevent third parties from violating it. The third duty is to fulfill the right to health, which requires states to provide, facilitate, and promote it.[48] With regard to reproductive health, states, according to the General Comment, must not circumscribe access to contraception methods or any "means of maintaining sexual and reproductive health."[49] In addition, they have an obligation to refrain from "withholding," "censoring" or deliberately "misrepresenting" information related to reproductive health, or preventing some individuals like doctors from taking part in "health-related matters."[50]

Given that the evaluation of states' obligations is based on the available resources of each state,[51] the Committee may not be able to discover the deliberate "denials of the available resources."[52] Therefore, in General Comment 14, the Committee states that the right to health must not be subjugated to intentional "retrogressive measures" or any kind of inattention.[53] In the event that any retrogressive measures are taken, the Committee will place the burden of proof on states to demonstrate the use of "maximum available

43 *Id.*
44 *Id.* para. 12(c).
45 *Id.* para. 12(b).
46 *Id.* para. 12(d).
47 *Id.* para. 33.
48 *Id.*
49 *Id.* para. 34.
50 *Id.*
51 *Id.* para. 12.
52 Lord, *supra* note 12, at 602.
53 General Comment 14, *supra* note 28, para. 32.

resources," "most careful considerations," and all alternative solutions.[54] Some commentators consider laws passed by some states to criminalize abortion as forms of retrogressive measures because they lead to massive increases in rates of maternal mortality.[55]

In General Recommendation 24, the CEDAW's Committee adopted the same approach as the ICESCR's Committee, noting that Article 12 of CEDAW imposes three main obligations on states to "respect, protect and fulfill women's rights to health care."[56] They must issue legislation and take measures in accordance with these obligations. In addition, the Committee emphasized that judicial action must be taken in cases of violations of a woman's right to health care.[57] Furthermore, states must take affirmative measures to promote "women's access to sexual and reproductive health services" in line with Article 12 of CEDAW.[58]

Moreover, the CEDAW's Committee clarified the relationship between restrictive abortion laws and a woman's right to health. It declares that a woman must not be subjected to any discriminatory obstacles regarding her access to health services.[59] The criminalization of some medical procedures, such as abortion, is one of these obstacles. In other words, domestic laws that criminalize abortion are deemed discriminatory by the CEDAW's Committee because they prevent women from exercising their right to access health care services.[60] The Committee believes that these laws could force a woman to resort to health-threatening abortion methods.[61] Therefore, the Committee criticized countries, such as Colombia and Mexico, for enacting anti-abortion legislation.[62]

In Purohit and Moore v. Gambia,[63] the African Commission on Human and Peoples' Rights declared that the "enjoyment of the human right to health as it is widely known is vital to all aspects of a person's life and

54 *Id.*

55 Lord, *supra* note 12, at 602.

56 General Rec. 24, *supra* note 28, para. 13.

57 *Id.*

58 Comm. on the Elimination of Discrimination Against Women, Concluding Comments: Nicaragua, 37th Sess., U.N. Doc. CEDAW/C/NIC/CO/6 (Feb. 2, 2007) [hereinafter CEDAW 37th Session].

59 General Rec. 24, *supra* note 28, para. 14.

60 *Id.*

61 *Id.*

62 U.N. Comm. on the Elimination of Discrimination Against Women, Report of the Committee on the Elimination of Discrimination Against Women (18th and 19th Sessions), Part I, 354–427 (1998).

63 Purohit & Moore v. Gambia, 11 IHRR 257 (Afr. Comm'n on Human and Peoples' Rights 2003).

well-being, and is crucial to the realisation of all the other fundamental human rights and freedoms."[64] In addition, the Commission emphasized that the right to health includes access to health services that must be available to everyone without any kind of discrimination.[65]

a *Comparison between the Right to Life in Article 6 of the ICCPR and Reproductive Rights under CEDAW*

Many human rights advocates believe that Article 6(1) of the ICCPR is superior to CEDAW's articles on maternal health "when fighting for the implementation of reproductive rights."[66] Despite the fact that CEDAW's articles are more specific to women's reproductive rights, Article 6(1) of the ICCPR, which focuses on the right to life in general, provides greater protection for the following reasons:[67]

b *Reservations to CEDAW's Maternal Health Articles*

The number of CEDAW member states exceeds the number of the ICCPR member states.[68] However, a large number of CEDAW's member states have made reservations to Articles 11, 12, 14 and 16 protecting women's reproductive rights.[69] For example, Egypt made a reservation to Article 16.[70] On the other hand, there is no reservation made to Article 6(1) of the ICCPR, which protects the inherent right to life.[71]

---

64 *Id.* para. 80. The events of the case started when two mental health advocates brought a claim against Gambia challenging the country's treatment of mental health patients. They argued that the law regulating mental health in Gambia was outdated. The Commission found that Gambia, due to its treatment of persons with disabilities, violated Articles 2, 3, 5, 7(1)(a) and (c), 13(1), 16, and 18(4) of the African Charter on Human and Peoples' Rights. *Id.* para. 85.

65 *Id*

66 Dina Bogecho, *Putting It into Good Use: The International Covenant on Civil and Political Rights to Reproductive Health,* 13 S. Cal. Rev. L. & Women's Stud. 229, 238 (2004).

67 *Id.*

68 Office of the U.N. High Comm'r for Human Rights, Status of Ratifications of the Principal International Human Rights Treaties, http://www2.ohchr.org/english/bodies/docs/status.pdf (last visited Aug. 5, 2024).

69 U.N. Division for the Advancement of Women, Convention on the Elimination of All Forms of Discrimination Against Women: Reservations, U.N., http://www.un.org/womenwatch/daw/cedaw/reservations.htm (last visited Aug. 5, 2024).

70 *Id.*

71 *See* Declarations and Reservations to the ICCPR, http://www2.ohchr.org/english/law/cat-reserve.htm (last visited Aug. 7, 2024).

c *The Issue of Enforcement*

The First Optional Protocol to the ICCPR allows individuals and groups to bring complaints before the HRC, the body whose function is to monitor compliance with the ICCPR.[72] However, the Optional Protocol to CEDAW allows the complaints of individuals and groups to be brought to the attention of the CEDAW's Committee, the body that monitors the compliance of CEDAW's member states with the Convention's provisions.[73] The number of states that have ratified the First Optional Protocol to the ICCPR is larger than the number of states ratifying the Optional Protocol to CEDAW.[74] Consequently, in cases of violations of reproductive rights, a greater number of individuals and groups have access to filing complaints before the HRC than before the CEDAW's Committee.

d *Broadening of the Right to Life under the ICCPR*

Article 6 of the ICCPR provides a comprehensive description of the right to life protection.[75] This article obviously supports a woman's right to have an abortion in the case of a life-threatening pregnancy. In addition, this article's broad statements may constitute a strong endorsement of the right to health, including the right to reproductive health.[76] In other words, Article 6 is sufficiently inclusive to enable individuals and groups to file complaints against any violations of their right to health, including their right to reproductive health.[77] For example, in K.L. v. Peru,[78] the argument of the petitioner, who was prevented from having an abortion, was based on

72 Optional Protocol to the International Covenant on Civil and Political Rights, *opened for signature* Dec. 19, 1966, 999 U.N.T.S. 171 (entered into force Mar. 23, 1976).

73 Optional Protocol to the Convention on the Elimination of All Forms of Discrimination Against Women, *adopted* Oct. 6, 1999, 2131 U.N.T.S. 83 (entered into force Dec. 22, 2000).

74 Office of the U.N. High Comm'r for Human Rights, Status of Ratifications of the Principal International Human Rights Treaties, http://www2.ohchr.org/english/bodies/docs/status.pdf (last visited Aug. 1, 2024).

75 ICCPR, *supra* note 10, art. 6.

76 Bogecho, *supra* note 66, at 240–41.

77 *Id.*

78 U.N. ESCOR, Human Rights Comm., Views of the Human Rights Committee under Article 5, Paragraph 4, of the Optional Protocol to the International Covenant on Civil and Political Rights Concerning Communication No. 1153/2003, U.N. Doc. CCPR/C/85/D/1153/2003 (Oct. 24, 2005) [hereinafter K.L. v. Peru].

the violation of her right to health in the context of the protection of the right to life under Article 6 of the ICCPR.[79]

e *The Human Rights Committee Annual Abortion Review*

The HRC is the oldest existing treaty monitoring body that receives complaints and issues recommendations and observations.[80] The HRC's views are not binding; however, they do carry some legal weight in clarifying the proper interpretation of the ICCPR's articles.[81]

The HRC's Concluding Observations on Countries' Annual Reports include abortion, but their emphasis has shifted from past to present reports. From 1987 to 1998, its reports on abortion "were fairly sparse."[82] In other words, the Committee did not focus on the issue of abortion; it merely included brief descriptions on the procedure and domestic laws criminalizing it.[83]

In its 1988 annual report, the HRC commented negatively on the general ban on abortion in Colombia, clarifying that it stemmed from Catholic cultural traditions.[84] In its 1992 annual report, the HRC criticized Austria's criminalization of abortion. The Committee noted that ICCPR member states demanded that the Country legalize the procedure.[85] In the same report, the HRC also criticized Ecuador for prosecuting women who had abortions.[86] Furthermore, in its 1996 annual report, the HRC observed the relationship between the high rate of maternal mortality and abortion criminalization in Zambia.[87]

Since 1999, the majority of the HRC's annual reports have addressed abortion.[88] In its 1999 annual report, the HRC recommended that Chile

---

79 *Id.* para. 33 (this case will be discussed later).
80 Bogecho, *supra* note 66, at 241.
81 *Id.*
82 Tom Venzor, *Protecting the Unborn Child: The Current State of Law Concerning the So-Called Right to Abortion and Intervention by the Holy See*, 89 Neb. L. Rev. 1132, 1145 (2011).
83 *Id.*
84 Rep. of the Human Rights Comm., para. 523, U.N. Doc. A/43/40; GAOR, 43d Sess., Supp. No. 40 (Sept. 28, 1988). Cultural traditions of Catholicism support the fetus's right to life, assuring that it gains a soul at the moment of conception. Catechism of the Catholic Church, 2270.
85 Rep. of the Human Rights Comm., para. 94, U.N. Doc. A/47/40; GAOR, 47th Sess., Supp. No. 40 (Oct. 9, 1992).
86 *Id.* para. 234.
87 Rep. of the Human Rights Comm., P 195, U.N. Doc. A/51/40 (Vol. 1); GAOR, 51st Sess., Supp. No. 40 (Apr. 13, 1997).
88 Venzor, *supra* note 82, at 1146.

"introduce exceptions to the general prohibition of all abortions and protect the confidentiality of medical information," ensuring that medical professionals do not reveal information related to a woman's private life.[89] In addition, the HRC pointed out its concern with the law of Lesotho that introduced only a single exception for abortion if a pregnancy is an outcome of rape or incest.[90] The HRC recommended that the State "review the abortion law in order to provide for situations where the life of the woman is in danger."[91] With regard to Costa Rica, the Committee criticized the high rate of clandestine abortions and recommended that the State "introduce exceptions to general prohibition of all abortion."[92] Concerning Poland, the HRC recommended that the State introduce policies and programs in order to change the discriminatory access related to "methods of family planning."[93]

In its 2000 annual report, the HRC criticized Morocco because its criminalization of abortion led to unsafe and clandestine abortions.[94] The HRC recommended that the Country ensure "that women have full and equal access to family planning services and to contraception."[95] The HRC criticized Kuwait because its domestic law has no exceptions for abortions even on "humanitarian grounds."[96] Additionally, it criticized Ireland because its law does not allow an abortion unless pregnancy endangers a woman's life.[97] The HRC recommended that the State help a woman avoid unwanted pregnancy and ensure that she will never seek unsafe abortions.[98]

In its 2001 annual report, the HRC recommended that two states, Trinidad and Tobago, repeal their abortion laws.[99] Additionally, it found that the practices of abortion in both countries should be reexamined.[100] Reporting on Argentina, the HRC criticized the medical professionals who refused to provide abortion services even if a pregnant woman's life was threatened

89 Rep. of the Human Rights Comm., para. 211, U.N. Doc. A/54/40 (Vol. I); GAOR, 54th Sess., Supp. No. 40 (Oct. 21, 1999).
90 *Id.* para. 254.
91 *Id.*
92 *Id.* para. 280.
93 *Id.* para. 344.
94 Rep. of the Human Rights Comm., para. 100, U.N. Doc. A/55/40 (Vol. I); GAOR, 55th Sess., Supp. No. 40 (Oct. 10, 2000).
95 *Id.*
96 *Id.* para. 466.
97 *Id.* para. 444.
98 *Id.* para. 134.
99 Rep. of the Human Rights Comm., para. 72(18), U.N. Doc. A/56/40 (Vol. I); GAOR, 56th Sess., Supp. No. 40 (Oct. 26, 2001).
100 *Id.*

by pregnancy or if pregnancy was an outcome of rape.[101] The HRC recommended that "in cases where abortion procedures may lawfully be performed, all obstacles to obtaining them should be removed."[102] Concerning Peru, the HRC criticized the criminal penalties against abortions. It noted that these penalties are in contradiction with Article 3 (the right to equality), Article 6 (the inherent right to life), and Article 7 (the prohibition of torture or other cruel, inhuman or degrading treatment or punishment) of the ICCPR.[103] Furthermore, the HRC decided that such legislation should be amended to introduce exceptions that allow medical abortions.[104] With respect to Venezuela, the HRC recommended that the State introduce exceptions in its domestic laws banning "all non-therapeutic abortions."[105]

In its 2003 annual report, the HRC commented on the clandestine abortion practices in Mali, considering them a violation of Article 6 of the ICCPR.[106] It recommended that the State help women "avoid unwanted pregnancies," improve "family planning and sexual education programs," and ensure that a woman would never be compelled to undergo unsafe clandestine abortions.[107]

In its 2004 annual report, the HRC commented on Sri Lankan laws prohibiting abortion except if a woman's life is endangered by pregnancy.[108] It recommended that the State "ensure that women are not compelled to continue with pregnancies, where this would be incompatible with obligations arising under the Covenant and repeal the provisions criminalizing abortion."[109] In addition, the HRC recommended that Equatorial Guinea amend its law restricting family planning services in order to reduce the maternal mortality rate.[110] With regard to Colombia, the HRC recommended that the State amend its law banning abortion and allow a woman in cases of rape, incest or life-threatening pregnancies to have access to the procedure.[111]

101 *Id.* at 74, para. 14.
102 *Id.*
103 *Id.* at 76, para. 20.
104 *Id.*
105 *Id.* at 77, para. 19.
106 Rep. of the Human Rights Comm., para. 81(14), U.N. Doc. A/58/40 (Vol. 1), GAOR, 76th–78th Sess.,Supp. No. 40 (Oct. 24, 2003).
107 *Id.*
108 Rep. of the Human Rights Comm., para. 66(12), U.N. Doc. A/59/40 (Vol. 1), GAOR, 79th–81st Sess., Supp. No. 40 (Jan. 10, 2004).
109 *Id.*
110 *Id.* at 77, para. 9.
111 *Id.* at 67, para. 13.

In its 2005 annual report, the HRC highlighted the criminalization of abortion in Albania.[112] It recommended that the State "take steps to ensure that abortion is not used as a method of family planning and take appropriate measures to reduce infant mortality."[113] Concerning Morocco, the Committee recommended that the State provide women with access to an abortion and "relax the legislation relating to abortion" in order to be in line with its obligations under ICCPR's Article 6 (the inherent right to life) and Article 7 (the prohibition of torture or cruel, inhuman or degrading treatment or punishment).[114] With regard to Poland, the Committee was concerned with the "unavailability of abortion in practices."[115] In this country, the law allows abortions in certain cases such as rape; however, medical practitioners refuse to conduct legal abortions due to "the lack of information on the use of the conscientious objection clause."[116] The Committee recommended that the State "liberalize its legislation and practice on abortions" and provide further information on the use of the conscientious objection clause by doctors."[117]

In its 2006 annual report, the HRC commented on Paraguay's law that led "women to seek unsafe, illegal abortions, at potential risk to their life and health."[118] The Committee recommended that the State amend the law in order to bring it into conformity with the ICCPR.[119]

In its 2007 annual report, the HRC commented on abortion practices in Chile, Madagascar, and Honduras, where abortion is prohibited except in cases of life-threatening pregnancies.[120] The Committee recommended that

---

112 Rep. of the Human Rights Comm., para. 82(14), U.N. Doc. A/60/40 (Vol. 1), GAOR, 82d–84th Sess., Supp. No. 40 (Mar. 10, 2005).

113 *Id.*

114 *Id.* at 84, para. 29.

115 *Id.* at 85, para. 8.

116 *Id.* In some states, a "conscience clause" allows medical practitioners to refuse to use certain medical facilities for reasons of conscience or religion. For example, Washington's statute stipulated that "[n]o individual health care provider, religiously sponsored health carrier, or health care facility may be required by law or contract in any circumstances to participate in the provision of or payment for a specific service if they object to so doing for reason of conscience or religion. No person may be discriminated against in employment or professional privileges because of such objection." Wash. Rev. Code § 48.43.065(2)(a) (2008).

117 *Id.*

118 Rep. of the Human Rights Comm., para. 77(10), U.N. Doc. A/61/40 (Vol. 1), GAOR, 85th–87th Sess., Supp. No. 40 (Jan. 1, 2006).

119 *Id.*

120 Rep. of the Human Rights Comm., para. 79(8), 84(14), 84(8), U.N. Doc. A/62/40 (Vol. 1), GAOR, 88th-90th Sess., Supp. No. 40 (Jan. 11, 2007).

these states modify their domestic laws in order to comply with the Covenant's obligations.[121]

In its 2008 annual report, the HRC commented on the Panamanian law restricting abortion to the first two months of rape-related pregnancies.[122] The HRC recommended that the State "amend its legislation so that it effectively helps women avoid unwanted pregnancies and so that they do not have to resort to illegal abortions that could endanger their lives."[123]

In its 2009 annual report, the Committee criticized the "general ban on abortion" in Nicaragua that banned abortion even in cases of "rape, incest" or "pregnancies threatening the life of the mother."[124] The HRC recommended that the Country "bring its legislation into line with" the ICCPR and take measures that enable a woman to "avoid unwanted pregnancies" so that she need not resort to illegal abortions that may threaten her life.[125] Furthermore, the Committee required the State to "avoid penalizing medical professionals in the conduct of their professional duties."[126]

In its 2010 report, the Committee criticized Moldova, Mexico, Argentina, Colombia and Cameroon.[127] With regard to Moldova, the Committee noted that although abortion is not legally banned, some women were "prosecuted for murder or infanticide" because they had abortions; in addition, they did not receive proper health care in prison.[128] The Committee recommended that the State take steps to release women who are imprisoned for having abortions and provide them with "appropriate health care."[129] Concerning Mexico, the Committee recommended that the State "bring its legislation into line" with the ICCPR and take appropriate measures to help a woman "avoid unwanted pregnancy" so that she does not need to resort to unsafe and illegal abortions that endanger her life.[130] With respect to Argentina, the Committee recommended that the State abolish Article 86 of the Penal Code that criminalized abortion and modify its domestic legislation to help

121 *Id.*
122 Rep. of the Human Rights Comm., para. 79(9), U.N. Doc. A/63/40 (Vol. I), GAOR, 91st–93rd Sess., Supp. No. 40 (Jan. 10, 2008).
123 *Id.*
124 Rep. of the Human Rights Comm., para. 86(13), U.N. Doc. A/64/40 (Vol. I), GAOR, 94th–96th Sess., Supp. No. 40 (Aug. 19, 2010).
125 *Id.*
126 *Id.*
127 Rep. of the Human Rights Comm., U.N. Doc. A/65/40 (Vol. I), GAOR, 97th-99th Sess., Supp. No. 40 (Oct. 11, 2010).
128 *Id.* at 66, para. 17.
129 *Id.*
130 *Id.* at 70, para. 10.

a woman avoid unwanted pregnancies that may threaten her life.[131] Regarding Colombia, the Committee lauded the country's "progress in implementing the earlier recommendation made by the Committee in 2004."[132] However, the Committee recommended that the State ensure that women "avoid unwanted pregnancies" and facilitate their access to legal and safe abortions.[133] Concerning Cameroon, the Committee recommended that the State ensure that a woman has access to "reproductive health services" and amend its legislation to help a woman "avoid unwanted pregnancies" and protect her from resorting to illegal abortion that may endanger her life.[134]

In its 2011 report, the Committee criticized El Salvador, Poland and Kazakhstan in relation to abortion.[135] To start with, the Committee criticized articles of El Salvador's Penal Code criminalizing all forms of abortion even if a pregnancy endangers a woman's life.[136] In addition, the Committee noted that women seeking the procedure were "reported to judicial authorities by medical staff."[137] The Committee recommended that the State bring its legislation into line with the ICCPR, take measures to prevent a woman "from being reported by the medical or administrative staff for the offence of abortion," and "open a national dialogue on women's rights to sexual and reproductive health."[138] As for Poland, the Committee was extremely concerned about the lack of "reproductive health services."[139] It highlighted the prevalence of illegal abortions that endanger a woman's life. In addition, the Committee recommended that the State help women avoid unwanted pregnancies, conduct research, and compile statistics on the use of illegal abortions.[140] Furthermore, the Committee recommended that the State ensure the absence of restrictions imposed by medical personnel on women seeking abortion, make "a comprehensive range of contraceptives widely available" at low cost, and include them "on the list of subsidized medicines."[141] In relation to Kazakhstan, the Committee was gravely alarmed by the rise in

---

131 *Id.* at 71, para. 13.

132 *Id.* at 76, para. 19. The Colombian Constitutional Court decriminalized abortion in certain cases, such as when the pregnancy is an outcome of "rape or incest," when pregnancy threatens a woman's life, and "when the fetus displays signs of serious malformations" that make its life impossible outside a woman's womb. *Id.*

133 *Id.*

134 *Id.* at 77, para. 13.

135 Rep. of the Human Rights Comm., U.N. Doc. A/66/40 (Vol. 1), GAOR, 100th-102nd Sess., Supp. No. 40 (Jan. 6, 2012).

136 *Id.* at 83, para. 10.

137 *Id.*

138 *Id.*

139 *Id.* at 84, para. 12.

140 *Id.*

141 *Id.*

"teenage pregnancies and clandestine abortions" that result in a high death rate.[142] The Committee recommended that the State take effective measures in order to help a woman avoid unsafe abortions, "raise awareness" and ensure a woman's access to "reproductive health services."[143]

Consistent with the aforementioned reports, the HRC continues to urge nations to decriminalize abortion, assist women in avoiding unintended pregnancies, and expand access to safe and legal abortions in subsequent reports.

iii Protection of the Right to Gender Equality

Gender equality, according to pro-choice supporters, cannot be achieved without the legalization of abortion because women, and not men, worry about every imaginable difficulty associated with bearing and raising children.[144] For this reason, it is crucial to include a discussion of the importance of protecting the right to equality as a pro-choice argument.

The right to equality is typically included among the initial articles of international human rights instruments. Article 2 of the UDHR, the ICCPR, and the ICESCR all confirm the necessity of the right to equality and the eradication of gender discrimination. According to Article 2 of the UDHR:

> Everyone is entitled to all the rights and freedoms set forth in this Declaration, without distinction of any kind, such as race, colour, sex, language, religion, political or other opinion, national or social origin, property, birth or other status. Furthermore, no distinction shall be made on the basis of the political, jurisdictional or international status of the country or territory to which a person belongs, whether it be independent, trust, non-self-governing or under any other limitation of sovereignty.[145]

Under Article 2 of the ICCPR, state parties should take necessary measures to "respect and to ensure to all individuals within its territory and subject to its jurisdiction the rights recognized in the present Covenant, without distinction of any kind, such as race, colour, sex, language, religion, political or other opinion, national or social origin, property, birth or other status."[146]

---

142 *Id.* at 94, para. 11.
143 *Id.*
144 Roy, *supra* note 2, at 356.
145 UDHR, *supra* note 9, art. 2.
146 ICCPR, *supra* note 10, art. 2.

According to Article 2 of the ICESCR, state parties should ensure that rights enshrined in the Covenant "will be exercised without discrimination of any kind as to race, colour, sex, language, religion, political or other opinion, national or social origin, property, birth or other status."[147]

CEDAW addresses the fact that some national constitutions and domestic laws may have negative impacts on women's right to equality. Under Article 2 (F) of the CEDAW, member states are required to "take all appropriate measures, including legislation, to modify or abolish existing laws, regulations, customs and practices which constitute discrimination against women."[148] In addition, under paragraph (G) of this article, member states should "repeal all national penal provisions which constitute discrimination against women."[149] According to pro-abortion advocates, domestic laws criminalizing abortions could restrict women's access to lifesaving procedures, thereby violating the Convention's principle of gender equality.[150]

Furthermore, with regard to the ICCPR, the HRC in General Comment 28 clarifies that there is an inseparable relation between access to reproductive health services and gender equality.[151]

Concerning regional protection, Article 18(3) of the Banjul Charter states that states should "ensure the elimination of every discrimination against women and also ensure the protection of the rights of the woman and the child as stipulated in international declarations and conventions."[152] Egypt made a reservation on this article, claiming that it may violate provisions of the Islamic Code. It stipulated that the application of this article must adhere to Islamic Shari'a.[153]

In Resource Foundation v. Zambia, the African Commission clarified the meaning of Article 2 and Article 3 of the Banjul Charter, highlighting the great importance of non-discrimination and equal protection before the law.[154] The significance of the right to equality was emphasized for two

147 ICESCR, *supra* note 24, art. 2.

148 CEDAW, *supra* note 25, art. 2.

149 *Id.*

150 Lord, *supra* note 12, at 600.

151 General Comment 28, *supra* note 18, para. 10.

152 African Charter, *supra* note 11, art. 18, para. 3.

153 *Id.* (under Article 2 of the Egyptian Constitution, Islamic Shari'a is the main source of legislation). Constitution of the Arab Republic of Egypt, art.2, Sept. 11, 1971 [hereinafter 1971 Constitution].

154 Legal Resource Foundation v. Zambia, para. 63, Comm. No. 211/98 (2001) AHRLP 84. Article 2 of the Banjul Charter stipulates that "every individual shall be entitled to the enjoyment of the rights and freedoms recognised and guaranteed in the present Charter without distinction of any kind such as race, ethnic group, colour, sex, language, religion, political or any other opinion, national and social origin, fortune, birth or any

reasons. The first is to ensure that all citizens are treated "fairly and justly" in African countries' legal systems and that everyone enjoys equal rights. The second reason is that the lack of equality will hinder the enjoyment of other Charter- guaranteed rights.[155]

iv Prohibition of Torture and Other Cruel, Inhuman, or Degrading Treatment

The study will briefly examine the right against torture and other cruel, inhuman, or degrading treatment since many pro-choice advocates believe that legalized abortion preserves that right.[156]

Regarding international protection, Article 5 of the UDHR stipulates that "no one shall be subject to torture or other cruel or inhuman treatment or punishment."[157] The same protection has been provided in identical language under Article 7 of the ICCPR.[158]

With respect to regional protection, Article 5 of the Banjul Charter states that everyone shall "have the right to the respect of the dignity inherent in a human being and to the recognition of his legal status. All forms of exploitation and degradation of man particularly slavery, slave trade, torture, cruel, inhuman or degrading punishment and treatment shall be prohibited."[159]

Pro-choice commentators argue that Article 7 of the ICCPR is violated when a pregnant woman is in a state of distress and has no access to abortion due to laws restricting it.[160] The case of K.L v. Peru supports this argument because the HRC linked laws criminalizing abortion to the violation of Article 7 of the ICCPR.[161]

In this case, K.L was a pregnant teenager in Peru.[162] She sought to have an abortion because the fetus had no chance of survival outside the womb due to its condition.[163] However, the domestic law of Peru restricted a woman's access to an abortion except in cases of life- or health-threatening

status." African Charter, *supra* note 11, art. 2. Article 3 of the Charter states that "every individual shall be equal before the law" and "shall be entitled to equal protection of the law." African Charter, *supra* note 11, art. 3.

155 Legal Resource Foundation v. Zambia, *supra* note 154.

156 Lord, *supra* note 12, at 604.

157 UDHR, *supra* note 9, art. 5.

158 Article 7 of the ICCPR stipulates that "no one shall be subjected to torture or to cruel, inhuman or degrading treatment or punishment. In particular, no one shall be subjected without his free consent to medical or scientific experimentation." ICCPR, *supra* note 10, art. 7.

159 African Charter, *supra* note 11, art. 5.

160 Lord, *supra* note 12, at 604.

161 K.L. v. Peru, *supra* note 78, paras. 2.1, 2.2.

162 *Id.* at 2.7.

163 *Id.*

pregnancies.[164] Therefore, K.L was not permitted to have the procedure and was compelled to give birth to a kid who lived for only four days.[165] In the aftermath, K.L was psychologically shocked and suffered from serious depression.[166] The petitioners argued that K.L's right to health was violated by depriving her of access to abortion. Because the ICCPR has no articles protecting one's right to health, the petitioners' main line of argument was based on the violation of the right to health in the context of the protection of the right to life enshrined in Article 6 of the ICCPR.[167] The Committee agreed that K.L's right to health was violated; however, its resolution was based on the violation of Article 7 of the ICCPR[168] In other words, since Peru refused to heal K.L, she suffered mental trauma and was subjected to cruel and inhuman treatment.[169] Moreover, the Committee decided that Peru had to provide K.L with an effective remedy and compensation.[170] Additionally, it demanded that Peru take precautions to ensure that a similar violation never occurs again.[171]

v Protection of the Right to Autonomy

The right to autonomy includes a woman's ability to make decisions regarding her sexual and reproductive health.[172] Although the right to autonomy is not mentioned in any international or regional human rights instruments, it is linked to other rights such as the right to privacy, the right to liberty, and the right to security of person.[173]

Some commentators consider that the right to autonomy in making decisions related to individuals' health in general, and sexual and reproductive health in particular, is originally derived from the fundamental right to liberty.[174] According to this point of view, everyone has the right to freedom of

164 *Id.* at 2.3.
165 *Id.* at 2.6.
166 *Id.*
167 *Id.* at 3.3.
168 *Id.* at 3.4, 6.3.
169 *Id.*
170 *Id.* at 8.
171 *Id.*
172 Ebenezer Durojaye, *Realizing Access to Sexual Health Information and Services for Adolescents through the Protocol to the African Charter on the Rights of Women*, 16 Wash. & Lee J. Civil Rts. & Soc. Just. 135, 168 (2009).
173 *Id.*
174 Carmel Shalev, *Rights to Sexual and Reproductive Health: The International Conference on Population and Development and the Convention on the Elimination of All Forms of Discrimination Against Women*, 4 Health & Hum Rts. 38, 46 (2000).

choice with regard to his or her reproductive health.[175] In other words, based on the right to liberty, everyone has the autonomy and capacity to make decisions related to his or her body including those related to his or her reproductive rights.[176]

In addition, autonomy in decision-making should be attained in a private setting in order to preserve one's dignity and prestige. In other words, privacy embodies the norm of personal autonomy;[177] "it manifests a right that, by its very nature, cannot be separated from the individual and thus cannot be exercised by another."[178]

In General Recommendation 24, the CEDAW's Committee emphasizes the importance of sexual and reproductive autonomy for women and girls.[179] Additionally, in some concluding observations, the Committee requires states to recognize women's and girls' rights to be "autonomous decision makers." It recommended that states take actions to eradicate any obstacles that may hinder the accomplishment of this aim.[180]

a *The Right to Liberty and Security of Person*

Article 3 of the UDHR and Article 9 (1) of the ICCPR stipulate that "everyone has the right to liberty and security of person."[181]

Regarding regional protection, Article 6 of the Banjul Charter requires states to ensure that "everyone has the right to liberty and security of his person. No one may be deprived of his freedom except for reasons and conditions previously laid down by law."[182]

Pro-choice commentators claim that the absence of access to legal abortion may endanger a pregnant woman's life and lead to mental and physical

---

175 Durojaye, *supra* note 172, at 169.

176 Isaiah Berlin, *Two Concepts of Liberty*, in Four Essays on Liberty, 120–23 (1969).

177 Radhika Rao, *Property, Privacy, and the Human Body*, 80 B.U. L. Rev. 359, 445 (2000).

178 *Id.*

179 General Rec. 24, *supra* note 28, para. 14.

180 U.N. Committee on CEDAW, Concluding Observations: Greece, 20th Sess., 415th–416th mtgs., para. 207, U.N. Doc. A/54/38 (January 28, 1999); *see also* U.N. Committee on CEDAW, Concluding Observations: Mauritius, 268th & 271st mtgs., para. 211, U.N. Doc. A/50/38 (January 20, 1995).

181 Article 3 of the UDHR states that "everyone has the right to life, liberty and security of person." UDHR, *supra* note 9, art. 3. Article 9 of the ICCPR stipulates that "everyone has the right to liberty and security of person. No one shall be subjected to arbitrary arrest or detention. No one shall be deprived of his liberty except on such grounds and in accordance with such procedure as are established by law." ICCPR, *supra* note 10, art. 9.

182 African Charter, *supra* note 11, art. 6.

complications.[183] This may induce anxiety, fear, and depression in her. In addition, a woman may resort to an unsafe or backstreet abortion leading to health complications or psychological trauma.[184] Hence, she may have irrational fear of marriage, pregnancy, and childbirth, and that makes her lose her sense of security.[185] This argument clarifies that reproductive integrity is a part of a woman's security.[186] Furthermore, according to the pro-choice perspective, reproductive self-determination is a main part of a woman's liberty because domestic laws restricting abortions may violate a woman's right to liberty by circumscribing her ability to have access to health services.[187] According to these lines of argument, legal and safe abortions promote a woman's right to liberty and security of person.[188]

b *The Right to Privacy*

Article 12 of the UDHR and Article 17 of the ICCPR stipulate that "no one shall be subjected to arbitrary interference with his privacy, family, home or correspondence, nor to attacks upon his honour and reputation. Everyone has the right to the protection of the law against such interference or attacks."[189]

In its General Comment 16, the HRC defined the word "unlawful" enshrined in Article 17 of the ICCPR as "no interference can take place except in cases envisaged by the law" and "interference authorized by states can only take place on the basis of law, which itself must comply with the provisions, aims and objectives of the Covenant."[190] It further stated that the term "arbitrary interference" aims at ensuring that any interference, even if provided by a law, must be in line with the "provisions, aims, and objective of the Covenant and should be, in any event, reasonable in the particular circumstances."[191] In other words, the interference should be strictly limited

183 Rebecca J. Cook, *International Protection of Women's Reproduction Rights*, 24 N.Y.U. J. Int'l L. & Pol'y 256 (1992).
184 *Id.* at 646.
185 *Id.*
186 Audrey E. Haroz, *South Africa's 1996 Choice on Termination of Pregnancy Act: Expanding Choice and International Human Rights to Black South African Women*, 30 Vand. J. Transnat'l L. 863, 901–902 (1997).
187 *Id.*
188 *Id.*
189 UDHR, *supra* note 9, art. 12; ICCPR, *supra* note 10, art.17.
190 U.N. GAOR Hum. Rts. Comm., 32d Sess. (1988), U.N. Doc. CCPR/C/21/Rev.1 (1989), para. 3.
191 *Id.* para. 4.

to serve the state's interests and reduce restrictions on the fundamental freedom of choice.

With regard to sexual and reproductive health, if abortion is criminalized, doctors and other health personnel might have a legal duty to report cases of women who have had an abortion.[192] In turn, a woman would avoid dealing with doctors and seek other approaches to terminate her pregnancy. Hence, not only would her right to privacy be violated, but her life and health may also be at risk. Therefore, the HRC acknowledged that the right to life in this case would be derogated and clarified the causal relationship between laws circumscribing abortion and violations committed against a woman's rights to privacy and life.[193] In addition, the HRC required state parties to report "any law, public or private action" restricting equal enjoyment of a woman's right to privacy enshrined in Article 17 of the ICCPR[194] and to protect women from any form of interference violating their privacy.[195]

Concerning regional protection, the right to privacy is not enshrined in the Banjul Charter[196] as it is explicitly stated in the other regional conventions. For example, the right to privacy has been squarely addressed in detail in Article 8 of the European Convention on Human Rights.[197] Nevertheless, the lack of explicit provisions does not prevent the African Commission on Human and Peoples' Rights from protecting rights not specifically mentioned in the Charter, as long as they are connected to other rights provided in it.[198] That is, the Committee protects the unmentioned rights in the context of the mentioned ones, synthesizing the absent right from the present.[199] The Commission has not yet interpreted one of the rights in the Charter to protect the right to privacy.[200]

192 General Comment 28, *supra* note 18, para. 20.

193 *Id.*

194 ICCPR, *supra* note 10, art.17.

195 General Comment 28, *supra* note 18, para. 20.

196 African Charter, *supra* note 11.

197 European Convention for the Protection of Human Rights and Fundamental Freedoms, art.8, *opened for signature* Nov. 4, 1950, Europ. T.S. No. 5, 213 U.N.T.S. 221 (entered into force Sept. 3, 1953) [hereinafter European Convention].

198 Soc. and Econ. Rts. Action Ctr. v. Nigeria, Comm. No. 155/96 (Oct. 2001), Fifteenth Annual Activity Report of the ACHPR, 2001–2002, at 31–44, para. 60, available at http://www.achpr.org/english/_doc_target/documentation.html?../activity_reports/activity15_en.pdf (last visited Jul. 25, 2024).

199 Sebastian Maguir, *the Human Rights of Sexual Minorities in Africa*, 35 Cal. W. Int'l L.J. 1, 51 (2004).

200 *Id.*

Due to the significance of the right to privacy in relation to abortion, it has been used repeatedly by the European Court of Human Rights to provide women with the right to abortion.[201] This study will shed light on the European legal system with regard to abortion and discuss notable cases in this context.

1 Bruggeman and Scheuten v. Federal Republic of Germany (1977)

In Bruggeman and Scheuten v. Federal Republic of Germany, the German Federal Constitutional Court repealed a law permitting an abortion during the first twelve weeks of pregnancy.[202] The Court ruled that such a law was unconstitutional because it violated the fetus's right to life.[203] In turn, two German women, Bruggeman and Scheuten, brought a claim before the European Commission of Human Rights to challenge this rule.[204] Their argument was based on the violation of Article 8 of the ECHR (the right to respect for private and family life).[205] Nevertheless, the European Commission found that abortion was not solely a matter of privacy; therefore, it did not create an automatic violation of Article 8 of the Convention.[206] In addition, the Commission declared that when the ECHR entered into force, all member states' abortion-restrictive laws were "at least as restrictive as the one now complained of by the applicants."[207] Therefore, the Commission acknowledged that the ruling of the German Constitutional Court did not violate the right to privacy.[208]

2 Paton v. U.K. (1979)

In Paton v. the U.K., Paton claimed that she suffered from a deteriorating condition and severe mental distress due to her pregnancy.[209] Therefore, she followed the required procedures specified by the British Abortion Act

201 A., B. and C. v. Ireland, Eur. Ct. H.R. 2032 (2010); R.R. v. Poland, Eur. Ct. H.R., para. 64 (2011).
202 Bruggemann and Scheuten v. Federal Republic of Germany, App. No. 6959/75, 10 Eur. Comm'n H.R. Dec. & Rep. 92 (1977).
203 *Id.*
204 *Id.* at 107–08.
205 *Id.*
206 *Id.* at 116.
207 *Id.* at 117.
208 *Id.* at 116–18.
209 Paton v. British Pregnancy Advisory Serv., 1979 Q.B. 281 (1978).

of 1967[210] in order to undergo an abortion.[211] In turn, her husband, Mr. Paton, applied for an injunction to prevent her from having an abortion.[212] The British courts refused the injunction, stating that a "foetus has no right of action, no right at all, until birth."[213] Nevertheless, Mr. Paton brought a petition before the European Commission of Human Rights.[214] One of his main arguments was that the 1967 Act violated his right to respect for private and family life enshrined in Article 8 of the ECHR.[215] In addition, he argued that the Act violated the unborn child's right to life, which is protected under Article 2 of the Convention.[216]

Regarding the admissibility of the case, the Commission found that the applicant, as the fetus's father, was closely affected by the 1967 Act, under which abortion is allowed in certain cases.[217] Thus, Mr. Paton qualified as a victim according to Article 25 of the ECHR, and his case was admissible.[218]

Regarding the violation of Article 8 protecting the right to privacy, the Commission ruled that the potential father's rights under this article could not override a pregnant woman's right to respect for private and family life.[219] Concerning the violation of the unborn child's right to life, the Commission examined Article 2 protecting the right to life to determine whether it could be applicable to the fetus or not.[220] The Commission found that in the case of life threating pregnancy, if the unborn child's right to life were protected, a pregnant woman's right to life could be violated.[221] The Commission avoided issuing a resolution that would cause a violation of a pregnant woman's right to life if a pregnancy endangers her life, and therefore, it determined that the fetus had no legal rights under Article 2 of the

---

210 Abortion Act 1967, c. 87 (Eng.) (allowing abortions when two doctors find that "the continuance of the pregnancy would involve risk to the life of the pregnant woman, or of injury to the physical or mental health of the pregnant woman or any existing children of her family, greater than if the pregnancy were terminated; or (b) that there is substantial risk that if the child were born it would suffer from such physical or mental abnormalities as to be seriously handicapped").

211 Paton v. British Pregnancy Advisory Serv., *supra* note 209.

212 *Id.* at 277.

213 *Id.* at 282–83.

214 X. v. United Kingdom, App. No. 8416/78, 19 Eur. Comm'n H.R. Dec. & Rep. 244, 3 Eur. H.R. Rep. 408 (1980).

215 *Id.* at 253.

216 *Id.* at 247.

217 *Id.* at 248.

218 *Id.*

219 *Id.* at 253.

220 *Id.* at 252.

221 *Id.*

ECHR.[222] In addition, the Commission found that Mrs. Paton's abortion was lawful under the domestic law of the U.K. because it was "carried out at the initial stage of the pregnancy… in order to avert the risk of injury to the physical or mental health of the pregnant woman."[223] Therefore, the Commission concluded that Article 2 of the Convention was not violated.[224]

The applicant's arguments did not address the question of whether Article 2 protects the fetus's right to life in a general context.[225] Rather, his arguments only focused on whether the protection of the fetus's right to life could outweigh a pregnant woman's right to have an abortion if a pregnancy threatens her life.[226] Therefore, the Commission avoided issuing a general standard clarifying its point of view regarding the fetus's right to life. In other words, the Commission stated that its view was based on the applicant's concern only, which was not related to the "broad question [of] whether Article 2 recognises a right to life of the foetus during the whole period of the pregnancy."[227]

3 Open Door and Dublin Well v. Ireland (1991)

Open Door and Dublin Well v. Ireland is the first case related to the unborn child's right to life brought before the European Court of Human Rights.[228] In addition, this case established a link between the unborn child's right to life and the right to freedom of expression.[229]

The unborn child's right to life is a fundamental right under the Irish Constitution.[230] The petitioners, two women's health clinics in Ireland, were prevented by the Irish Attorney General from distributing campaign information related to the advantages of abortion because of the high level of protection given to the fetus's right to life under Irish law.[231] In turn, the petitioners brought a claim before Ireland's courts seeking to appeal this injunction; however, domestic courts upheld the ban, finding that it served a legitimate aim.[232]

---

222 *Id.*
223 *Id.* at 252–53.
224 *Id.*
225 *Id.* at 253.
226 *Id.*
227 *Id.*
228 Open Door Counselling & Dublin Well Woman Centre v. Ireland, Apps. No. 14234/88, 14235/88, Report of the Commission (Mar. 7, 1991).
229 *Id.*
230 Ir. Const., art. 40.3.3 (Eighth Amendment).
231 Att'y Gen. ex rel. Soc'y for the Protection of Unborn Children v. Open Door Counseling & Dublin Wellwoman Ctr., 1988 I.R. 593, 595 (Ir. H. Ct. 1986).
232 *Id.* at 613.

In the aftermath, the petitioners brought a claim before the European Commission of Human Rights.[233] The Commission ruled that the injunction failed to accomplish its purpose and unjustifiably violated Article 10 of the ECHR protecting the right to freedom of expression because the public could obtain the same information from other sources.[234] Therefore, it referred the application to the European Court of Human Rights.[235]

The European Court of Human Rights upheld the Commission's decision confirming that the ban was disproportionate and ineffective in achieving its objective.[236] Therefore, it found that such a ban violated the petitioners' right to freedom of speech enshrined in Article 10 of the ECHR.[237] Nevertheless, the Court stipulated that "in the present case it was not called upon to examine whether a right to abortion [was guaranteed] under the Convention or whether the foetus was encompassed by the right to life as contained in Article 2."[238]

In summary, both the Commission and the Court avoided revealing their views on abortion and the fetus's right to life. Rather, they confined their opinions to the right to freedom of expression, sidestepping the more complicated questions of abortion and fetal rights protection.

4 D v. Ireland (2006)

In June 2006, the ECtHR held that D. v. Ireland was inadmissible because the applicant did not exhaust domestic remedies in her country.[239] The study will discuss this rule in detail since the exhaustion of domestic remedies was Ireland's main argument in the landmark case in the area of reproductive rights in Europe, A, B & C v. Ireland.[240]

The events of the case started when D, a woman in her fourteenth week of pregnancy with twins, learned that one of her fetuses had stopped developing weeks earlier.[241] Three weeks later, in the seventeenth week of pregnancy, she was informed that the other fetus had started to suffer from a severe "chromosomal abnormity."[242] Therefore, D sought an abortion in

233 Open Door Counseling & Dublin Well Woman Ctr., Rep. of the Comm'n, *supra* note 228.
234 *Id.* at 13.
235 *Id.*
236 Open Door & Dublin Well Woman Ctr., 246 Eur. Ct. H.R. (ser. A) at 30–31.
237 *Id.* at 32.
238 *Id.* at 28.
239 D v. Ireland, 43 E.H.R.R. SE16 at 191 (2006).
240 A., B. and C. v. Ireland, App. No. 25579/05, Eur. Ct. H.R. 2032 (2010).
241 D, 43 E.H.R.R. SE16 at 191.
242 *Id.*

Ireland but was prevented from undergoing the procedure.[243] In turn, she went to England to have an abortion and upon her return to Ireland, she brought a case before the ECtHR claiming that her rights enshrined in Articles 3, 5, 10, and 14 of the ECHR were violated.[244] Regarding Article 8, she argued "that there was a disproportionate interference with an intimate and personal aspect of her private and family life and/or a failure to fulfill a positive obligation to protect those Art. 8 rights."[245]

Ireland's principal argument was that the applicant had not exhausted domestic remedies.[246] Ireland asserted that D "should have initiated an action in the High Court, pursued if unsuccessful to the Supreme Court …."[247] In response to this argument, D contended that her own psychological, economic and temporal circumstances prevented her from taking this action.[248]

In reviewing the admissibility of the case, the ECtHR applied a two-part test. The Court first reviewed the domestic remedies' accessibility and capability of "providing redress" and "reasonable prospects of success." Second, the Court reviewed "whether, in all the circumstances of the case, the applicant did everything that could reasonably be expected of her to exhaust domestic remedies."[249]

Regarding the first part, the ECtHR found that Ireland's courts were accessible, since D could have complained before them.[250] In addition, the Court reasoned that domestic courts were capable of providing redress and a "reasonable prospect of success."[251] According to its view, if Ireland's courts had the chance to review the case, they could have allowed D to have an abortion, since there was "a feasible argument to be made that the [Irish constitution created a] balance between the right to life of the mother and of the foetus."[252] In addition, the ECtHR found that this argument "could have shifted in favour of the mother when the unborn suffered from an abnormality incompatible with life."[253]

243 *Id.* at 191–92.
244 *Id.* at 212.
245 *Id.*
246 *Id.* at 213.
247 *Id.*
248 *Id.*
249 *Id.* at 221.
250 *Id.*
251 *Id.*
252 *Id.* at 222.
253 *Id.*

Concerning the second part of the question, the applicant argued that she had no chance to seek domestic remedies due to the imminence of her pregnancy, the preservation of her privacy, and her expectation that Irish courts would issue a ruling against her.[254] However, the Court rejected that argument, reasoning that the applicant could at least have attempted "to take legal proceedings" in her country.[255] Since the applicant was incapable of satisfying such a burden, her case was deemed inadmissible, and therefore the ECtHR did not discuss the merits of the case.

5 Tysiac v. Poland (2007)

In Tysiac v. Poland, Alicia Tysiac was a pregnant woman who suffered from health problems and was advised to have an abortion in order to avoid further deterioration.[256] Although abortion is legal in Poland to protect a pregnant woman's health, doctors refused to perform the procedure.[257] After giving birth, Tysiac suffered from health problems that led her to become almost blind.[258] In turn, she brought a claim before the European Court of Human Rights.[259] Tysiac's argument was mainly based on the violation of her right to health.[260] In addition, she argued that preventing her from having an abortion violated her right to privacy enshrined in Article 8 of the ECHR.[261]

The Court acknowledged that Tysiac's right to health was violated. Since the ECHR does not explicitly protect such a right, the Court's ruling was based on the violation of the right to "physical and psychological integrity," which derives from the right to privacy.[262] The Court stated that "while the Convention does not guarantee such a right [the right to health] to any specific level of medical care, ... private life includes a person's physical and psychological integrity."[263] Therefore, "the State [Poland] is also under a positive obligation to secure to its citizens their right to effective respect for this integrity,"[264] and "once the legislature decides to allow abortion, it must not structure its legal framework in a way which would limit real

254 *Id.*
255 *Id.* at 225–26.
256 *See* Tysiac v. Poland, No. 5410/03, 2007-IV Eur. Ct. H.R. para. 9.
257 *Id.* at 13–15, 38.
258 *Id.* at 146.
259 *Id.* at 1.
260 *Id.*
261 *Id.* at 77.
262 *Id.* at 107.
263 *Id.*
264 *Id.*

possibilities to obtain it."[265] Additionally, the Court reasoned that domestic laws restricting abortions, in some countries like Poland, might result in "high numbers of clandestine abortions with attendant risks to life and health of women."[266] The Court demanded that Poland compensate Tysiac for the violation of her rights. However, doctors in Poland were still permitted to determine on a case-by-case basis whether a woman required an abortion for medical reasons.[267]

6 A., B., & C. v. Ireland (2010)

The events of A, B and C v. Ireland[268] started when three pregnant women, A, B, and C, sought abortions in Ireland; however, they could not have access to the procedure due to its prohibition under Irish law.[269] A was an indigent woman who became pregnant unintentionally while already having four other children. Due to her alcoholism, her children were in foster care.[270] Following her pregnancy, she traveled to England for an abortion.[271] When she returned to Ireland, "she experienced pain, nausea and bleeding for eight to nine weeks, but was afraid to seek medical advice because of the prohibition on abortion."[272]

B experienced a similar situation when she became pregnant unintentionally and decided to have an abortion due to a possible ectopic pregnancy, which occurs when the fetus grows outside of the uterus.[273] She also went to England to have an abortion and returned to Ireland with health complications.[274] Due to the prohibition on abortion in Ireland, B could not seek medical advice there.[275] Therefore, she returned to England for a checkup, incurring significant expenses.[276] Ultimately, she brought a case before the ECtHR claiming that she suffered from health complications and

---

265 *Id.* at 116.
266 *Id.* at 48.
267 Hilary Hammel, *From Page to Practice: Broading the Lengs for Reproductivw and Sexual Rights: Is the Right to Health a Necessary Precondition for Gender Equality*? 35 N.Y.U. Rev. L. & Soc. Change 131, 161 (2011).
268 A., B., & C. v. Ireland, App. No. 25579/05, Eur. Ct. H.R. 2032 (2010).
269 *Id.* at 11–12.
270 *Id.* at 13–17.
271 *Id.*
272 Statement of Facts, A., B., & C. v. Ireland, App. No. 25579/05, Eur. Ct. H.R. (2008), available at http://www.eclj.org/PDF/081118_ECLJ_StatementofFacts7May2008.pdf (last visited Aug. 19, 2024).
273 A., B., & C., Eur. Ct. H.R. 2032, at 19.
274 *Id.* at 20–21.
275 *Id.* at 19.
276 *Id.*

trauma and had also incurred major costs because of Ireland's abortion ban.[277]

With regards to C, the facts that surround her case are different from those of A and B because she unintentionally became pregnant while suffering from cancer. C needed to receive cancer treatment, but the side effects would be detrimental during her pregnancy.[278] Because no physician in Ireland was willing to perform an abortion, she went to England to have the procedure.[279] She faced medical complications when she returned to Ireland, and therefore she filed a claim with the ECtHR challenging Ireland's abortion ban.[280]

The applicants' arguments were based on the violation of their rights enshrined in Articles 8 (the right to privacy), and Article 3 (the right to be free from torture or degrading treatment or punishment) of the ECHR.[281] In addition, C argued that Article 2 of the Convention, under which the right to life is protected, was violated.[282]

Before discussing the merits of the case, the ECtHR first reviewed its admissibility based on whether the applicants exhausted their country's domestic remedies. The Court adopted the two-part test as discussed in D's case. In the first part, the Court focused on whether Irish courts were accessible or "capable of providing a redress" and a "reasonable prospects of success."[283] If these requirements were met, the Court would review the second part of the test, which is whether each applicant did everything that could reasonably be expected to exhaust domestic remedies.[284]

Regarding the first part of the question, the Court found that all applicants had no opportunity to get relief from the Irish Courts due to the high level of protection given to the fetus's right to life by domestic laws.[285] As for A and B, it was clear that they would never get relief from the courts of Ireland because they faced no serious risks to their lives; rather, they sought

277 *Id.* at 18–21.
278 *Id.* at 23.
279 *Id.* at 22.
280 *Id.* at 25–26.
281 *Id.* at 113.
282 *Id.*
283 D v. Ireland, 43 E.H.R.R. SE16, 191, 221 (2006).
284 *Id.*
285 The ECtHR reviewed the Irish courts' position in Open Door v. Ireland, in which, as discussed above, Ireland's courts supported the injunction of the Irish Attorney General to ban two women's clinics from disseminating information about the benefits of abortion. Open Door Counselling & Dublin Well Woman Centre v. Ireland, Apps. No. 14234/ 88 and 14235/88, Report of the Commission (Mar. 7, 1991).

abortion only for health and well-being concerns.[286] Similarly, with respect to applicant C, despite her suffering from cancer and the imminent risk to her life, the ECtHR found that it was difficult for her to obtain relief due to the lack of domestic legislation implementing the right to an abortion if a pregnancy endangers a woman's life.[287] The ECtHR distinguished this case from D v. Ireland, in which the twin fetuses suffered fatal conditions and had no chance of survival outside a woman's womb. Because the fetuses were inevitably doomed, there was no need for protection of their right to life. Therefore, it could be strongly argued that Irish courts would grant D relief enabling her to have an abortion in Ireland.[288] In contrast, in the case of A, B and C, the fetus of each woman was in good health. Due to the high level of protection given to the fetus under Irish law, it would be very difficult for the applicants to obtain relief from the domestic courts. That is, domestic courts would not provide effective and sufficient redress, nor offer reasonable prospects of success. As a result, the ECtHR found this case admissible without handling the second part of the test.[289]

Since the case was deemed admissible, the ECtHR started reviewing its merits. The Court rejected the claim of the third applicant concerning the violation of Article 2 of the ECHR, which protects the right to life, for the reason that "there was no legal impediment to the third applicant travelling for an abortion abroad."[290] In addition, the applicants' claim of the violation of Article 3 of the Convention, which requires states to ensure that no one is subject to torture, degrading treatment or punishment was rejected because the ECtHR found that the "facts [of the case did] not disclose a level of severity falling within the scope" of this article.[291]

Regarding the alleged violation of Article 8 of the ECHR protecting the right to privacy, the ECtHR reached a different conclusion for applicant C than for A and B. Concerning applicant C, the Court unanimously agreed that her right to privacy enshrined in Article 8 was violated.[292] However,

---

286 A., B., and C., Eur. Ct. H.R. 2032, para. 147.

287 *Id.*

288 *Id.* at 148.

289 Shannon K. Calt, *Note and Comment: A., B. & C. V. Ireland: "Europe's Roe V. Wade"?* 14 Lewis & Clark L. Rev. 1189, 1219–20 (2010). Unlike D's case, in which the Court addressed the second part of the test, in the A., B., & C. case, the Court found the case admissible without reviewing the second part because the requirements of the first part were not met. *Id.*

290 *Id.* at 158.

291 *Id.* at 164.

292 Fiona de Londras, *Ireland Is Still in Denial Over Abortion*, The Guardian, Dec. 16, 2010, at 6; Carl O'Brien, *State Loses Case on Woman's Abortion Right*, Irish Times, July 15, 2009.

with respect to A and B's scenarios, the Court found that their rights were not violated.[293]

Concerning applicant C, the Court recalled the legal precedent established in Tysiac v. Poland,[294] wherein it was stipulated that even though the right to health is not protected under the ECHR, Article 8 "may impose on a State certain positive obligations"[295] that require "the implementation, where appropriate, of specific measures in an abortion context."[296] The ECtHR noted some factors that reflected the uselessness of Irish abortion law if a woman's life is endangered by pregnancy. The ECtHR had "a number of concerns as to the effectiveness of [the medical consultation] procedure as a means of establishing the third applicant's qualification for a lawful abortion in Ireland."[297] The Court then stated that there was no legal framework that existed for situations "whereby any difference of opinion between the woman and her doctor or between different doctors consulted, or whereby an understandable hesitancy on the part of a woman or doctor, could be examined and resolved."[298] In addition, the ECtHR noted the existence of severe criminal abortion sanctions that "constitute a significant chilling factor for both women and doctors in the medical consultation process."[299] Therefore, the ECtHR declared that the Irish courts were not "the appropriate *fora* for the primary determination as to whether a woman qualifies for an abortion which is lawfully available in a State" and that "it would be wrong to turn the High Court into a 'licensing authority' for abortions."[300] Lastly, according to the Court, "it would be equally inappropriate to require women to take on such complex constitutional proceedings when their underlying constitutional right to an abortion in the case of a qualifying risk to life was not disputable."[301] As a result, the Court found that Ireland failed to provide applicant C, whose life was at risk because of the pregnancy, with adequate measures through which she could have a legal abortion in Ireland, and therefore the Court decided that C's rights enshrined in Article 8 were violated.[302]

293 *Id.*
294 *See* Tysiac v. Poland, No. 5410/03, 2 007-IV Eur. Ct. H.R. (2007).
295 A., B. & C., Eur. Ct. H.R. 2032, para. 244.
296 *Id.* at 245.
297 *Id.* at 253.
298 *Id.*
299 *Id.* at 254.
300 *Id.*
301 *Id.* at 259.
302 *Id.* The Irish Constitution allows abortion in certain circumstances, such as when a woman's life is in danger during pregnancy. Thus, Ireland's interference in a woman's private life was not prescribed by law, as required by Article 8(2) of the ECHR. *Id.*

With regard to applicants A and B, the ECtHR found that "the prohibition of the termination of the first and second applicants' pregnancies sought for reasons of health and/or well-being amounted to an interference with their right to respect for their private lives."[303] Therefore, the Court acknowledged that Ireland's interference was in line with Article 8(2) of the Convention. According to this article, three requirements should be fulfilled for the State to interfere in people's right to privacy: such interference should be in accordance with the law, show a legitimate aim, and be necessary in a democratic society.[304]

Regarding the first requirement, the ECtHR simply relied on its ruling in Open Door v. Ireland affirming that the ban on abortion was based on the Irish Constitutional Law.[305] As for the second requirement, the Court reasoned that the fetus's right to life was based on "profound moral values concerning the nature of life which were reflected in the stance of the majority of the Irish people against abortion during the 1983 referendum and which have not been demonstrated to have relevantly changed since then."[306] Therefore, the Court found that Ireland's interference had a legitimate aim: to protect moral values.[307]

Concerning the third requirement, the Court noted that the State must choose between two conflicting values. The first was the respect for the applicants' private and family lives. The second value was the respect for the Irish people's morals and ethics that gave tremendous protection for the unborn child. If the first value is adopted, abortion could be allowed. On the contrary, if the alternative is chosen, the State could intervene to ban the procedure.[308] In addition, the Court found that its role is to "examine whether the prohibition of abortion in Ireland for health and/or well-being reasons struck a fair balance between, on the one hand, the first and second applicants' right to respect for their private lives under article 8 and, on the other hand, profound moral values of the Irish people."[309] Nevertheless, the Court decided that the Country could have a "broad margin of appreciation" to determine between the two conflicting values. As a result, the Court

303 *Id.* at 216.
304 European Convention, *supra* note 197, art. 8(2).
305 Open Door Counseling v. Ireland, App. No. 14234/88 & 14235/88, 246 Eur. Ct. H.R. (ser. A), para. 73 (1992)
306 *A., B., & C.*, Eur. Ct. H.R. 2032, para. 226.
307 *Id.*
308 *Id.* at 230.
309 *Id.*

found that Ireland did not violate Article 8 of the Convention in relation to applicants A and B.[310]

7 R.R. v. Poland (2011)

In this case, the ECtHR decided that Poland should grant R.R. compensation for preventing her from having an abortion.[311] The events of this case started when R.R., a 29-year old woman, learned during a medical checkup in a Polish hospital that she was in her sixth or seventh week of pregnancy.[312] A short time later, she was informed that her fetus suffered from an "unidentified malformation."[313] She proceeded to undergo an ultrasound scan that showed the same result.[314] Therefore, R.R. sought an abortion. However, she faced several burdens because doctors refused to perform the procedure informing her that she should undergo genetic testing as required by domestic law.[315] After experiencing difficulties due to domestic classical and bureaucratic procedures, she had the genetic testing done and the result of this test confirmed that her fetus suffered from Turner syndrome. This result gave her the opportunity to have an abortion under domestic law.[316] Nevertheless, doctors refused to perform the procedure because her pregnancy had reached a late stage that exceeded the legal time limit for an abortion.[317] Ultimately, after enduring severe suffering, she gave birth to a baby who had Turner syndrome.[318]

Unlike the previous cases, D v. Ireland and A, B, & C v. Ireland, R.R. brought a complaint before domestic courts seeking both criminal and civil relief.[319] As for the criminal relief, her case was denied.[320] Regarding the civil relief, she received compensation because her right to privacy had been violated.[321] Apparently, one of the physicians divulged some information about her health and private life.[322] Due to the inadequate compensation she was granted, she brought a case before the ECtHR.[323]

310 *Id.*
311 R.R. v. Poland, App. No. 27617/04, Eur. Ct. H.R. (2010), para. 64 (2011).
312 *Id.*
313 *Id.* at 9.
314 *Id.* at 13.
315 *Id.* at 14.
316 *Id.* at 33.
317 *Id.*
318 *Id.* at 37.
319 *Id.* at 38.
320 *Id.* at 39–42.
321 *Id.* at 43.
322 *Id.*
323 *Id.* at 1.

Because R.R. sought relief in her country, the ECtHR found that R.R. clearly qualified as a victim.[324] The Court noted that the relief given to R.R. by the Polish courts could not "be regarded as financial redress commensurate with the nature of the damage."[325] In addition, the Court found that the applicant did not complain about the law; rather, she complained about "the way in which the laws were applied in practice."[326]

Concerning the merits of the case, the Court found that R.R.'s rights enshrined in Article 8 (the right to privacy), and Article 3 (the right to be free from torture or degrading treatment or punishment)[327] of the ECHR were violated, as follows:

Concerning the violation of Article 8, the Court stated that the interference in R.R.'s private life should be in accordance with "the second paragraph [of Article 8]," because "the interference corresponds to a pressing social need ... proportionate to one of the legitimate aims pursued by the authorities."[328] In addition, the Court addressed Poland's positive obligations to protect the "right to effective respect for their physical and psychological integrity."[329] Therefore, the Court concluded that Poland violated Article 8 of the Convention. According to the Court, the State had a positive obligation to "safeguard the applicant's right to respect for her private life in the context of controversy over whether she should have had access to, firstly, prenatal genetic tests and subsequently, an abortion, had the applicant chosen this option."[330] Furthermore, the ECtHR criticized bureaucratic procedures in Poland that R.R. was forced to endure until she reached the expiration of the legal time limit for an abortion.[331]

Concerning Article 3 (the right to be free from torture or degrading treatment or punishment), the ECtHR used this article to provide the petitioner with relief. The Court clarified that the concept of "ill-treatment requires a minimum level of severity" and should depend on the circumstances and facts of the applicant's particular case.[332] Besides, the Court stated that such treatment need not be deliberately humiliating; rather, it depends on how the applicant was dealt with.[333] To support its reasoning, the Court

324 *Id.* at 38.
325 *Id.* at 108.
326 *Id.* at 116.
327 *Id.* at 121.
328 *Id.* at 183.
329 *Id.* at 185.
330 *Id.* at 211.
331 *Id.* at 203.
332 *Id.* at 148.
333 *Id.* at 151.

addressed the applicant's feelings. The Court noted that R.R. "suffered acute anguish through having to think about how she and her family would be able to ensure the child's welfare, happiness and appropriate long-term medical care."[334] In addition, the Court stated that other facts increased R.R.'s suffering such as "the diagnostic services which she requested early on were at all times available and that she was entitled as a matter of domestic law to avail herself of them."[335]

c *The Right to Control Reproduction*

Abortion may be used as a technique of controlling reproduction when there are no other effective methods, hence this might be cited as an argument in favor of the pro-choice opinion.

Article 10 of CEDAW requires states to allow women, on the basis of equality with men, to have access to "specific educational information" related to well-being and family health matters including information related to family planning.[336]

Article 12(1) of CEDAW stipulates that states must take measures to eradicate any discrimination against women in the sphere of health care. In addition, states must "ensure, on a basis of equality of men and women, access to health care services, including those related to family planning."[337]

Article 16 of CEDAW requires states to take measures to guarantee the elimination of discrimination between men and women in the sphere "relating to marriage and family relations."[338] In particular, member states should ensure, on the basis of equality with men, that women have the same rights "to decide freely" on "the number and spacing of their children," so that they could have "access to information and education and means to enable them to exercise these rights."[339] In the context of this study, it is worth mentioning that Egypt made a reservation to this article, claiming that it violates the provisions of the Islamic Code.[340]

The CEDAW's Committee directly addresses a woman's right to control reproduction, requiring states to take measures to prevent "unwanted preg-

---

334 *Id.* at 159.
335 *Id.* at 160.
336 CEDAW, *supra* note 25, art. 10(h).
337 *Id.* art. 12(1).
338 *Id.* art. 16.
339 *Id.* art. 16(e).
340 U.N. Women, Reservations to cedaw (2004), http://www.un.org/womenwatch/daw/cedaw/reservations.htm (last visited Aug. 19, 2024).

nancies" and disseminate information related to family planning.[341] In addition, they must take strict actions to ensure that a woman does not undergo "unsafe medical procedures" including an "illegal abortion" due to "the lack of family planning and contraceptive services."[342] Furthermore, the Committee found that if a woman is provided with access to control of reproduction, she will be able to participate in the "society through employment," and that reflects "a positive implication on equality between men and women."[343]

The ICESCR's Committee interpreted Article 12 of the ICESCR (protecting the right to health) to require state parties to take measures to improve "sexual and reproductive health services."[344] This issue includes "access to family planning," "access to information," "pre-and post-natal care," and "emergency obstetric services."[345]

vi The Protocol to the African Charter

The first human rights instrument that explicitly stated a woman's right to an abortion is the Protocol to the African Charter on Human and Peoples' Rights on the Rights of Women in Africa.[346] Prior to the adoption of this Protocol, the right to an abortion was only derived from human rights treaty

341 CEDAW 37th Session, *supra* note 58, at 18.

342 *Id.*

343 Comm. on the Elimination of Discrimination against Women, General Recommendation 21: Equality in Marriage and Family Relations, 1–10, U.N. Doc. A/49/38 (Apr. 14, 1994).

344 General Comment 14, *supra* note 28, at 14. Article 12 of the ICESCR states:

1. States Parties to the present Covenant recognize the right of everyone to the enjoyment of the highest attainable standard of physical and mental health.
2. The steps to be taken by the States Parties to the present Covenant to achieve the full realization of this right shall include those necessary for:
   (a) The provision for the reduction of the stillbirth-rate and of infant mortality and for the healthy development of the child;
   (b) The improvement of all aspects of environmental and industrial hygiene;
   (c) The prevention, treatment and control of epidemic, endemic, occupational and other diseases;
   (d) The creation of conditions which would assure to all medical services and medical attention in the event of sickness.

ICESCR, *supra* note 24, art.12.

345 General Comment 14, *supra* note 28, at 14.

346 Protocol to the African Charter on Human and Peoples' Rights on the Rights of Women in Africa, adopted July 11, 2003 (entered into force Nov. 25, 2005), reprinted in Martin Semalulu Nsibirwa, *A Brief Analysis of the Draft Protocol to the African Charter on Human and Peoples' Rights in Africa*, 1 afr. hum. rts. L.J. 40, 53 (2001) [hereinafter African Women's Protocol].

bodies' interpretation of the provisions protecting other rights.[347] The establishment of the African Protocol is considered as one of the great events for a woman in Africa.[348] In addition, it is ranked as one of the best human rights documents protecting and promoting the rights of women.[349] This Protocol was formed for the sake of women and focused on the protection of their rights[350]; it is considered the Africans' CEDAW and the "first instrument of its kind" that was "developed by Africans, for Africans."[351]

The African Protocol was established to rectify the shortcomings of the African Charter regarding the respect, protection, and promotion of a woman's rights.[352] The Charter did not mention the word "woman" except in Article 18(3), which requires the elimination of discrimination against women.[353] In addition, Article 2 of the African Charter did not specifically focus on the elimination of discrimination against women; rather, it highlighted the principle of non-discrimination in a very general context stating that all grounds of discrimination should be eradicated.[354]

Article 14 of the Protocol, which refers to a woman's right to an abortion, is divided into two sections.[355] The first section states the necessary protection of a woman's right to health in general, and sexual and reproductive health in particular.[356] This protection includes the right to control fertility, a woman's right to determine whether to have children, their number, the spacing between them, and a woman's right to use any method of contraception.[357] Moreover, it includes a woman's right to be informed about her

---

347 Chad M. Gerso, *Toward an International Standard of Abortion Rights: Empirical Data from Africa*, 18 Pace Int'l L. Rev. 373 (2006).

348 Kristin Davis, *The Emperor Is Still Naked: Why the Protocol on the Rights of Women in Africa Leaves Women Exposed to More Discrimination*, 42 Vand. J. Transnat'l L. 949, 952 (2009).

349 Center for Reproductive Rights (Crr), Briefing Paper: The Protocol on the Rights of Women in Africa; an Instrument for Advancing Reproductive and Sexual Rights 7 (2006).

350 African Women's Protocol, *supra* note 346, Pmbl.

351 Rose Gawaya & Rosemary Semafumu Mukasa, *The African Women's Protocol: A New Dimension for Women's Rights in Africa*, 13 Gender & Devel. 42 (2005).

352 Report of the Meeting of Experts on the Draft Protocol to the African Charter on Human and Peoples' Rights of Women in Africa, para. 110, Nov. 12–16, 2001, http://www.chr.up.ac.za/hr_docs/african/docs/oau/oau10.doc (last visited Aug. 17, 2024).

353 African Charter, *supra* note 11, art. 18(3).

354 *Id.* art.2.

355 African Women's Protocol, *supra* note 346, art. 14.

356 *Id.* art. 14, para. 1.

357 *Id.* at (a, b, c).

health status, in particular the "sexually transmitted diseases" such as "HIV/AIDS" and to have "family planning education."[358]

On the other hand, under the second section of Article 14, state parties must take measures to achieve three objectives.[359] The first one is to provide a woman with "adequate, affordable, and accessible health services."[360] The second objective is to establish and support "existing prenatal, delivery, post-natal health and nutritional services" for a woman during pregnancy and beyond.[361] The third objective is to permit a woman to undergo "medical abortion" in certain cases such as "sexual assault, rape" or "incest."[362] Additionally, if a pregnancy constitutes any danger to a woman's "medical or physical health" or her life or the fetus's life, a woman can undergo a medical abortion.[363]

Egypt did not sign or ratify the Protocol.[364] In addition, Egypt made a reservation to Article 18(3) of the African Charter stipulating the principle of non-discrimination against a woman in family matters.[365] As a result, regarding the regional protection of women's rights, Egypt is only bound by Article 2 of the Banjul Charter that discusses the principle of non-discrimination in very broad language.[366]

B *Pro-Life Arguments*

This study will clarify whether it is possible to turn the argument for the right to life on its head in favor of the fetus. In other words, can Article 3 of the UDHR,[367] Article 6 of the ICCPR,[368] and other articles of the regional conventions protecting the right to life be used to prohibit abortion?

To find an answer, the study will try to determine when the right to life is protected under international law: at fertilization, conception, or birth. If

358 *Id.* at (e, g).
359 *Id.* art. 14, para. 2.
360 *Id.* at (a).
361 *Id.* at (b).
362 *Id.*at (c).
363 *Id.*
364 *See* List of Countries Which Have Signed, Ratified/Acceded to the Protocol to the African Charter on Human and Peoples' Rights on the Rights of Women, available at http://www.africa-union.org/home/Bienvenue.htm (last visited Aug. 13, 2024).
365 African [Banjul] Charter on Human and Peoples' Rights: Ratification, available at http://afronet.org.za/links/banjul. ratifi.htm (last visited Aug 15, 2024).
366 African Charter, *supra* note 11, art. 2.
367 UDHR, *supra* note 9, art. 3.
368 ICCPR, *supra* note 10, art. 6.

international law protects the right to life from the moment of fertilization or conception, the fetus's right to life must not be violated. On the other hand, if international law protects the right to life from the moment of birth, the fetus has no right to life. This study will begin by reviewing international and regional human rights instruments for references to this issue. In addition, the study will examine the practices of international and regional treaty bodies to determine their perspective on the fetus's right to life.

i International Protection of the Fetus's Right to Life

Article 3 of the UDHR and Article 6 of the ICCPR protect the inherent right to life; however, they do not specify a minimum age at which a person is eligible for protection, or a point at which a person can enjoy this right.[369]

Article 6 of the CRC provides for the protection of a child's inherent right to life but it does not determine when childhood starts.[370] Thus, this study will examine other articles to determine whether the Convention clarifies the point at which a child can enjoy his or her inherent right to life. Article 1 of the Convention identifies a child as "every human being below the age of eighteen years, unless under the law applicable to the child, majority is attained earlier."[371] This article determines the maximum age of a child, but does not specify whether its minimum age is the moment of fertilization, conception, or birth. In addition, this article could be interpreted in different ways.[372] That is, two contradictory arguments could be based on this article: the first one supports abortion and the second prohibits it.[373] These two lines of argument are derived from Article 31(a) of the Vienna Convention on the Law of Treaties, which stipulates that "a treaty shall be interpreted in good faith in accordance with the ordinary meaning to be given to the terms of the treaty in their context and in the light of its object and purpose."[374]

---

369 UDHR, *supra* note 9, art. 3; ICCPR, *supra* note 10, art. 6.

370 U.N. Convention on the Rts. of the Child, art. 6, Nov. 20, 1989, G.A. Res. 44/25, U.N. GAOR 44th Sess., Supp. No. 49, at 167, U.N. Doc. A/44/736 (1989) [hereinafter CRC].

371 *Id.* art. 1.

372 Abby F. Janoff, *Rights of the Pregnant Child vs. Rights of the Unborn under the Convention on the Rights of the Child*, 22 B.U. Int'l L.J. 163, 166–67 (2004).

373 *Id.* at 167.

374 Vienna Convention on the Law of Treaties, art. 31, *opened for signature* May 23, 1969, 1155 U.N.T.S. 331 (Jan. 27, 1980) (entered into force Jan. 27, 1980) [hereinafter VCLT].

The first argument is that the CRC does not protect the unborn child.[375] It contends that if the unborn child were protected, the Convention's drafters would have explicitly included the fetus in the definition of the child enshrined in Article 1.[376] Since the drafters did not do so, they did not intend to protect the fetus.[377] In contrast, the second argument is based on the broad definition of a child under Article 1, which could be interpreted to include unborn children. Under this line of argument, if the Convention's drafters intended to limit the protection of the child to the moment of birth, this limitation would have been expressly stated.[378] However, this was not the case.

Another important point of the CRC deserves to be highlighted. Paragraph 9 of the preamble states that a child "needs special safeguard and care, including appropriate legal protection before and after birth."[379] The literal interpretation of this paragraph is that an unborn child is entitled to legal protection. Nonetheless, the preamble of a treaty is not regarded as a binding law by the majority of international law scholars.[380] Therefore, the preamble of paragraph 9 does not define the term "child" for the purpose of the Convention.[381] This position is supported by the International Court of Justice's rules clarifying the binding legal force of the U.N. Charter.

In its 1993 decision, the ICJ clarified that in order to avoid the ambiguity and uncertainty in the U.N. Charter's preamble, member states must specify their aims, objectives, declarations and determinations in light of Article 1 of the Charter.[382] In addition, in its 1966 decision, the ICJ stipulated that the preamble parts of the U.N. Charter, although they constitute the basis of morality and politics "for the specific legal provisions thereafter set out ..., [s]uch considerations, do not ... in themselves amount to rules of law."[383] Thus, they are not binding on member states of the U.N. According to this

375 Janoff, *supra* note 372, at 167.

376 The United Nations Convention on the Rights of the Child: A Guide to the "Travaux Preparatoires" 109 (Sharon Detrick ed. 1992).

377 Janoff, *supra* note 372, at 167.

378 *Id.*

379 CRC, *supra* note 370, Pmbl. para. 9.

380 Philip Alston, *The Unborn Child and Abortion Under the Draft Convention on the Rights of the Child*, 12 Hum. Rts. Q. 156, 169 (1990).

381 *Id.*

382 Application of the Convention on the Prevention and Punishment of the Crime of Genocide, Provisional Measures, Order of April 8,1993, 1993 I.C.J. 325, 391 (Sept. 13).

383 South West Africa, Second Phase, Judgment (Eth. v. S. Afr.; Liber. v. S. Afr.), 1966 I.C.J. 6, 34 (July 18).

line of argument, paragraph 9 of the CRC's preamble does not carry legal weight or grant unborn children legal protection.[384]

Nevertheless, Article 31(2) of the Vienna Convention on the Law of Treaties states that the context for the purposes of interpretation should comprise, in addition to the text, the preamble.[385] Applying this provision to the CRC, paragraph 9 of its preamble would be taken into consideration and have legal weight.[386] Thus, the unborn child could be entitled to legal protection. This argument contradicts the previous one that depends on the ICJ's decisions.

Multiple contradictory arguments indicate that the CRC is ambiguous regarding the protection of the unborn child's right to life. Some commentators have clarified that this ambiguity has three major pillars,[387] as follows:

1. Article 1, which identifies the child without determining when the childhood starts.[388]
2. Paragraph 9 of the preamble, which affirms that the child is in need of "legal protection" before or after birth.[389]
3. Article 6(1), which protects the child's right to life.[390]

It could be argued that the drafters of the Convention deliberately did not specify the child's minimum age in order to encourage widespread ratification of the Convention.[391] In other words, the Convention's drafters sought ratification from states with divergent views on abortion.[392] Thereby, signatory states would have the option to interpret the term "child" based on their respective interpretations of the scope of the treaty. In addition, they would shape the Convention's goals and objectives based on their understanding.[393]

The study will present a concluding argument to end the discussion of the unborn child's protection under the CRC. Despite the ambiguity, logic suggests that the Convention does not grant protection to unborn children. On the one hand, if there were an under-eighteen pregnant girl, whose pregnancy endangered her life, the Convention, according to Article 6 protecting

384 Janoff, *supra* note 372, at 167.
385 VCLT, *supra* note 374, art. 31(2).
386 Alston, *supra* note 380, at 169–70.
387 Janoff, *supra* note 372, at 166.
388 CRC, *supra* note 370, art. 1.
389 *Id.* at Pmbl. para. 9.
390 *Id.* art. 6.
391 Alston, *supra* note 380, at 172.
392 *Id.*
393 *Id.*

the right to life,[394] would undoubtedly support the girl's right to have an abortion. On the other hand, the Convention is vague with regard to the protection of the unborn child's right to life. In other words, the Convention will strongly support the pregnant girl, whose right to life is explicitly protected by Article 6, over the fetus, whose right to life is not clearly protected under the Convention. This is the most sensible argument. Thus, the CRC does not protect the fetus's right to life or support arguments against abortion. If it were otherwise, the Convention would be contradicting itself. Therefore, if the Convention sought to protect the fetus's right to life, it would have focused on, organized and clarified this point. That is, when would a pregnant girl have the right to an abortion, and when would she not? But the Convention's opacity and lack of obviousness give greater weight to the clearer and more obvious right, which is the girl's right to life if her life is endangered by pregnancy.

ii Regional Protection of the Fetus's Right to Life

The African Charter on Human and Peoples' Rights states in Article 4 the protection of the right to life.[395] Additionally, the right to life is enshrined in Article 2 of the European Convention on Human Rights.[396] However, none of these articles may be utilized as acceptable justifications in favor of the fetus's right to life.[397] This is because they do not determine the moment at which a person can enjoy such a right.[398]

The American Convention on Human Rights, unlike other international and regional instruments, explicitly declares that the right to life is protected from the moment of conception.[399] Under Article 4 of the Convention, "every person has the right to have his life respected. This right shall be protected by law and, in general, from the moment of conception. No one shall be arbitrarily deprived of his life."[400]

Under this article, an argument could be made in favor of the fetus's right to life and domestic laws restricting abortion. According to this argument, abortion would be treated as a crime of murder that a woman could never be permitted to commit, even in life-threatening pregnancies. However,

394 CRC, *supra* note 370, art. 6.
395 African Charter, *supra* note 11, art. 4.
396 European Convention, *supra* note 197, art. 2.
397 *Id.*; African Charter, *supra* note 11, art. 4.
398 *Id.*
399 American Convention on Human Rights, art. 4, *opened for signature* Nov. 22, 1969, OEA/ser. K/XVYI.1, Doc. 65, Rev. 1, Corr. 1 O.A.S.T.S., No. 36 (1970) (entered into force July 18, 1978) (hereinafter American Convention).
400 *Id.*

such an argument is weak and refuted by pro-abortion advocates with the following points:[401]

1. Based on the standards of treaty interpretation enshrined in the Vienna Convention on the Law of Treaties, the statement of the American Convention related to the right to life should be reconciled with the articulation of the right to life under international treaties[402] such as the ICCPR.[403] Therefore, the Inter-American Commission on Human Rights must interpret the right to life in accordance with other international treaties.[404] Thus, in life-threatening pregnancies, the Commission must provide a pregnant woman with access to an abortion.[405]
2. The word "arbitrary" used by the Convention to describe the deprivation of life indicates that the Convention does not "support hard and fast prohibition of abortion."[406] Rather, the Convention's language suggests that there is a grey area in interpreting this provision.[407] This perspective was supported by the Inter-American Commission on Human Rights in its 1981 report, in which it clarified that the Convention's language does not affirm the prohibition of abortion but instead permits legal access to abortion within compelling circumstances.[408]

This study will examine some cases in the Inter-American Legal System in order to find a solution or eliminate the ambiguity surrounding the protection of the unborn child's right to life. First, the study will address the Inter-American Court's position on the unborn child, followed by the Commission's resolutions.

a *Inter-American Court of Human Rights*

There have been no decisions made by the Inter-American Court of Human Rights concerning challenges to the protection of the fetus's right to life under Article 4(1) of the American Convention. However, it is

---

401 Lord, *supra* note 12, at 594–95.
402 VCLT, *supra* note 374, art. 30(2).
403 ICCPR, *supra* note 10, art. 6.
404 Lord, *supra* note 12, at 596.
405 *Id.*
406 *Id.*
407 Inter-Am. Comm'n on Human Rights, Annual Report of the Inter-American Commission on Human Rights 1980–1981, OEA/Ser. L/V/II.54 (Mar. 6, 1981), available at http://www.cidh.org/annualrep/80.81eng/USA2141.htm (citing OAS General Secretariat, Conferencia Especializada Interamericana Sobre Derechos Humanos, OEA/Ser.K/XVI/1.2, at para. 159 (Sept. 26, 1969) (last visited Aug. 19, 2024).
408 *Id.*

important to note that the Court occasionally referred to the fetus as a baby, a child, or a minor.

In Gomez-Paquiyauri Brothers v. Peru,[409] the Inter-American Court granted reparations to a pregnant woman whose fetus was miscarried during the ninth month of pregnancy. This miscarriage resulted from a nervous disorder the mother suffered because of violations committed by her government.[410] In such a case, the Court referred to the fetus as a family member.[411] The Court reasoned that reparations were granted for the "devastating consequences of the facts of the instant case on the [victim's] family as a whole, and individually on each of its members."[412]

The second case is Sawhoyamaxa Indigenous Community v. Paraguay, in which a vulnerable community was suffering from the absence of health services. In its ruling, the Inter-American Court stated that vulnerable indigenous women must have access to health services, particularly during pregnancy, childbirth and breast-feeding.[413] In addition, the Court referred to unborn children as minors, citing Article 19 of the American Convention.[414] This article emphasizes the necessity of protecting minors' rights by the family, the society and the State.[415]

In the third case, Miguel Castro Prison v. Peru, three pregnant women in Castro-Prison in Peru, together with other prisoners, were harmed by military attacks on the prison.[416] Those women did not receive medical care either during pregnancy or after childbirth.[417] The Court provided them with reparations for their "non-pecuniary" losses.[418] In its ruling, the Court described the unborn as children and granted mothers compensation for their "feelings of anguish, despair, and fear for the lives of their children."[419]

409 Gomez-Paquiyauri Brothers v. Peru, Merits, Reparations, and Costs, Inter-Am. Ct. H.R. (ser. C) No. 110, para. 71 (Jul. 8, 2004).
410 *Id.* at 67(x).
411 *Id.* at 216.
412 *Id.*
413 Sawhoyamaxa Indigenous Community v. Paraguay, Merits, Reparations and Costs, Inter-Am. Ct. H.R. (ser. C) No. 146, 177 (March 29, 2006).
414 *Id.* at 177.
415 American Convention, *supra* note 399, art. 19.
416 Castro Prison v. Peru Merits, Reparations, and Costs, Inter-Am. Ct. H.R. (ser. C) No. 160 (Nov. 25, 2006).
417 *Id.* at 186(a)(6).
418 *Id.* at 292.
419 *Id.*

Goiburu et al. v. Paraguay is the fourth case regarding this point.[420] In this case, the Court decided to compensate Carlos Marcelo Rois for the losses he incurred when the government of his Country punished his father with forced disappearance, and that led him to be born and live in prison for three years.[421] Moreover, in its ruling, the Court referred to Carlos as a minor, despite still being unborn at that time.[422]

b *Inter-American Commission on Human Rights*

1 Baby-Boy v. U.S. (1981)

In this case, "Baby-Boy" is a fictional name for a fetus on whose behalf a petition was brought before the Inter-American Commission on Human Rights[423] to challenge the United States Supreme Court's ruling in Roe v. Wade[424] creating the fundamental right to abortion in the country. To avoid redundancy, this book will elaborate on the issue of abortion under American law in a later section. What is important for this part is that the Inter-American Commission determined that abortion, which is permissible in the United States, "due to the decision of the U.S. Supreme Court and the Supreme Judicial Court of Massachusetts ... [does not] constitute a violation of articles I, II, VII and XI of the American Declaration of the Rights and Duties of Man."[425] The Commission also pointed out that Roe v. Wade did not contradict the American Convention on Human Rights. In other words, the Commission ruled that the fundamental right to abortion in the United States established by Roe v. Wade was not incompatible with these regional instruments.

Thus, the American Commission's resolution indicates that neither the Inter-American Declaration nor the Convention prohibit abortion.[426] However, such a resolution does not necessarily imply that abortion is part of a

420 Goiburu et al. v. Paraguay, Merits, Reparations and Costs, Inter-Am. Ct. H.R (ser. C) No. 153 (Sept. 22, 2006).

421 *Id.* at 56(d).

422 *Id.* at 160(b)(III) (stating that "the amount mentioned in paragraph (I) shall be increased ......for Patricia Jazmín Goiburú Benítez, Claudia Anahí Mancuello Ríos, Carlos Marcelo Mancuello Ríos and Emilio Raúl Mancuello Bareiro, who were minors at the time of the forced disappearance of their fathers and brother, respectively, since the said sufferings were increased by their situation as minors and the lack of protection to which the State subjected them").

423 Baby Boy v. United States, Case 2141, Inter-Am. Comm'n H.R., Report No. 23/81, OEA/Ser.L/V/II.54, doc. 9 rev. 1, paras. 14(a), 19(b) (1981) [hereinafter Baby Boy].

424 Roe v. Wade, 410 U.S. 113 (1973).

425 *See* Baby Boy, *supra* note 423, at 15.

426 *Id.*

woman's rights, protected by the Convention or the Declaration, and that states should support it.

2 Paulina Ramirez v. Mexico (2007)

In Paulina Ramirez v. Mexico, a 14-year-old Mexican girl, Paulina Ramirez, was raped at her home by a burglar, and she became pregnant.[427] Although Mexican law permits abortions where a pregnancy is an outcome of rape, public officials prevented Paulina from having an abortion, and that led her to give birth.[428] In the aftermath, the girl brought a claim against Mexico before the Inter-American Commission.[429] Her line of argument was based on the violation of her personal integrity and her right to emotional and mental health.[430] NGO s across Latin America interfered and supported Paulina's claim.[431] Their argument was based on the violation of the right to health; they claimed that the right to an abortion should be considered a part of a woman's right to health.[432] Nevertheless, the Inter-American Commission did not issue a resolution because Paulina reconciled with the government of Mexico.[433] Thus, in this case, the Inter-American Commission did not clarify its view on the fetus's right to life according to the American Convention.

3 James Demers v. Canada (2007)

In Demers v. Canada, there was a link between the right to freedom of expression and an unborn child's right to life.[434] The Inter-American Commission was requested to investigate alleged violations of two rights, the right to freedom of expression and the fetus's right to life.[435] The events of the case started when Demers, a pro-life activist, protested outside one of the abortion clinics.[436] As a result, Demers was arrested for violating the

427 Paulina Del Carmen Ramirez Jacinto v. Mexico, Case 161–02, Inter-Am. Comm'n H.R., Report No. 21/07, OEA/Ser.L/V/II.130, doc. 22, rev. 1, para. 9 (2007) [hereinafter Paulina v. Mexico].

428 *Id.* at 10–13.

429 *Id.*

430 *Id.*

431 *Letter from 70 Latin American NGO s to the Inter-Am. Comm'n on Human Rights (Sept. 23, 2003)*, in Grupo de Informacion en Reproduccion Eligida, Paulina: Five Years Later 78, 81 (2005).

432 *Id.*

433 Paulina v. Mexico, *supra* note 427, at 16.

434 James Demers v. Canada, Petition 225–04, Inter-Am. Ct. H.R., No. 85/06 (2006) [hereinafter Demers v. Canada].

435 *Id.* at 3.

436 *Id.* at 12–13.

zone regulation that prohibited individuals from distributing materials and information or causing any disturbance within thirty meters of abortion clinics.[437]

After Demers exhausted Canadian domestic remedies, he brought a petition before the American Commission claiming a violation of his right to freedom of speech and the right to life of thousands of unborn children and their mothers.[438] Since Canada is not a member of the American Convention,[439] the Commission applied only the American Declaration of Rights and Duties of Man to this case.[440] The Commission found that the petition was admissible with regard to the argument of freedom of speech.[441] In addition, it declared that Demers' right to freedom of speech enshrined in Article IV of the American Declaration was violated.[442] Nevertheless, the Commission decided that the petition related to the unborn children's right to life was inadmissible due to its lack of specificity. The petitioner's claim was considered vague since it was filed on behalf of thousands of unidentified fetuses and mothers.[443] The Commission stated that "thousands of unborn children and their mothers as referred to by the Petitioner do not constitute sufficiently specific, defined and identifiable groups for the purpose of Article 32 of the Commission's Rules of Procedure."[444]

4 Amelia v. Nicaragua (2010)

On February 26, 2010, the Inter-American Commission issued a precautionary measure against Nicaragua in Amelia v. Nicaragua.[445] The events of the case started when Amelia became pregnant while she had cancer.[446] Because the two major approaches of curing cancer, chemotherapy and radio-

437 *Id.* at 13.
438 *Id.* at 2.
439 *See* Basic Documents-Ratification of the Convention, Inter-Am. Comm'n H.R., available at http://www.cidh.oas.org/Basicos/English/Basic4.Amer.Conv.Ratif.htm (last visited Apr. 25, 2024).
440 Demers v. Canada, *supra* note 434, at 40.
441 *Id.* at 62.
442 *Id.*
443 *Id.* at 45.
444 *Id.*
445 Precautionary Measures Granted by the Commission in 2010, "Amelia," Nicaragua, PM 43–10 Inter-Am. Comm'n H.R., http://www.cidh.oas.org/medidas/2010.eng.htm (last visited Apr. 21, 2024).
446 *Id.*

therapy, may terminate pregnancy and cause a spontaneous abortion, the government prevented her from receiving these treatments.[447]

After reviewing the case, the Commission requested Nicaragua to take necessary measures to ensure that Amelia would obtain adequate treatment. In response, Nicaragua informed the Commission that Amelia started receiving her treatment five days later.[448] Noticeably, in its resolution, the Commission did not require Nicaragua to enable Amelia to have a therapeutic abortion; rather, it asked the Country to protect Amelia's right to health and intervene to allow her to receive the necessary cancer treatment.[449]

5 Costa Rica's Ban on IVF (2010)

In August 2010, the Commission issued a report condemning Costa Rica for banning In Vitro Fertilization (IVF). Costa Rica's Supreme Court banned IVF because it causes the destruction of a high proportion of embryos.[450] Since domestic law in Costa Rica protects human life from the moment of conception, the Supreme Court ruled that IVF was illegal because each IVF trial results in the termination of at least six embryos.[451]

According to the Inter-American Commission, the ban violated Article 11 (the right to privacy in family life), Article 17 (the right to raise a family), and Article 24 (the right to equal protection before the law) of the American Convention on Human Rights.[452] In addition, the Commission found that such a ban would have a disproportionate impact on a woman preventing her from using scientific approaches in order to overcome "disadvantaged situations."[453] Furthermore, the Commission rejected Costa Rica's main argument that the ban was in line with Article 4(1) of the American Convention.[454]

C *Comparison between Regional Systems*

A close review of the regional systems' perspectives reveals that the European System of Human Rights could be the most pro-choice regional legal system supporting women's right to choose an abortion. This is clearly

447 *Id.* After Amelia went to physicians in order to find the proper treatment for her disease, they refused, arguing that the treatment may induce a spontaneous abortion, which was illegal under Nicaraguan law. *Id.*

448 *Id.*

449 Alvaro Paul, *Controversial Conceptions: The Unborn and the American Convention on Human Rights,* 9 Loy. U. Chi. Int'l L. Rev. 209, 235 (2012).

450 Gretel Artavia Murillo et al. (In Vitro Fertilization), Costa Rica, Case 12.361, Inter-Am. Comm. H.R., Report No. 85/10 (2010).

451 *Id.*

452 *Id.*

453 *Id.*

454 *Id.* at 96.

manifested through a series of cases in which the European Court of Human Rights deduced a woman's right to an abortion mainly from the right to privacy enshrined in Article 8 of the European Convention on Human Rights. However, the Court stated that abortion is not merely a matter of privacy, and therefore preventing a woman from having an abortion does not automatically violate Article 8 of the Convention.[455] In other words, according to the Court, preventing a woman from having an abortion, if she seeks the procedure for only serious and compelling reasons, could result in violating the right to privacy enshrined in Article 8 of the ECHR. For example, in life-threatening pregnancies, the Court frequently derived a woman's right to abortion from the right to privacy stated in Article 8 of the Convention.[456]

From a historical perspective, this study argues that the whole matter emerged gradually. Initially, the ECtHR did not make an overt decision advocating a woman's right to choose to have an abortion; however, over time, the Court started to uphold that right. In 2007, the Court, for the first time, declared its support for a woman's right to choose to terminate her pregnancy and have an abortion. This was the case of Tysiac v. Poland, where a pregnancy had a significant negative impact on the woman's health.[457] The Court clarified that the private life of a pregnant woman includes "physical and psychological integrity," and the State has to take necessary measures "to secure to its citizens their right to effective respect for this integrity."[458]

Later, in 2010, the Court recalled its decision in Tysiac, adopting a similar approach in A, B and C v. Ireland.[459] Concerning applicant C, whose life was threatened by pregnancy, the Court concluded that her right to privacy, protected in Article 8 of the ECHR, was violated.[460] The ECtHR reasoned that Article 8 of the Convention might impose on a State a positive obligation that requires the implementation of "specific measures in an abortion context."[461] Nevertheless, the Court had a different viewpoint concerning applicants A and B, who were banned from having the procedure while pregnant with malformed fetuses.[462] The Court decided that their prevention from having an abortion did not violate Article 8 of the Convention

455 Bruggemann, 6959/75, 10 Eur. Comm'n H.R, at 116.
456 Tysiac, 5410/03, 2007-IV Eur. Ct. H.R. at 107; *A., B. & C.*, 25579/ 05, 2010-Eur. Ct. H.R, at 244–45.
457 *Id.* at 9.
458 *Id.* at 107.
459 A., B., & C., 25579/ 05, Eur. Ct. H.R.
460 *Id.* at 244–45.
461 *Id.* at 245.
462 *Id.* at 216–26.

protecting the right to privacy or Article 3 protecting the right to be free from torture or degrading treatment or punishment.[463] The Court reasoned that the State has a wide "margin of appreciation" to choose between the two opposing values: the protection of applicants' private and family lives on the one side, and the respect of Irish people's morals protecting the unborn child's right to life on the other side.[464]

Unlike the previous case, one year later, in R.R. v. Poland, the Court declared that a woman's suffering from carrying an abnormal fetus should be entitled to the right to abortion.[465] In that case, the Court found that preventing a pregnant woman from having an abortion in the case of fetal deformity violated Article 8 of the ECHR, which imposes positive obligations upon states to secure individuals' right to "physical and psychological integrity."[466] It could be argued that the Court in R.R. v. Poland treated a pregnant woman who suffered from an abnormal fetus the same way it treated a woman whose life was endangered by pregnancy in the cases of Tysiac v. Poland and A, B and C v. Ireland. Furthermore, the Court found that R.R.'s psychological pain during her pregnancy because of her grave fears of giving birth to an abnormal child violated Article 3 of the ECHR protecting the right to be free from torture or degrading treatment or punishment.[467]

In short, the ECtHR has progressively ruled in favor of a woman's right to abortion and against the fetus's right to life. Based on the right to privacy, the Court regularly granted a woman the right to an abortion in the event of a life-threatening pregnancy, and subsequently granted her the right to an abortion in the case of an abnormal fetus. Furthermore, the Court recently used Article 3 of the ECHR, protecting the right to be free from torture or degrading treatment, to give a woman the right to an abortion. This demonstrates that the Court's pro-choice stance has developed over time.

On the other hand, it could be argued that the Inter-American system of human rights is the most protective system for the fetus's right to life. This argument is based on Article 4 of the American Convention, protecting the right to life from the moment of conception and stipulating that "no one shall be arbitrarily deprived of his life."[468] Nevertheless, in its 1981 report, the Inter-American Commission on Human Rights refuted this argument, declaring that the American Convention could not be applied to prevent a woman from having an abortion; rather, a woman is permitted to have legal

---

463 *Id.* at 164, 230.
464 *Id.* at 230.
465 R.R., 27617/04, Eur. Ct. H.R, at 211.
466 *Id.* at 185.
467 *Id.* at 151–60.
468 American Convention, *supra* note 399, art. 4.

access to abortion under compelling circumstances.[469] What is more confusing in the Inter-American system is that the Inter-American Court of Human Rights described the fetus as a "child,"[470] a "minor,"[471] or a "family member."[472] Although the Court has not yet issued a decision regarding abortion applying Article 4 of the Convention, its portrayal of the fetus could be a foundation for pro-life advocates to support the unborn child's right to life and, as a result, prevent women from terminating their pregnancies and having abortions.

2 Abortion under American Law

In the United States of America, the ban on abortion developed gradually.[473] Initially, abortion was legal in the early stages of pregnancy.[474] However, Connecticut took the initiative and outlawed abortion in 1821.[475] The State's ban on abortion was inspired by a law passed in England in 1803 that made abortion illegal after quickening.[476] New York was the second State to ban abortion, classifying post-quickening abortions as felonies and pre-quickening abortions as misdemeanors.[477]

In the middle of the nineteenth century, several states enacted statutes banning abortion, except to save a pregnant woman's life.[478] Most of these states focused more on abortions after quickening than before quickening.[479] By 1960, the great majority of the American states had adopted statutes banning abortion.[480] In addition, the penalty for abortion began to increase regardless of the period of pregnancy. However, abortion was only allowed to protect a pregnant woman's life.[481]

469 1981 Rep., Inter-Am. Comm'n on Human Rights, *supra* note 407.
470 Inter-Am. Ct. H.R. (ser. C) No. 160, *supra* note 416, at 292.
471 Inter-Am. Ct. H.R. (ser. C) No. 146, *supra* note 413, at 177.
472 Inter-Am. Ct. H.R. (ser. C) No. 110, *supra* note 409, at 216.
473 Roe, 410 U.S. at 138.
474 *Id.*
475 Conn. Gen. Stat. § 20, 14 (1821), *cited in* Roe, 410 U.S. at 138.
476 *Id.*
477 N.Y. Rev. Stat., pt. 4, ch. 1, tit. 2, art. 1, § 9, 661, and tit. 6 § 21, 694, (1829), *cited in* Roe, 410 U.S. at 138.
478 *See, e.g.*, Me. Rev. Stat. Ann. ch. 160, §§ 13–14 (1840); Mo. Rev. Stat. § 10 (1835), quoted in *The Evolution of the Right to Privacy after Roe v. Wade*, 13 Am. J. L. & Med. 368, 371 (1987).
479 *Id.*
480 Roe, 410 U.S. at 139.
481 *Id.*

In 1962, the American Law Institute issued a Model Penal Code,[482] under which abortion was permitted in three cases: (1) if a woman was gravely endangered by pregnancy'[483] (2) if the fetus had a serious defect,[484] and (3) if a pregnancy was a result of rape or incest.[485]

Nevertheless, some liberal movements and trends supported a woman's right to choose abortion.[486] These trends were based on scientific standards.[487] For example, in 1970, the American Medical Association (AMA) considered abortion a safe medical procedure that did not violate its medical principles.[488] According to these views, a woman may still be forced to undergo risky and unlawful abortion treatments, notwithstanding the Model Penal Code.[489]

A *The Legal Basis of Women's Right to Abortion*

The right to abortion was derived from the right to privacy, which was derived from the right to freedom of choice enshrined in the Fifth[490] and the Fourteenth[491] Amendments to the American Constitution.[492] The issue was divided into two stages. First, the Supreme Court expanded the right to freedom of choice to include the right to privacy.[493] Second, in the well-known

482 Model Penal Code 230.3 (Proposed Draft 1962). According to the Penal Code, "abortion is allowed by a licensed physician under the following circumstances:" (1)" if the physician believes that there is a substantial risk to the mother's health or that her mental health would severely deteriorate if pregnancy were to continue; or (2) if the child would be born seriously crippled in mind or body; or (3) if the pregnancy were the result of forcible rape or incest." (quoted in *The Evolution of the Right to Privacy, supra* note 478, at 33).

483 *Id.* at 1.

484 *Id.* at 2.

485 *Id.* at 3.

486 *The Evolution of the Right to Privacy, supra* note 478, at 37.

487 *Id.*

488 American Med. Ass'n, Proceedings of the Ama House of Delegates 220 (June 1970), *cited in* Roe, 410 U.S. at 143–44.

489 *The Evolution of the Right to Privacy, supra* note 478, at 37.

490 U.S. Const. amend. v:

> No person shall be held to answer for a capital, or otherwise infamous crime, unless on a presentment or indictment of a grand jury, except in cases arising in the land or naval forces, or in the militia, when in actual service in time of war or public danger; nor shall any person be subject for the same offense to be twice put in jeopardy of life or limb; nor shall be compelled in any criminal case to be a witness against himself, nor be deprived of life, liberty, or property, without due process of law; nor shall private property be taken for public use, without just compensation.

491 *Id.* amend. xiv(1) (stipulating that no person should be deprived of his right to "life, liberty, or property, without due process of law").

492 Tamara F. Kushnir, *Comment: It's My Body, It's My Choice: The Partial-Birth Abortion Ban Act of 2003*, 35 Loy. U. Chi. L.J. 1117, 20 (2004).

493 Griswold v. Connecticut, 381 U.S. 479 (1965).

case of Roe v. Wade,[494] the Supreme Court granted women, for the first time, the right to an abortion, considering it a regular exercise of their right to privacy.[495]

i Freedom of Choice Cases

The U.S. Supreme Court recognizes freedom of choice as a fundamental right.[496] Through its decisions, it emphasizes that any legislation should not violate the right to freedom of choice.[497] The Court often conducts a scrutiny analysis to examine whether the State has a compelling interest in enforcing legislation that restricts the freedom of choice.[498] If this requirement is met, the legislation must be narrowly tailored to serve the state's compelling interests and impose the least possible restrictions on an individual's fundamental freedom of choice.[499]

The study will discuss two cases embodying the right to freedom of choice regarding education. The first case is Meyer v. Nebraska,[500] in which the Supreme Court declared the unconstitutionality of a statute preventing students from learning in the German language and forcing them to learn in English only.[501] The second case is Pierce v. Society of Sisters, in which the Supreme Court held that the fundamental right to freedom of choice related to education should be reaffirmed.[502] It declared the unconstitutionality of a statute that prevented students from attending private schools and required them to attend only public schools.[503] In both cases, the Court's decisions were based on the Fourteenth Amendment of the Constitution protecting the fundamental right to freedom of choice.[504] In other words, the Court declared the unconstitutionality of statutes restricting the right to freedom of choice in both cases where there was no compelling state interest.[505]

In a third case, Skinner v. Oklahoma,[506] the fundamental right to freedom of choice was once again upheld; the Supreme Court declared the

494 Roe, 410 U.S. 113.
495 *Id.* at 164.
496 Pierce v. Soc'y of Sisters, 268 U.S. 510, 534–35 (1925); Meyer v. Nebraska, 262 U.S. 390, 403 (1923).
497 *Id.*
498 Kushnir, *supra* note 492, at 1121.
499 *Id.* (citing United States R.R. Ret. Bd. v. Fritz, 449 U.S. 166, 175 (1980); Craig v. Boren, 429 U.S. 190, 197 (1976)).
500 Meyer, 262 U.S. 390.
501 *Id.* at 403.
502 Pierce, 268 U.S. 510.
503 *Id.* at 535.
504 Meyer, 262 U.S. at 403; Pierce, 268 U.S. at 535.
505 *Id.*
506 Skinner v. Oklahoma, 316 U.S. 535 (1942).

unconstitutionality of a law enforcing sterilization of persons who had committed two crimes involving moral turpitude.[507] In addition, the Court stated that an individual has the full right to choose whether to have children or not, without interference from the State.[508]

ii The Modern Right to Privacy as Defined by the Supreme Court

a *Justice Harlan's Dissent in Poe v. Ullman (1961)*

Poe v. Ullman[509] was the first case in which the right to privacy appeared.[510] Although such a right was not elucidated in the majority ruling of the Court, Justice Harlan's dissent argued that the right to privacy could be deduced from principles of the Third[511], Fourth[512], and Fourteenth Amendments of the Constitution.[513] In that case, based on the right to privacy, Justice Harlan suggested the unconstitutionality of a Connecticut statute banning the use of contraceptives.[514]

b *Griswold v. Connecticut (1965)*

In Griswold v. Connecticut,[515] the Supreme Court for the first time acknowledged the protection of the right to privacy.[516] To begin with, the Connecticut Statute prevented the use of contraceptives and the assistance of others in their use.[517] The appellants were doctors who recommended contraceptives for married couples.[518] The majority opinion of the Court, written by Justice Douglas, held that the Statute violated married couples' right to privacy.[519] The Court deduced the right to privacy from the scope of guarantees

---

507 *Id.* at 535.
508 *Id.*
509 Poe v. Ullman, 367 U.S. 497 (1961).
510 *Id.* at 536 (Harlan, J., dissenting).
511 U.S. Const. amend. III (No soldier should be quartered in any house except in cases of emergency).
512 *Id.* amend. IV (banning unreasonable seizures and searches).
513 *Id.* amend. XIV(1) (protecting the right to life, liberty, property, and due process).
514 Poe v. Ullman, 367 U.S. 497, 505 (1961) (Harlan, J., dissenting). The majority opinion of the Court did not discuss the constitutionality of the Connecticut statute and ruled that none of the plaintiffs' submitted events presented a justiciable issue. According to the majority opinion, the plaintiffs failed to demonstrate that they were stakeholders in the case and that they were harmed by the criminalization of contraceptive use. *Id.* at 504–05.
515 Griswold v. Connecticut, 381 U.S. 479 (1965).
516 Debra L. Dippel, *Someone to Watch over Me: Medical Decision Making for Hopelessly Ill Incompetent Adult Patients*, 24 Akron L. Rev. 639, 644 (1991).
517 Griswold, 381 U.S. at 480.
518 *Id.*
519 *Id.* at 485.

enshrined in the Bill of Rights.[520] The Court reasoned that the right to privacy could be derived in light of the penumbras of the First,[521] Third,[522] Fourth,[523] Fifth,[524] and Ninth[525] Amendments of the Constitution. To support its argument, the Court cited the case of NAACP v. State of Alabama,[526] in which it broadened the scope of the First Amendment to include the right to freedom of association.[527]

The Court further noted that state regulations must not violate the intimate relationships between wives and husbands where medical consultancies play a significant role in supporting and enhancing such relationships.[528] In addition, the Court described that relationship as having a sacred nature.[529] Although the majority opinion of the Court decided the unconstitutionality of the Connecticut Statute because it violated the individual's right to privacy,[530] this decision was followed by three concurrences and two dissents.[531]

The first concurrence was written by Justice Goldberg and was based on the Ninth Amendment of the American Constitution, stating that rights guaranteed by the Constitution are not limited to those explicitly listed as protected.[532] The Ninth Amendment clarifies that the Constitution does not merely protect rights specifically enumerated in the Bill of Rights; rather, other rights, such as the right to privacy, could be granted protection.[533] According to his view, the Ninth Amendment was "proffered to quiet expressed fears that a bill of specifically enumerated rights could not be sufficiently broad to cover all essential rights and that the specific mention

520 *Id.* at 484.

521 U.S. Const. amend. I (Congress should not promulgate laws respecting an establishment of religion, or banning the free practice of religion ... and the right of people to peaceably assemble should be protected...).

522 *Id.* amend. III.

523 *Id.* amend. IV.

524 *Id.* amend. V (protecting the right to freedom from self-incrimination).

525 *Id.* amend. IX ("The enumeration in the Constitution, of certain rights, shall not be construed to deny or disparage others retained by the people.").

526 NAACP v. State of Alabama, 351 U.S. 449 (1958).

527 Griswold, 381 U.S. at 483 (citing NAACP, 351 U.S. at 462).

528 *Id.* at 482.

529 *Id.*

530 *Id.* at 485–86.

531 *See id.* at 480–86; *id.* at 486–99 (Golberg, J., concurring); *id.* at 499–502 (Harlan, J. concurring); *id.* at 502–07 (White, J., concurring); *id.* at 507–27 (Black, J., dissenting); *id.* at 527–31 (Stewart, J., dissenting).

532 *Id.* at 488 (Goldberg, J., concurring).

533 U.S. Const. amend. IX.

of certain rights would be interpreted as a denial that others were protected."[534] In short, Justice Goldberg concluded that "the right of privacy in the marital relation is fundamental" and could be granted to people "within the [context] of the Ninth Amendment."[535]

The second concurrence was written by Justice Harlan,[536] whose view was mainly based on the text of the Fourteenth Amendment's Due Process Clause stating that states should not violate individuals' right to liberty.[537] According to his view, the "Connecticut statute infringes the Due Process Clause of the Fourteenth Amendment because the enactment violates basic values implicit in the concept of ordered liberty."[538] He added that judicial restraint, in light of interpreting the Fourteenth Amendment's Due Process Clause, must be in accord with the teachings of history and the basic values dominating the society.[539] Furthermore, it must not violate the doctrines of federalism or the principle of separation of powers.[540]

The third concurrence by Justice White agreed with the previous conclusion that the Connecticut Statute violated the Fourteenth Amendment's Due Process Clause.[541] His argument was not based on the violation of the right to privacy; rather, he saw that the Connecticut Statute was overbroad to the extent that it violated the "right to liberty without due process of law, as that concept is used in the Fourteenth Amendment."[542] He affirmed that in the "realm of family life ... the state cannot enter without substantial justification."[543] In addition, the State does not have an interest in banning the use of contraceptives because the Connecticut Statute, as applied to married couples, does not prohibit sexual relations.[544]

534 Griswold, 381 U.S. at 488–89 (Goldberg, J., concurring).
535 *Id.* at 489 (Goldberg, J., concurring).
536 Griswold, 381 U.S. at 500 (Harlan, J., concurring).
537 U.S. Const. amend. XIV(1) (affirming that states should not deprive any person of life, liberty, or property, without due process of law).
538 Griswold, 381 U.S. at 500 (Harlan, J., concurring).
539 *Id.* at 501 (Harlan, J., concurring).
540 *Id.* (Harlan, J., concurring).
541 *Id.* at 502 (White, J., concurring).
542 *Id.* (White, J., concurring).
543 *Id.* (White, J., concurring).
544 *Id.* at 505 (White, J., concurring).

The two dissents were written by Justices Stewart and Black.[545] According to their view, the Bill of Rights comprises an exhaustive list.[546] Since the right to privacy is not explicitly stated in the Bill of Rights, such a right cannot be protected. Besides, if the drafters intended to protect the right to privacy, the Bill of Rights would include it expressly.[547] According to Justice Black's view, the Constitutional standards are fixed and unchangeable.[548] On the other hand, Justice Stewart affirmed that "the function of this Court [is not] to decide cases on the basis of community standards, [but] to decide cases agreeably to the Constitution and laws of the United States."[549]

c *Eisenstadt v. Baird (1972)*

Eisenstadt v. Baird[550] was decided seven years after Griswold. A Massachusetts statute banned the use of contraceptives for unmarried persons and permitted it for married couples.[551] The Court used the same rationale as in Griswold.[552] It declared that the Massachusetts statute should not violate the right to privacy of persons whether they are married or not.[553] According to the Court, "If under Griswold the distribution of contraceptives to married persons cannot be prohibited, a ban on distribution to unmarried

---

545 *Id.* at 507 (Black, J., dissenting) (stating that "there is no single one of the graphic and eloquent strictures and criticisms fired at the policy of this Connecticut law either by the Court's opinion or by those of my concurring Brethren to which I cannot subscribe – except their conclusion that the evil qualities they see in the law make it unconstitutional."); *id.* at 527 (Stewart, J., dissenting). Stewart stated in his dissent:

> I think professional counsel about methods of birth control should be available to all, so that each individual's choice can be meaningfully made. But we are not asked in this case to say whether we think this law is unwise, or even asinine. We are asked to hold that it violates the United States Constitution. And that I cannot do.

Id.

546 *Id.* at 527 (Black, J., dissenting) (stating that "Connecticut's law as applied here is not forbidden by any provision of the Federal Constitution as that Constitution was written ...."); *id.* at 528 (Stewart, J., dissenting) ("I can find nothing in any of [the Amendments] to invalidate this Connecticut law, even assuming that all those Amendments are fully applicable against the States.").

547 *Id.*

548 *Id.* at 522 (Black, J., dissenting).

549 *Id.* at 530 (Stewart, J., dissenting).

550 Eisenstadt v. Baird, 405 U.S. 438 (1972).

551 *Id.* at 454–55.

552 *Id.* at 453.

553 *Id.* ("If the right of privacy means anything, it is the right of the individual, married or single, to be free from unwarranted governmental intrusion into matters so fundamentally affecting a person as the decision whether to bear or beget a child.").

persons would be equally impermissible."[554] The Court's decision was based on the violation of the Equal Protection Clause of the Fourteenth Amendment.[555] The Court stated that any statute circumventing Griswold's ruling is unconstitutional.[556]

d *Roe v. Wade (1973)*

Roe v. Wade[557] is the landmark case in the area of reproductive rights, in which the Supreme Court recognized the right to abortion as a fundamental right.[558] The facts of the case started when an unmarried pregnant woman challenged the constitutionality of Texas abortion laws allowing abortion only if pregnancy jeopardizes a woman's life.[559] The District Court for the Northern District of Texas struck down that law as unconstitutional.[560] In 1973, the Supreme Court upheld that ruling, declaring that the fundamental right to privacy includes a woman's right to choose whether or not to have an abortion.[561]

The Supreme Court's ruling was based on the violation of the Fourteenth Amendment's Due Process Clause. The Supreme Court held that any legislation regulating abortion should be justified by a compelling state interest.[562] Because the American Constitution does not provide any protection for the lives of unborn children,[563] the Court determined a point at which the interest of the State becomes compelling to ban abortions.[564] This point was viability, "which is usually placed at about seven months (28 weeks) but may occur earlier, even at 24 weeks."[565] At viability, the unborn child can live and grow outside a woman's uterus, and therefore the state's interest becomes compelling to protect potential human life.[566]

In addition, the Court affirmed that, regarding the health of the mother, the compelling point at which the State could interfere is after the end of

---

554 *Id.*
555 *Id.* at 454–55.
556 *Id.* at 450.
557 Roe v. Wade, 410 U.S. 113 (1973).
558 *Id.* at 164.
559 Tex. Penal Prob. Code Ann. arts. 1191–94, 1196, *cited in* Roe, 410 U.S. at 117.
560 Roe v. Wade, 314 F. Supp. 1217 (N.D. Tex. 1970).
561 Roe, 410 U.S. at 164.
562 *Id.* at 163.
563 *Id.* at 157.
564 *Id.* at 163.
565 *Id.* at 160.
566 *Id.* ("This is so because [according to medical facts,] the fetus then presumably has the capability of meaningful life outside the mother's womb. State regulation protective of fetal life after viability thus has both logical and biological justifications.").

the first trimester because, according to medical facts,[567] "until the end of the first trimester mortality in abortion may be less than mortality in normal childbirth."[568] Therefore, during the second trimester, states could regulate abortion for the protection and preservation of a woman's health.[569] Thus, the Court made a timetable dividing the period of pregnancy into three parts, or trimesters, taking into consideration the protection of a woman's health and life.[570]

During the first trimester, the Court stated that states have no interest in regulating abortion.[571] Thus, abortion at this time must be fully subjected to a pregnant woman's choice only.[572] During the second trimester, the Court reasoned that, despite the absence of viability, states could control abortion because they have a legitimate interest in protecting a woman's health.[573] During the third trimester, post-viability, the Court declared that states have a compelling interest in banning abortion to protect potential human life; however, abortion should be allowed in cases jeopardizing a pregnant woman's life or health.[574]

Moreover, the Court referred to the significant role played by medical professionals who offer advice to a pregnant woman.[575] According to the Court's decision, "if an individual practitioner abuses the privilege of exercising proper medical judgment, the usual remedies, judicial and intra-professional, are available."[576]

Justice Rehnquist's dissent affirmed that the majority exceeded its power as a judiciary and formulated a "rule of constitutional law broader than is

567 *Id.* at 149. The Court referred to Modern medical techniques stating that, prior to the end of the first trimester,

> mortality rates for women undergoing early abortions, where the procedure is legal, appear to be as low as or lower than the rates for normal childbirth. Consequently, any interest of the State in protecting the woman from an inherently hazardous procedure, except when it would be equally dangerous for her to forgo it, has largely disappeared.

Id.

568 *Id.*

569 *Id.*

570 *Id.* at 153.

571 *Id.* at 163.

572 *Id.*

573 Roe, 410 U.S. at 163.

574 *Id.* at 163–64 ("If the State is interested in protecting fetal life after viability, it may go so far as to proscribe abortion during that period, except when it is necessary to preserve the life or health of the mother").

575 *Id.* at 166.

576 Roe, 410 U.S. at 166.

required by the precise facts."[577] According to his view, before the adoption of the Fourteenth Amendment, on which the majority based their ruling, most of the states had issued statutes banning abortion.[578] Therefore, it is possible that the drafters of the Fourteenth Amendment did not intend for the legislation to extend to abortion.[579] In addition, he argued that the plaintiff, Roe, would not make use of such a ruling because "at the time of filing her complaint [, Roe] was a pregnant woman; for aught that appears in this record, she may have been in her last trimester of pregnancy as of the date the complaint was filed."[580]

Furthermore, Justice Rehnquist affirmed that the right to privacy could not be involved in this case because, in the precedents of the Court, such a right used to be relative to "the freedom from searches and seizures protected by the Fourth Amendment to the Constitution."[581]

iii Applications of Roe

In Doe v. Bolton,[582] the petitioners challenged a law permitting abortion in only three cases, as follows: (1) if a pregnancy jeopardizes a woman's health or life, (2) if the fetus suffers from a serious disorder, and (3) if a pregnancy is an outcome of rape.[583] In this case, the Supreme Court's decision was in favor of the petitioners, striking down the Statute on the basis of Roe v. Wade.[584] Thus, the Court reaffirmed that abortion law should not regulate the first trimester of pregnancy.

In Planned Parenthood v. Danforth,[585] the Supreme Court considered a law prohibiting a particular procedure of abortion, a woman's use of saline amniocentesis during the first trimester of pregnancy, as unconstitutional.[586] The Court stated that states have no legitimate interest in restricting a woman's choice to have an abortion during the first trimester of pregnancy.[587] In other words, the Court declared that any restriction on abortion during the first trimester constitutes a violation of Roe.[588]

---

577 *Id.* at 172. (Rehnquist, J., dissenting) (quoting New York & Philadelphia S. S. Co. v. Comm'rs of Emigration, 113 U.S. 33, 39 (1885)).
578 *Id.* (Rehnquist, J., dissenting).
579 *Id.*
580 *Id.* at 171 (Rehnquist, J., dissenting).
581 *Id.* at 172 (Rehnquist, J., dissenting) (quoting Katz *v.* United States, 389 U.S. 347 (1967)).
582 Doe v. Bolton, 410 U.S. 159 (1973).
583 *Id.*
584 *Id.* at 164.
585 Planned Parenthood of Cent. Mo. v. Danforth, 428 U.S. 52 (1976).
586 *Id.* at 79.
587 *Id.* at 76–79.
588 *Id.*

The Court upheld other laws requiring a woman's consent before having an abortion.[589] The Court did not find that such a requirement, even during the first trimester violated Roe.[590] The Court acknowledged that the State has a legitimate interest in promulgating such a statute, because women's "awareness of the decision [of abortion] and its significance may be assured."[591] According to the Court, the procedure was imperative and desirable because it helped a woman make her decision "with full knowledge of its nature and consequences."[592]

In Hodgson v. Minnesota,[593] the Court struck down a Minnesota abortion statute requiring pregnant minors to obtain consent from their parents before having an abortion.[594] The statute had a judicial bypass if an abortion without notice was in a pregnant minor's best interest.[595] The Court's decision was based on the obstacles the "statute places in the pregnant minor's path to an abortion."[596] Thus, the Court emphasized that the statute "cannot be sustained [under any analysis], if the obstacles it imposes are not reasonably related to legitimate state interests."[597]

In Maher v. Roe,[598] two women challenged Connecticut's statute limiting the funding for abortions that were not "medically necessary."[599] The Court upheld such a statute, considering it compatible with Roe.[600] It reasoned that there was "a basic difference between direct state interference with a protected activity and state encouragement of an alternative activity consonant with legislative policy."[601]

In City of Akron v. Akron Center for Reproductive Health,[602] the Court ruled that the requirement that doctors provide a woman with information and counseling regarding a pregnancy before performing an abortion was unconstitutional because it was "unreasonable for a state to insist that only a physician is competent to provide the information and counseling."[603] In addition, the Court deemed the requirement that physicians study specific

589 *Id.* at 65.
590 *Id.* at 66.
591 *Id.*
592 *Id.* at 67.
593 Hodgson v. Minnesota, 497 U.S. 417 (1990).
594 *Id.* at 435.
595 *Id.* at 427.
596 *Id.* at 436.
597 *Id.*
598 Maher v. Roe, 432 U.S. 464 (1977).
599 *Id.* at 467.
600 *Id.* at 475.
601 *Id.*
602 City of Akron v. Akron Ctr. for Reprod. Health, 462 U.S. 416 (1983).
603 *Id.* at 444.

materials addressing pregnancy and abortion before conducting abortions to be unconstitutional.[604] The Court considered such requirements as an "obstacle in the path of the doctor upon whom [a woman was] entitled to rely for advice in connection with her decision."[605] Thus, the Court declared the unconstitutionality of such procedures that represent a governmental intrusion into a woman's fundamental right to an abortion during the first trimester of pregnancy.[606]

iv Planned Parenthood v. Casey (1992)

In Planned Parenthood v. Casey,[607] the majority opinion, written by Justice O'Connor, moved away from Roe's trimester framework, while reaffirming the central holding of such a ruling that allowed states to restrict only post-viability abortion because their interest in potential life is compelling at that point.[608]

To reach this ruling, the Court revamped the trimester system because medical studies undermined the trimester analysis enshrined in Roe.[609] In addition, the Court adopted the undue burden standard, considering it the most appropriate means "of reconciling the State's interest with the woman's constitutionally protected liberty."[610]

The Court stated that states should not place an undue burden concerning pre-viability abortion on a pregnant woman's path to an abortion.[611] According to the Court, "viability marks the earliest point at which the State's interest in fetal life is constitutionally adequate to justify a legislative ban on nontherapeutic abortions."[612] The Court stipulated that the point of the fetus's viability is not fixed; rather, a doctor treating a pregnant woman should determine it.[613]

This ruling reaffirmed Roe's holding regarding the protection of a woman's life or health.[614] The Court reaffirmed that a woman, at any time of

604 *Id.* at 445.
605 *Id.*
606 *Id.*
607 Planned Parenthood v. Casey, 505 U.S. 833 (1992).
608 *Id.* at 846.
609 *Id.* at 873.
610 *Id.* at 877.
611 *Id.* at 860.
612 *Id.*
613 *Id.*
614 *Id.* at 879.

pregnancy, should have access to an abortion if her life or health is jeopardized by pregnancy.[615] According to the Court, "the State in promoting its interest in the potentiality of human life may, if it chooses, regulate, and even proscribe, abortion except where it is necessary, in appropriate medical judgment, for the preservation of the life or health of the mother."[616]

In addition, the Court reaffirmed that the right to privacy is protected under the Fourteenth Amendment's Due Process Clause.[617] In other words, since the State has no compelling interest in regulating abortions during the first trimester of pregnancy, the Supreme Court concluded that a woman has the absolute right to make this decision as a private matter without intervention from the government.

Justice Rehnquist's dissent was based on two lines of argument. First, Roe's case was erroneously decided because the right to privacy could not be applicable to abortion.[618] He added that a woman cannot have the right to abortion because the decision is not related to her alone; rather, it is more related to the fetus.[619] According to his view, "[o]ne cannot ignore the fact that a woman is not isolated in her pregnancy, and that the decision to abort necessarily involves the destruction of a fetus."[620] Second, Justice Rehnquist argued that the core of Casey's case was different from that of Roe.[621] The central point of Casey was abortion regulation, whereas the core of Roe was abortion prohibition.[622] Thus, there was no need to discuss or reaffirm Roe's ruling.[623] He added that the majority ruling lacked the use of "stare decisis" because it upheld Roe's core finding while ignoring a critical aspect of the ruling, the trimester system.[624]

v Stenberg v. Carhart (2000)

Stenberg v. Carhart[625] is considered one of the most significant cases with regard to abortion under American law. In that case, the Supreme

615 *Id.*
616 *Id.* (quoting Roe, 410 U.S. at 164–65).
617 *Id.* at 847.
618 *Id.* at 944 (Rehnquist, J., dissenting).
619 *Id.* at 952 (Rehnquist, J., dissenting).
620 *Id.* (Rehnquist, J., dissenting).
621 *Id.* (Rehnquist, C.J., dissenting).
622 *Id.* at 944 (Rehnquist, C.J., dissenting).
623 *Id.* (Rehnquist, C.J., dissenting).
624 *Id.* at 944 (Rehnquist, C.J., dissenting); *id.* at 993 (Scalia, J., dissenting).
625 Stenberg v. Carhart, 530 U.S. 914 (2000).

Court ruled that Nebraska Statute,[626] banning partial birth abortion was unconstitutional.[627]

Before discussing the case, the study will briefly explain the medical procedures that were cited in the Court's reasoning, as follows:

During the first trimester of pregnancy, physicians always use D & C Procedures, Dilation and Suction Curettage.[628] This method is called Vacuum Aspiration; it is the safest and most common form of abortion and it typically does not cause any complications.[629] After the first trimester, the most commonly used method is D & E, Dilation and Evacuation.[630] Using this procedure, because fetal tissues are friable and easily broken into tiny pieces, physicians do not remove the fetus intact and are obliged to check the uterus to ensure that no fetal tissues remain.[631]

After the fifteenth week of pregnancy, two different methods are used, intact D & E and D & X procedures, that is, Dilation and Extraction.[632] Both methods employ the non-medical term, partial birth abortion that Nebraska Statute bans. Since intact D & E and D & X procedures are similar, the Court indicated that it would use both terms "interchangeably."[633] Intact D & E procedure "involves removing the fetus from the uterus through the cervix intact, *i.e.*, in one pass, rather than in several passes. It is used after sixteen weeks at the earliest, as vacuum aspiration becomes ineffective and the fetal skull becomes too large to pass through the cervix."[634] Physicians use this procedure if the skull of the fetus is "too large to pass through the cervix."[635] This procedure has two variations depending on the fetus's "presentation" inside a woman's uterus. "If the fetus presents head first (a vertex presentation), the doctor collapses the skull; and the doctor then extracts the entire fetus through the cervix." On the other hand, "If the fetus presents

626 Neb. Rev. Stat. § 28–328(1) (1999). ("No partial birth abortion shall be performed in this state, unless such procedure is necessary to save the life of the mother whose life is endangered by a physical disorder, physical illness, or physical injury, including a life-endangering physical condition caused by or arising from the pregnancy itself.").

627 Stenberg, 530 U.S. at 922.

628 *Id.* at 923 (citing Ctrs. for Disease Control & Prevention, *Abortion Surveillance - United States, 1996*, MMWR Weekly, at 41 (July 30, 1999)).

629 *Id.*

630 *Id.* at 924–25.

631 *Id.*

632 *Id.* at 928.

633 *Id.* (stating that "intact D&E and D&X are sufficiently similar for us to use the terms interchangeably").

634 *Id.* at 927.

635 *Id.*

feet first (a breech presentation), the doctor pulls the fetal body through the cervix, collapses the skull, and extracts the fetus through the cervix."[636]

According to the majority opinion of the Court, the Nebraska Statute was unconstitutional for several reasons: (1) in certain cases, D & X procedure might have greater benefits than other methods of abortion[637]; (2) the Statute lacked a health exception allowing a woman to undergo abortion, at any time, if a pregnancy jeopardized her health[638]; (3) the Nebraska Statute might impose an undue burden on a woman seeking a pre-viability abortion because its language did not clearly differentiate between the banned D & X and other abortion procedures.[639]

---

636 *Id.*

637 *Id.* at 931–46.

638 *Id.* at 930–46. The absence of a health exception in any statute regulating abortion is considered a violation of the two precedents, Roe and Casey, in which the Supreme Court required that all abortion laws include a health exception. Roe, 410 U.S. at 164–65; Casey, 505 U.S. at 879.

639 *Id.* at 930. The State of Nebraska tried to prove the constitutionality of this Statute using the following eight lines of argument: First, the State argued that women rarely undergo the D & X method; thus, it was not necessary for the Statute to contain a health exception. *Id.* at 933. Second, the State claimed that just a few doctors use the procedure. *Id.* Third, the State contended "that D&E and labor induction are at all times safe alternative procedures"; therefore, there was no need for a woman to resort to the prohibited procedure, D&X. *Id.* Fourth, the prohibition of D & X method would not increase women's "risk of several rare abortion complications." *Id.* Fifth, the elements of D & X procedures have their own special risks that are not present in other procedures. *Id.* Sixth, no studies have confirmed the safety of the D & X technique. *Id.* Seventh, the State adopted the view of the American Medical Association (AMA) that the D & X method was not the only appropriate procedure for abortion. *Id.* at 944 (citing the AMA statement stating that "there does not appear to be any identified situation in which intact D&X is the only acceptable procedure to induce abortion.") AMA Policy H-5.982 (1997). Eighth, the State adopted the statement of the American College of Obstetricians and Gynecologists that circumstances never required that D & X method be the only option to protect and maintain a woman's life and health; therefore, a woman should have alternative solutions to D & X. *Id.*

The Court found all of these lines of argument insufficient. Refuting the first and second arguments, the Court indicated that they are not "highly relative" because the State could not prevent a woman from obtaining a certain treatment, claiming that a woman or a doctor rarely uses it. *Id.*

In response to the third argument, the Court relied on the District Court's reasoning that the D & X procedure, in some cases, would be safer for a woman than other methods. *Id.* The fourth argument was rejected by the Court on the grounds that other expert testimony indicated that prohibiting the D & X procedure would increase the risk of a number of rare abortion complications. This testimony stated that "another advantage of the intact D&E [D&X] is that it eliminates the risk of embolism of cerebral tissue into the woman's blood stream." *Id.* at 935. (quoting Hearing on H. R. 1833 before

The Court reaffirmed Roe and Casey regarding the preservation of a woman's health declaring the unconstitutionality of any statute that lacks a health exception for a woman.[640] In addition, the Court preferred to permit the D & X procedure in spite of the absence of medical consensus, and therefore federal courts would not leave a "margin of error for legislatures to act in the face of medical uncertainty."[641]

B *The Partial-Birth Abortion Ban Act of 2003*

Although the Nebraska statute was unconstitutional, Congress made several attempts to pass similar legislation.[642] In 1995, fifty-four percent of senators voted in favor of a draft law banning partial birth abortion.[643] Thus, the approval percentage did not exceed two-thirds of senators. Therefore, the draft did not overturn the presidential veto, and President Clinton vetoed it due to the absence of a health exemption for a pregnant woman.[644] In 1997, Congress attempted to pass similar legislation again, but it never received more than two-thirds of the vote and was subject to the presidential veto.[645] It was vetoed once again by President Clinton.[646]

In 2002, Congress reintroduced another bill to prohibit partial birth abortions, but it failed to obtain the support of more than two-thirds of

---

the Senate Committee on the Judiciary, 104th Cong., 1st Sess., 260 (1995) (statement of W. Hern).

In relation to the fifth argument, D & X poses unique risks; the Court relied on the view of the American College of Obstetricians and Gynecologists that other methods would pose greater risks than D & X. *Id.* As for the sixth argument that no studies confirm the safety of the D & X procedure, the Court did not reject the argument; rather, it stated that medical studies did not convince the Court of the necessity of the banned procedure. *Id.* In rejecting both the seventh and the eighth arguments that D & X was never the only appropriate procedure for an abortion and that circumstances never required D & X to be the only solution for a woman, the Court simply stated that medical testimonies mattered but were contradictory. *Id.*

640 *Id.* at 930–46.

641 Gonzales v. Carhart, 127 S. Ct. 1610, 1638 (2007) (Ginsburg, J., dissenting).

642 Alex Gordon, *The Partial-Birth Abortion Ban Act of 2003*, 41 Harv. J. Legis. 501 (2004).

643 Alissa Schecter, *Note: Choosing Balance: Congressional Powers and the Partial-Birth Abortion Ban Act of 2003*, 73 Fordham L. Rev. 1987, 1997 (2005) (citing Senate Bill Clerk, U.S. Senate Roll Call Votes 104th Congress, 1st Session, at http://www.senate.gov/legislative/LIS/roll call lists/roll call vote cfm.cfm?congress=104&session=1&vote=00596 (clarifying that the two-thirds percentage could place a draft law into force without being subject to the presidential veto).

644 Kushnir, *supra* note 492, at 1149 (citing Carol Jouzaitis, *Clinton Vetoes Late-term Abortion Curb*, Chi. Trib., Apr. 11, 1996, at 3).

645 *Id.* at 1150.

646 *Id.*

senators.[647] After being subjected to President Bush's approval, he signed the bill into law.[648] The PBABA of 2003 was subsequently promulgated. It stated that "any physician who, in or affecting interstate or foreign commerce, knowingly performs a partial-birth abortion and thereby kills a human fetus shall be fined under this title or imprisoned not more than two years, or both. This subsection does not apply to a partial-birth abortion that is necessary to save the life of a mother whose life is endangered by a physical disorder, physical illness, or physical injury, including a life-endangering physical condition caused by or arising from the pregnancy itself. This subsection takes effect one day after the enactment."[649] Thus, the PBABA lacked a health exception for women, as it only provided an exception for life-threatening pregnancies.[650]

To prove its capacity to issue the PBABA, Congress included a section of findings at the end of the Act.[651] In this Section, Congress cited the Supreme Court's rulings in Anderson v. Bessemer City,[652] Katzenbach v. Morgan,[653] and Turner Broadcasting System, Inc. v. FCC cases, as precedents.[654] Thus, the Supreme Court would afford great deference to such findings.[655]

In the first case, Anderson, the petitioner was not recruited as a recreation director.[656] She filed a complaint alleging that she was not hired due to her gender.[657] The trial court ruled in favor of the petitioner reasoning that she was the best candidate.[658] On the other hand, the court of appeals concluded that the trial court's findings were "clearly erroneous."[659] Therefore, it ruled against the petitioner, stating that she was not the most qualified candidate for the position.[660] Nevertheless, the Supreme Court declared that the court of appeals incorrectly used the "clearly erroneous" standard.[661] The Supreme Court emphasized that appellate courts should

647 *Id.* at 1151.
648 *Id.* at 1118.
649 Partial-Birth Abortion Ban Act of 2003, Pub. L. No. 108–105, §3(a), 117 Stat. 1201, 1206.
650 *Id.*
651 *Id.* at § 2.
652 Anderson v. Bessemer City, 470 U.S. 564 (1985).
653 Katzenbach v. Morgan, 384 U.S. 641 (1966).
654 Turner Broad. Sys., Inc. v. FCC, 512 U.S. 622 (1994) [hereinafter Turner I]; Turner Broad. Sys., Inc. v. FCC, 520 U.S. 180 (1997).
655 Partial-Birth Abortion Ban Act § 2(6), (9), (11).
656 Anderson, 470 U.S. at 566.
657 *Id.* at 567.
658 *Id.* at 570.
659 *Id.* at 571.
660 *Id.*
661 *Id.* at 580–81.

accept the determinations of trial courts unless they have a "firm conviction" that these determinations were "clearly erroneous."[662] Thus, Congress relied on the "clearly erroneous" standard in order to require courts to accord substantial deference to its PBABA determinations.[663]

In the second case, Katzenbach v. Morgan, Congress passed a law in 1965 providing that states should not require English literacy as a condition for voters in elections.[664] In evaluating the constitutionality of such a law, the Supreme Court found that Congress had a margin of appreciation to choose between two conflicting interests.[665] The first was the interest of the State in encouraging Spanish speakers to learn English; the second was the interest of American Spanish speakers in exercising their fundamental right to vote.[666] The Court affirmed that Congress might choose to support one interest over the other in accordance with its own perception.[667] Thus, the Court upheld the constitutionality of the law.[668] Congress included this case in the PBABA's section of findings as a deferential standard for courts.[669]

The last two cases emphasized by Congress to prove its capacity to legislate the PBABA were Turner Broadcasting System, Inc. v. FCC cases (Turner I)[670] and (Turner II).[671] In Turner I, the Supreme Court evaluated the constitutionality of a law enforcing cable companies to carry a certain number of television stations.[672] The Court ruled that the law was constitutional, declaring that congressional findings of facts should be accorded great deference.[673] Similarly, in Turner II, the Supreme Court reaffirmed that Congress's factual findings should be afforded great deference.[674]

662 *Id.*
663 Partial-Birth Abortion Ban Act of 2003 § 2(6). In applying the clearly erroneous standard to the PBABA, and in the absence of medical consensus ensuring the safety of D&X procedure, Congress has the capacity to make a decision based on its own factual findings. In addition, federal courts should accept the findings of Congress unless they have a firm conviction that its assessment of the facts was clearly erroneous.
664 Katzenbach, 384 U.S. at 643.
665 *Id.* at 655–56.
666 *Id.*
667 *Id.* at 653.
668 *Id.* at 657–58.
669 Partial-Birth Abortion Ban Act § 2(9).
670 Turner I, 512 U.S. 622, 630 (1994).
671 Turner II, 520 U.S. 180, 185 (1997).
672 Turner I, 512 U.S. at 634.
673 *Id.* at 665.
674 Turner II, 520 U.S. at 195.

C *Gonzales v. Carhart* (2007)

In Gonzales v. Carhart, the Supreme Court upheld the constitutionality of the PBABA, affirming that it was neither unconstitutionally vague nor posed an impediment to a woman seeking a pre-viability abortion.[675]

In the majority opinion, Justice Kennedy reiterated the Court's commitment to Roe's three basic standards, which were reaffirmed in Casey:

1) Before viability, a woman should have the full right to choose whether to have an abortion without any interference from the State since it has no compelling interest to ban abortion at that time.
2) Reaffirming the state's power to circumscribe abortions after fetal viability for the protection and preservation of women's health or life.
3) Confirming that the State has a legitimate interest in protecting women's health and the fetus's life.[676]

The Supreme Court found that the PBABA was not vague because it specified illegal operations and explicitly distinguished between prospective criminal conduct and lawful abortion treatments.[677] The Court held that the CRC did not prohibit D & E procedures and that physicians facing criminal charges must meet two conditions:

1) performing the D & X procedure on purpose.
2) Performing an overt act other than completing the delivery that kills the partially delivered, still-alive fetus.[678]

According to the Court, the PBABA is different from the Nebraska Statute because it "provides doctors of ordinary intelligence a reasonable opportunity to know what is prohibited,"[679] then it "defines the unlawful abortion in explicit terms."[680] In addition, the Court reasoned that a physician would

---

675 Gonzales v. Carhart, 127 S. Ct. 1610 (2007).
676 *Id.* at 1626 (quoting Casey, 505 U.S. at 864).
677 *Id.* at 1627–28.
678 *Id.* at 1629.
679 *Id.* at 1628.
680 *Id.* at 1627. The PBABA defines illegal abortion

> as an abortion in which the person performing the abortion...
>
> (A) deliberately and intentionally vaginally delivers a living fetus until, in the case of a head-first presentation, the entire fetal head is outside the body of the mother, or, in the case of breech presentation, any part of the fetal trunk past the navel is outside the body of the mother, for the purpose of performing an overt act that the person knows will kill the partially delivered living fetus; and
>
> (B) performs the overt act, other than completion of delivery, that kills the partially delivered living fetus.

Partial-Birth Abortion Ban Act, § B(1).

avoid criminal liability by performing the D & E procedure.[681] Besides, a physician is allowed to perform the D & X procedure if necessary; however, he or she should inject the fetus with potassium chloride or dioxin in order to be demised before starting the procedure.[682] Thus, the Court found that the petitioners "failed to show that the Act should be invalidated on its face because it encourages arbitrary or discriminatory enforcement."[683]

The Court did not follow its rulings in Roe, Casey, and Stenberg. It affirmed the constitutionality of the PBABA, despite the absence of a health exception. It declared that "the medical uncertainty over whether the Act's prohibition creates significant health risks provides a sufficient basis to conclude in this facial attack that the Act does not impose an undue burden."[684]

The Court stated that a "zero tolerance policy would strike down legitimate abortion regulations ... if some part of the medical community were disinclined to follow the proscription. This is too exacting a standard to impose on the legislative power, exercised in this instance under the Commerce Clause, to regulate the medical profession."[685] The Court added that "considerations of marginal safety, including the balance of risks, are within the legislative competence when the regulation is rational and in pursuit of legitimate ends."[686] According to the Court, when standard medical choices are obtainable, "mere convenience does not suffice to displace them; and if some procedures have different risks than others, it does not follow that the State is altogether barred from imposing reasonable regulations."[687] Therefore, the Court found that the PBABA was not unconstitutional on its face if "there is uncertainty over whether the barred procedure is ever necessary to preserve a woman's health, given the availability of other abortion procedures that are considered to be safe alternatives."[688]

According to the Court, the "facial attacks" on the PBABA should not be considered in the first instance because "the proper means to consider exceptions is by as-applied challenge."[689] The Court clarified that the "government has acknowledged that preenforcement, as-applied challenges to the

681 Carhart, 127 S. Ct. at 1621, 1629, 1637.
682 *Id.*
683 *Id.* at 1628.
684 *Id.* at 1637.
685 *Id.* at 1638.
686 *Id.*
687 *Id.*
688 *Id.*
689 *Id.* at 1638.

Act can be maintained. This is the proper manner to protect the health of the woman if it can be shown that in discrete and well-defined instances a particular condition has or is likely to occur in which the procedure prohibited by the Act must be used."[690] Therefore, the Court declared that "[i]n an as-applied challenge the nature of the medical risk can be better quantified and balanced than in a facial attack."[691] Nevertheless, in line with the reasoning of the Court, the application of the Statute might be unconstitutional in specific cases. For example, if partial-birth abortion is the only means to save a pregnant woman's health, the prohibition of the Statute could violate the Constitution. This argument may only take place in the application of the Statute, but not in the Statute's general and abstract formulation.

In short, the Court disregarded Stenberg, which prohibited the D & X procedure. Furthermore, it was not committed to Roe, Casey, and Stenberg, in which the Supreme Court stated that abortion statutes must contain a health exception allowing a woman to have an abortion if a pregnancy endangers her health.

In her dissent, Justice Ginsburg rejected the ruling of the Court, describing it as a violation of women's right to "make an autonomous choice, even at the expense of their safety."[692] According to her view, because the PBABA has no health exception, it is unconstitutional according to Stenberg, Casey, and Roe, in which the Supreme Court affirmed that abortion statutes must contain a health exception.[693] In short, Justice Ginsburg concluded that the Court's hostility to "the right Roe and Casey secured is not concealed"[694]

Prior to this case, legal scholars, supporters, and opponents to the PBABA, expected that the main argument the Supreme Court would review was whether an abortion constitutes an economic activity potentially regulated by the Commerce Clause.[695] However, the Supreme Court did not review such a complicated issue. Rather, it simply stated, without clarification, that the PBABA is a mere use of the power given to Congress by the Constitution to "regulate the medical profession."[696]

---

690 *Id.*
691 *Id.* at 1638–39.
692 *Id.* at 1649 (Ginsburg, J., dissenting).
693 *Id.* at 1642.
694 *Id.* at 1650.
695 *See* Robert J. Pushaw, Jr., *Does Congress Have the Constitutional Power to Prohibit Partial-Birth Abortion?* 42 Harv. J. Legis. 319, 333–34 (2005).
696 *Id.*

D *Dobbs v. Jackson Women's Health Org.* (2022)

In Dobbs v. Jackson Women's Health Org., the Supreme Court, unexpectedly and in contrast to its previous rulings, decided that a woman's right to abortion is not guaranteed or protected by the United States Constitution.[697] The Court overruled its decisions in Roe v. Wade and Planned Parenthood v. Casey, enabling individual states to set their own abortion regulations and granting "the people and their elected representatives" the power to control and regulate abortion.[698]

The judgment was issued in response to a lawsuit filed by an abortion clinic, Jackson Women's Health Organization, against the Mississippi Gestational Age Act, which bans abortions after 15 weeks of pregnancy except in cases of medical emergency or serious fetal defects or abnormalities.[699]

This judgment overturns the fundamental and constitutional right to abortion that had been in place for nearly half a century and specifies that state abortion laws will henceforth be examined by courts using the "rational basis" test, which requires judges to only determine that the state abortion statute is logically connected to a legitimate government interest.[700] However, this decision does not ban or otherwise limit abortions under any federal constitutional or legal framework, does not create rights for the unborn, does not restrict access to contraception or overturn previous Supreme Court decisions upholding such access, and does not modify or alter any other federal or state health care legislation or regulation.[701]

In summary, based on Roe and Casey, this section concludes that the Supreme Court has clearly distinguished between abortion before and after fetal viability. Before fetal viability, the right to terminate a pregnancy was considered guaranteed by the federal Constitution; after viability, abortion could be prohibited, with very few exceptions. In Dobbs v. Jackson, however, this federal right was found wanting, and both Roe v. Wade and Planned Parenthood v. Casey were overruled. The individual states now may regulate abortion in exercise of their sovereign discretion.

---

697 Dobbs v. Jackson Women's Health Org., 142 S. Ct. 2228, 2234 (2022).

698 *Id.* at 2284.

699 Miss. Code Ann. §41-41-191 (2018). the Mississippi's Gestational Age Act states that "[e]xcept in a medical emergency or in the case of a severe fetal abnormality, a person shall not intentionally or knowingly perform or induce an abortion of an unborn human being if the probable gestational age of the unborn human being has been determined to be greater than fifteen (15) weeks." *Id.*

700 Dobbs v. Jackson Women's Health Org., 142 S. Ct. 2228, 2234 (2022).

701 *Id.* at 2234–40.

3 Abortion under Shari'a

A *The Prohibition of Murder in Islam*

Murder is strictly forbidden in Islam. According to the first major source of Shari'a, the Qur'an, murder is extremely prohibited in several instances. For example, the Qur'an states: "Whoever kills a believer intentionally – his recompense is Hell, wherein he will abide eternally, and Allah has become angry with him and has cursed him and has prepared for him a great punishment."[702] In addition, the Qur'an says: "And those who invoke not any other ilah (god) along with Allah, nor kill such life as Allah has forbidden, ... and whoever does this shall receive the punishment."[703] On the other hand, in respect of the second main source of Shari'a, the Sunna, Prophet Mohammad said: "Avoid the seven great destructive sins." The people asked, what are they? He said: ".... (3) to kill the life which Allah has forbidden ..."[704]

In particular, Shari'a forbids the murder of children. In other words, children's right to life is strongly protected under Shari'a. In the pre-Islamic era, female infants were being killed, slaughtered and even buried alive. This inhuman practice was widespread in the Arabian Peninsula owing to the fear of shame. Nevertheless, Islam came to dismantle and criminalize such a brutal act. The Qur'an says: "When the female infant is buried alive, the question is for what crime she was killed."[705] In another verse, the Qur'an says: "He hides himself from the people because of the ill of which he has been informed. Should he keep it in humiliation or bury it in the ground? Unquestionably, evil is what they decide."[706] In addition, some Arabs in the pre-Islamic era used to kill their infants out of dread of poverty. Islam strongly prohibits this heinous conduct. The Qur'an says: "Do not kill your children for fear of want."[707] Furthermore, another horrific tradition among Arabs was exemplified in slaughtering their newborns in sacrifice to the so-called idols, which was entirely prohibited and refuted by Islam. The Qur'an says: "They are losers indeed who kill their children foolishly without knowledge, and forbid that which Allah has provided

702 QUR'AN, *Surat Al- Nisa'* 4:93.
703 QUR'AN, *Surat Al-Furqan*, 25:68.
704 Sahih Al-Bukhari (Vol. 8, Book 82, Hadith 840).
705 QUR'AN, *Surat Al-Takweer* 81:8–9.
706 QUR'AN, *Surat Al-Nahl* 16:59.
707 QUR'AN, *Surat Al- Isra'* 17:31.

for them, forging a lie against Allah. They indeed go astray, and are not guided."[708]

Nevertheless, a crucial question must be raised: Does Shari'a recognize the fetus as a human being who enjoys the right to life? If the answer is yes, then Islam strictly opposes abortion. All the above-mentioned Qur'anic

---

708 QUR'AN, *Surat Al- An'am* 6:140. Under Shari'a, children enjoy many other rights. Children's right to health is fundamental, as parents are responsible for their children's health. It is narrated that Prophet Mohammad urged his companions to "seek treatment" and said: "Indeed Allah has not sent any illness without sending a cure for it." Sunan Ibn Majah (Vol. 4, Book 31, Hadith 3436). In addition, under Shari'a, breastfeeding is a fundamental right for a newborn child. The Qur'an says: "And mothers shall breast-feed their children for two full years." QUR'AN, *Surat Al-Baqarah* 2:233.

Furthermore, children's right to education is clearly protected under Shari'a. The first word revealed to Prophet Mohammad was the command verb "Read". QUR'AN, *El-'Alak* 96:1. Other verses glorify education and knowledge-seeking, such as: "Allah will exalt those of you who believe, and those who are given knowledge, to high ranks." QUR'AN, *Surat Al-Mujadelah* 58:11. In another similar verse, the Qur'an says: "Are those equal, those who know and those who do not know?" QUR'AN, *Surat Az- Zumar* 39:10. In addition, children's rights against sexual abuse are protected under Shari'a. In other words, sexual abuse is considered a serious crime in Islam. The Qur'an makes an indirect reference to this crime when it says, "My Lord has only prohibited indecencies, those of them that are apparent as well as those that are concealed." QUR'AN, *Surat Al-A'raf* 7:33.

Moreover, the right to have well-chosen parents is granted to children under Islam. According to the Sunna, each parent should carefully choose his or her partner and future child's parent. In other words, men and women have to seek marriage from those who can help them raise their children better. It is narrated that Prophet Mohammad said: "The best of you is the best among you in conduct." Riyad As-Salihin (Book 1, Hadith 625).

Similarly, Islam grants children the full right to have pretty names. This right is referred to in the Sunna. It is narrated that Prophet Mohammad said: "On the Day of Resurrection, you will be called by your names and by your father's names, so give yourselves good names." Abu Dawood (Book 42, Hadith 4930). In addition, the right to be welcomed at birth is granted to children under Islam. According to the Sunna, once a child is born, a great feast is prepared to commemorate his coming birth, and an animal sacrifice, known as aqeeqah, is performed for the newborn. It is narrated that Prophet Mohammad performed aqeeqah for his grandsons, Al-Hassan and Al-Husayn. Sunan Al-Nasa'i (Vol. 5, Book 4, Hadith 4218).

Children are also provided with special care in Islam. It is narrated that Prophet Mohammad said: "The pen has been lifted for three persons (meaning they are not held accountable for what they do): one who is sleeping until he wakes up, a child until he reaches the age of puberty, and an insane person until he becomes sane." Sunan Tirmidhi (Vol. 4, Book 32, Hadith 1423). According to this Hadith, children are neither held accountable for their actions nor given difficult tasks, but are instead lavished with love and care.

verses may thus be used to prohibit abortion. Alternatively, if the fetus is not regarded as a human being, another basic question would arise: Is abortion lawful, or is it legally contested?

To answer these questions, the study must examine the major sources of Shari'a and discuss how abortion is handled.

With regard to the Qur'an, abortion is never discussed or mentioned explicitly.[709] Regarding the Sunna, Prophet Mohammad said, in an authentic Hadith narrated by Bukhari, "(as regards your creation) every one of you is collected in the womb of his mother for the first forty days, and then he becomes a clot for another forty days, and then a piece of flesh for another forty days, then Allah sends an angel to give soul to him."[710] From this Hadith, one can notice that the fetus is given the spirit of life after four months of pregnancy, that is, 40 × 3 = 120 days.[711]

---

709 The primary sources of Shari'a, in order, are as follows: (1) the Qur'an, the sacred book of Allah; (2) the Sunna, the actions and utterances of Prophet Mohammad; (3) Fiqh, the Islamic jurisprudence; and (4) Qiyas, analogical deduction.

In order to determine the proper Islamic perspective on a certain subject, one must first consult the Qur'an. If this topic is explicitly addressed in the Qur'an, the whole matter is resolved, and there is no need to check other sources of Shari'a. In contrast, if this topic is not covered or explicitly referenced in the Qur'an, the researcher has to consult the Sunna to see how it is addressed. If this issue is explicitly handled, then there is no need to search further. If not, the researcher has to investigate Fiqh. In cases where Muslim scholars are unanimous, the consensus view is applied. If, however, this subject is contested, the researcher has to adopt the most proper viewpoint. In the absence of an issue in the Qur'an, the Sunna and Fiqh, the researcher has to use Qiyas, which is defined as the process of applying the ruling of a stated issue to an unmentioned issue if there is a strict similarity between the two cases.

For example, since murder, as mentioned above, is clearly prohibited in the Qur'an, there is no need to investigate how it is addressed in other sources of Shari'a. With regard to female circumcision, it is not explicitly referred to in the Qur'an. Additionally, the Sunna does not provide a clear text addressing this issue. Therefore, the researcher has to check Fiqh, and due to the absence of consensus, he has to adopt the most proper view, which is, female circumcision is prohibited.

Another example is that of drugs. Drugs are never mentioned in the Qur'an, the Sunna or Fiqh. Therefore, one has to resort to Qiyas, bearing in mind a case similar to that of drugs, which is addressed in the Qur'an or the Sunna. In the context of using Qiyas to demonstrate how Shari'a treats drugs, wine is an appropriate example to consider. Since wine is prohibited by the Qur'an and Sunna but drugs are not stated, one may assume that drugs are likewise prohibited under sharia by adopting Qiyas.

710 SAHIH AL-BUKHARI (Vol. 4, Book 55, Hadith 549).

711 In addition to this Sunna, the Qur'an says:

O mankind, If ye have a doubt about the Resurrection, (consider) that We created you out of dust, then out of sperm, then out of a leech-like clot, then out of a morsel of flesh, partly formed and partly unformed, in order that We may manifest (Our

Although this Hadith did not clarify whether abortion is prohibited or allowed, it determined the stages of fetus formation, stipulating that it is given a soul after three stages, each of which lasts for 40 days. Thus, according to this Hadith, the fetus is transformed from an inanimate thing into a human being after 120 days, about four months from the moment of conception.

Since the Sunna of the Prophet differentiated between the first 120 days of pregnancy and subsequent periods, Islamic jurisprudence (Fiqh) differed in dealing with the two periods:[712]

B *The Juristic Consensus on the Prohibition of Abortion after the First 120 Days of Pregnancy*

Since, according to the Sunna, the fetus is endowed with life and soul after the first 120 days from conception, abortion is forbidden after this period. Therefore, all schools of Fiqh, Hanafia, Malikia, Shafi'a, and Hanabila affirm the prohibition of abortion beyond 120 days of pregnancy.[713] However, this juristic consensus has only one exception: when a pregnancy endangers a woman's life or health. In this case, the four schools of Fiqh permit abortion at any time of pregnancy.[714] Thus, in case of a contradiction between the two values, a pregnant woman's life and the fetus's life, Islamic Fiqh would prioritize the life of the pregnant woman.[715]

---

power) to you; And We cause whom We will to rest in the wombs for an appointed term, then We bring you out as babes, then (foster you) that ye may reach your age of full strength; and some of you are called to die, and some are sent back to the feeblest old age, so that they know nothing.

Qur'an, *Surat Al-Hajj* 22:5. This verse summarizes the stages of human creation, beginning with conception and ending with death.

712 Abd-Elfatah Mahmoud Idrees, Aleghad fe Do'a Al-Islam (Abortion in Light of Islam) 19 (1995) (trans. by author).

713 *Id.*

714 *Id.*

715 Under Shari'a, the fetus enjoys many rights. Regarding the right to life, the fetus is given that right after the passing of 120 days of pregnancy, and therefore late abortion is prohibited. *Id.* The only exception that allows late abortion is the presence of a threat to a mother's life because of pregnancy.

In addition, under Shari'a, the fetus's right to health is protected because a mother is required to maintain her health during pregnancy. Mohammad Hassan, Heqook El-Tefl Wa El-Ganeen Fi El-Islam Wa El-Kanoon El-Dawly (The Fetus and Child's Rights under Islam and International Law) 64 (2011) (trans. by author). For example, a pregnant woman is entitled to breakfast in Ramadan, the month of mandatory daily fasting in Islam, in order not to negatively affect her health or her fetus' health. Mohammad Emara, Altahreer Al-Islami Le-Almar'a, Al-Rad a'la Shobhat Al'gholah

The following verse might be cited to justify allowing an abortion in cases of life- or health-threatening pregnancies: "No mother shall be treated unfairly on account of her child."[716] Although this verse comes in the midst of the regulations on divorce,[717] the wording is perfectly general so that it may include other meanings.

C *The Juristic Dispute over Abortion during the First Four Months of Pregnancy*

The vast majority of Hanafia scholars believe that abortion is fully allowed during the first 120 days of pregnancy;[718] however, a few of them argue that abortion in early pregnancies is only permissible for compelling reasons such as a perceived threat to a pregnant woman's health or in cases of rape or fetal deformity.[719] Similarly, most Shafi'a scholars consider that abortion is permissible during the first four months of pregnancy, but not recommended unless there is an emergency.[720]

Nevertheless, the majority of Malikia scholars prohibit abortion from the moment of conception;[721] however, few of them permit the procedure only during the first 120 days of pregnancy in certain cases, such as rape or fetal deformity.[722] On the other hand, most Hanabila scholars allow abortion for justifiable reasons during only the first 40 days of pregnancy;[723] after this

(Women's Liberty in Islam against Some Wrongful Perceptions) 92 (2002) (trans. by author). Besides, a husband is required to keep the proper atmosphere for his pregnant wife so as not to negatively impact her mental health, which could have detrimental effects on the fetus. *Id.* at 32.

Furthermore, the fetus's right to inheritance is protected under Shari'a, but his or her proportion is kept until birth. Youssef Kasem, El-Hekook El-Mota'leka Be El-Terka Fe El-Feqh El-Islami (Inheritance Rights in Islamic Jurisprudence) 325 (Vol. 1) (Dar El-Nahda) (trans. by author). This is known as a posthumous birth. In other words, once the fetus is born, he or she will be granted the specified portion of inheritance. *Id.*

716 Qur'an, *Surat Al-Baqarah* 2:233.

717 Abi El-Feda' Ibn-Katheer, Tafseer El-Qur'an (Interpretation of the Qur'an) 249 (Vol. 1, 1994) (trans. by author).

718 Idrees, *supra* note 712 (trans. by author).

719 *Id.*

720 *Id.*

721 Mostafa Abd-El-Fataah, Gareemat El-Eghad (Crime of Abortion) 301 (1996) (trans. by author).

722 Idrees, *supra* note 712 (trans. by author).

723 *Id.* The Hadith of the Prophet divided the 120-day period into three parts, each of which lasted 40 days. Sahih Al-Bukhari (Vol. 4, Book 55, Hadith 549). The Hanabila scholars only allow abortion during the first part of that period.

period, they consider abortion illegal unless a pregnancy endangers a woman's life.[724]

Based on this juristic dispute, it is clear that Muslim scholars have divergent views concerning early abortions: some of them believe that abortion is strictly forbidden, while others argue that it is permissible under all circumstances, citing the absence of any Qur'anic or Sunni sources prohibiting early abortions.[725] Nevertheless, the vast majority of Muslim scholars agree that abortion is permissible only under reasonable circumstances, as a pregnant woman should not, for trivial reasons, change Allah's will and violate the potential life of the fetus, which in most cases will receive a soul and develop into a human being.[726]

---

724 Idrees, *supra* note 712 (trans. by author).

725 *Id.*

726 *Id.* It is agreed among Muslim scholars that a life-threatening pregnancy is a compelling reason for abortion, whether during the first 120 days of pregnancy or after such a term. Idrees, *supra* note 712 (trans. by author). Therefore, if a woman's life is threatened by pregnancy, abortion is fully allowed, regardless of the stage of pregnancy. *Id.*

In addition, many Muslim scholars consider fetal deformity a reasonable exception to the prohibition of abortion during the first 120 days of pregnancy, but few scholars hold the opposite position. *Id.* at 714. On the other hand, some Muslim scholars connect the whole matter with the extent of abnormalities, whether minor or serious. Mohammad El-Bar, El-Ganeen El-Moshawah Wa El-Amraad El-Werasia (The Abnormal Fetus and Genetic Diseases) 372 (1999) (trans. by author). This view is based on medical reports detecting the extent of the expected deformity. *Id.* According to this opinion, if the deformity is minor and the fetus could practice all life activities with few physical barriers, abortion would be impermissible. However, if the fetus will suffer during his life or live with a sustainable disability, abortion would be permissible. *Id.* In spite of these views, it should be noted that, under Shari'a, fetal abnormality is a very adequate and sufficient excuse for abortion during the first 120 days of pregnancy. Idrees, *supra* note 712, at 20 (trans. by author). The vast majority of Muslim scholars support this view because both the fetus and the mother would suffer greatly in the event of an incurable disease or disability. Youssef El-Karadawy, Fatawa Mo'asera (Contemporary Islamic Advisories) 606 (Vol. 2) (trans. by author).

Similarly, rape is an acceptable reason for abortion during the first 120 days of pregnancy. The vast majority of Muslim scholars allow early abortion if the pregnancy is an outcome of rape. *Id.* at 609. However, they see that abortion, in cases of rape, is optional, not obligatory, and therefore a pregnant woman is fully entitled to have the procedure or retain the fetus. *Id.* On the other hand, very few Muslim scholars view rape as an impermissible reason for abortion. Idrees, *supra* note 712, at 20 (trans. by author). They recognize no justifiable reasons for abortion under Shari'a. *Id.*

Regarding fornication, Muslim scholars disagree on whether it is a reasonable exception to the prohibition of abortion during the first 120 days of pregnancy. Many Muslim scholars consider fornication to be an inconsiderable excuse for abortion. El-Karadawy, *supra* note 726, at 610 (trans. by author). Their argument is based on the

In summary, the Hadith of the Prophet differentiates between the first 120 days of pregnancy and the subsequent period. During the first duration, abortion could be permissible for justifiable reasons, such as a perceived threat to the mother's life or health, if the mother was a victim of rape, or if the fetus is expected to be born with a physical disability. On the other hand, after the early four-month period, according to this Hadith, the fetus is transformed into a human being, and therefore abortion is prohibited. This provision applies to all cases with one exception: where a woman's life or health is threatened by pregnancy, regardless of whether she is in her first or later period.

4 Abortion under Egyptian Law

A *The Crime of Abortion in Egyptian Law*

The Egyptian Penal Code classifies abortion as a criminal act.[727] However, this crime is not related to murder[728]; it is an independent crime with its

---

interpretation of the Qur'an stating that "no bearer of burdens will bear the burden of another." Qur'an, *Surat Fater* 35:18; Qur'an, *Surat Al-An'am* 6:164. According to their point of view, both fornication and abortion are prohibited under Shari'a. Therefore, if a woman commits fornication as a sin, she is not required to commit another sin, which is abortion. El-Karadawy, *supra* note 726, at 610 (trans. by author). Nevertheless, it could be argued that in cases of fornication or adultery, a woman might have an abortion under Shari'a. This argument is based on the absence of any sources banning early abortions in the Qur'an or Sunna. The majority of Hanafia scholars allow abortion without justification during the first 120 days of pregnancy. Idrees, *supra* note 712 (trans. by author).

Regarding incest, it is classified to the same degree as rape by many Muslim scholars. El-Karadawy, *supra* note 726, at 612 (trans. by author). They argue that incest may occur through the use of force, and therefore abortion because of incest should be treated similarly to rape. *Id.* According to this argument, incest could be a reasonable exception to the prohibition of abortion during the first 120 days of pregnancy. *Id.* On the other hand, other scholars classify incest in the same category as fornication. *Id.* They consider that a Muslim woman cannot atone for one sin by committing another. *Id.*

727 Penal Code, Egypt, 5 Aug. 1937.

728 Under the Penal Code of Egypt, the punishment of the crime of murder is stipulated in nine articles, from Article 230 to Article 238, as follows:

Article 230 (stating that anyone who deliberately, with premeditation and surveillance, murders another person shall be sentenced to death). *Id.* art. 230.

Article 231 (defining premeditation as the deliberate intent to commit a crime). *Id.* art. 231.

own elements,[729] and its punishment is specified in five articles of the Egyptian Penal Code, articles 260 to 264.[730]

Under Egyptian law, in order for an act to be considered a crime, the perpetrator must have criminal intent. This requirement is necessary to distinguish intentional criminal behavior from accidental criminal behavior.[731] Concerning abortion, criminal intent requires that the perpetrator be aware of pregnancy and intend to induce a miscarriage.[732] The Egyptian Court of Cassation[733] acknowledged that criminal intent is a major element of the crime of abortion, without which abortion is not punishable.[734]

Nevertheless, criminal intent is not the only element of abortion as a crime; pregnancy and miscarriage are also required.[735] Unquestionably, if

Article 232 (defining surveillance as waiting for a victim at the scene of the crime). *Id.* art. 232.

Article 233 (stating that anyone who murders another person using drugs or poison shall be sentenced to death or to life imprisonment). *Id.* art. 233.

Article 234 (stating that anyone who deliberately, without premeditation and surveillance, murders another person shall be sentenced to life in prison or a term of years). *Id.* art. 234.

Article 235 (indicating that whoever aids or abets a person to murder another person shall be sentenced to death or to life imprisonment). *Id.* art. 265.

Article 236 (stating that anyone convicted of beating another person to death shall be sentenced to three to seven years in prison). *Id.* art. 236.

Article 237 (stipulating an exceptional case in which a husband who catches his wife in the act of adultery and kills her and her lover shall be sentenced to a maximum of three years in jail). *Id.* art. 237.

Article 238 (stating that anyone who negligently or accidentally injures another person is subject to a maximum of six months in jail and a maximum fine of two hundred Egyptian pounds). *Id.* art. 238.

729 Mohammad Abd-El-Tawab, Al Mowsooa'a al Genae'ia fi Sharh Kanoon el Okobat (Clarification of Crimes Under the Penal Code) 1883 (Vol. 4, 2011) (trans. by author).

730 Penal Code, *supra* note 727, arts. 260–64.

731 *Id.*

732 Mostafa Haraga, Sharh Kanoon El-Okobat (Clarification of the Penal Code) 358 (Vol. 2) (trans. by author).

733 According to the Egyptian legal system, the highest court is the Court of Cassation, which has jurisdiction over all criminal, civil, and commercial cases in Egypt. Luna Droubi, *The Constitutionality of the Niqab Ban in Egypt: A Symbol of Egypt's Struggle for a Legal Identity*, 56 N.Y.L. Sch. L. Rev. 687, 694 (2012).

734 Mahkamat al-Nakd [Court of Cassation], al-Masria, case No. 1829/1950 (Egypt) (trans. by author).

735 Ehab Abd-El-Moteleb, Al-Mawsooa'a Al-Genae'ia Fe Sharh Kanoon El-Okobat (An Explanation of Crimes Under the Penal Code) 676 (Vol.3, 2010) (trans. by author).

a woman is not pregnant, an abortion cannot occur.[736] Alternatively, a miscarriage is the artificial termination of a pregnancy.[737] These two elements are not difficult to verify.[738]

Under Article 262 of the Egyptian Penal Code, a pregnant woman who has an abortion is subject to a maximum prison sentence of three years.[739] According to this article, the ban on abortion applies to both early and late pregnancies.

The physician's punishment is outlined in Article 263 of the Penal Code. According to this article, a physician who conducts an abortion is subject to a prison sentence of three to fifteen years.[740] This article indicates that doctors who perform abortions are subject to severe punishment.[741]

B *Arguments for Exceptions*

A quick review of Egyptian law reveals that the Egyptian legislator did not adhere to Islamic Shari'a and created an entirely different system for addressing abortion.[742] Although Shari'a is regarded as the main source of legislation in Egypt,[743] the Egyptian legal system does not differentiate between early and late abortions. Under Egyptian law, abortion from the moment of conception is strictly prohibited and regarded as a crime.[744]

---

736 *Id.*

737 Haraga, *supra* note 732, at 357 (trans. by author).

738 *Id.*

739 Penal Code, *supra* note 727, art. 262.

740 *Id.* art. 263. Two situations involving abortion qualify as felonies: (1) if the abortion was performed by a medical professional, and (2) if the abortion was performed by physically abusing a pregnant woman against her will or without her consent. Haraga, *supra* note 732, at 359–61.

741 According to Egyptian law, crimes are classified into three categories: felonies, misdemeanors, and contraventions. With regard to felonies, Article 10 of the Penal Code defines a felony as a crime for which the offender is sentenced to the death penalty, life imprisonment, or interim imprisonment. Penal Code, *supra* note 727, art. 10.

In addition, Article 11 of the Penal Code defines a misdemeanor as a crime for which the offender is sentenced to less than three years or fined more than one hundred Egyptian pounds. *Id.* art. 11.

Furthermore, according to Article 12 of the Penal Code, contraventions are those crimes for which the offender is fined at most one hundred Egyptian pounds. *Id.* art. 12.

742 Abd-El-Tawab, *supra* note 729 (trans. by author).

743 Under Article 2 of the Egyptian Constitution, Shari'a is the main source of legislation. 1971 Constitution, *supra* note 153, art. 2.

744 Penal Code, *supra* note 727, at arts. 260–64 (trans. by author).

However, there are two potential arguments for the exemption of the punishment for the crime of abortion.[745]

The first argument is based on Article 60 of the Egyptian Criminal Code, which exempts from punishment anyone who engages in a Shari'a-compliant activity.[746] According to this argument, a woman would have the right to abortion during the early four months of pregnancy because Shari'a permits abortion for justifiable reasons during this time frame.[747] However, this argument was rejected by the Egyptian Court of Cassation, which viewed abortion as a debatable right under Shari'a due to the fact that Muslim scholars were divided on this topic.[748] The Court of Cassation neither supported nor denied a woman's right to an abortion under Shari'a, but stated that there is no consensus in Shari'a on this issue.[749]

The second argument is based on Article 61 of the Criminal Code, stipulating that anyone who commits a crime for the purpose of self-defense shall be exempt from punishment.[750] The precise language of this article reads as follows: "No penalty shall be imposed on a person who commits a crime to save him/herself or others from a fatal danger that is imminently threatening to harm him/herself or others".[751] In line with the terms used in this article, including "fatal danger" and "imminently threatening to harm,"

745 *Id.*
746 *Id.* art. 60.
747 Mahkamat al-Nakd [Court of Cassation], Al-Masria, case No. 1193/1929 (Egypt) (trans. by author).
748 *Id.* The Egyptian Court of Cassation responded to a very interesting challenge concerning abortion. The events of this case started when a pregnant woman seeking an abortion went to a surgeon during the first four months of her pregnancy. *Id.* Once the surgeon agreed and began the procedure, he unintentionally caused her death. *Id.* Therefore, the physician was sent to trial and accused of committing two crimes: the crime of abortion and the crime of unintentional murder. *Id.* Before the Egyptian Court of Cassation, he argued that he should not be punished for performing an abortion since it is allowed during the early four months of pregnancy under Shari'a, the main source of Egyptian legislation under the Constitution. In addition, he challenged the constitutionality of the Egyptian Penal Code's articles regulating abortion, since they are incompatible with the Constitution. *Id.* The Court of Cassation rejected his argument, declaring that he was guilty of committing the crime of abortion. *Id.* In addition, it affirmed that unlike Shari'a, Egyptian law does not allow abortion, whether during the first four months or later, except in cases of life-threatening pregnancies. *Id.* Moreover, the Court added that the fact that Shari'a allows abortion during the first four months of pregnancy is not based on a major source of Islam reaching a juristic consensus; rather, it is disputed. *Id.*
749 *Id.*
750 Penal Code, *supra* note 727, art. 61 (trans. by author).
751 *Id.*

it could be argued that a life-threatening pregnancy is the only exception under which an abortion would be legal and not punishable.[752] Despite the absence of rulings by the Egyptian high courts applying this article to the crime of abortion, the vast majority of Egyptian legal specialists agree on this issue.[753] However, there is no legal consensus regarding other situations, such as rape, incest, health-threatening pregnancies, or when the fetus has a serious deformity or genetic defect.[754]

In summary, according to Egyptian law, abortion is illegal from the moment of conception until birth, unless a woman's life is threatened by her pregnancy.

5 Concluding Analysis of Abortion Rights

Upon reading the whole exposition presented in this chapter addressing abortion under international law, American law, Islamic law and Egyptian law, one can infer the following points:

- Under international law, pro-choice arguments surpass pro-life arguments to some extent. International law gives a woman the right to abortion for compelling reasons. However, there is no distinction between early and late abortions because international law deals with the issue of abortion under one approach, from the moment of conception and throughout all phases of the fetus. Pro-life arguments, considering the fetus as a distinct human being, are feeble under international law. Similarly, arguments providing the pregnant woman with the right to elective abortion, without a foundation of urgent reasons, are hardly valid under that law.
- Under American law, until recently, abortion before and after the viability of the fetus was treated differently based on the Supreme Court's decisions in Roe and Casey. That is, before the fetus's viability, abortion was regarded as a constitutional right, whereas after viability, abortion was prohibited with very few exceptions. However, the Supreme Court changed its position in 2022, enabling each state to determine its own abortion regulations.
- Under Shari'a, the interpretation of the Prophetic Hadith differentiates between early and late abortions, the early 120-day period of pregnancy

752 Haraga, *supra* note 732, at 359 (trans. by author).
753 *Id.*
754 *Id.*

and the subsequent period. During the first period, abortion is permissible for justifiable reasons, whereas in the second period, abortion is prohibited unless a pregnancy threatens a woman's life or health.

- Under Egyptian law, abortion is illegal and regarded as a crime from the moment of conception until birth; however, exceptions for non-punishable abortions may exist only in one case: if a pregnant woman's life is threatened by pregnancy. Although Shari'a is the primary source of legislation according to the Egyptian Constitution, the Egyptian legislator did not follow its rules or its timetable system, in which early and late abortions are differentiated. Rather, the legislator adopted another approach toward abortion that is completely different from that of Islamic Shari'a.

Comparing the above-mentioned systems, the author argues that international law does not protect the fetus's right to life at any stage of pregnancy. That is, it never differentiates between early and late abortions. Moreover, under international law, a woman's right to autonomy and her right to have control over her body have managed to prevail against arguments advocating the fetus's right to life.

In contrast, Egyptian law does not respect a woman's right to choose to have an abortion, and pro-choice arguments are given no attention under this law. Egyptian law is similar to international law in that it makes no distinction between early and late abortions; however, it processes the whole matter in a myopic view, depriving a woman of her right to choose to have an abortion. Consequently, pro-life arguments predominate under Egyptian law over pro-choice ones. A pregnant woman has no right to choose to have an abortion, even if the fetus has abnormalities or was the result of incest or rape. Thus, a woman is compelled to give birth to her child in these cases. The author argues that this approach not only harms the fetus but also the woman, because in such cases it is in the best interests of both the woman and the fetus to have an abortion in order to avoid a number of physical and psychological complications that may arise.

On the other hand, the author argues that both the American legal system based on Roe and Casey, and Shari'a present a just legal system balancing between a woman's right to abortion and the fetus's right to life. These two systems share a timetable that permits the pregnant woman to have an abortion within a certain time frame, after which abortion is restricted to avoid violating the fetus's right to life. In addition, in both systems, if a conflict arises between the woman's life and the fetus's life, the woman's life takes precedence. In other words, the two systems give a woman the right to an abortion at any time of pregnancy if her life or health is in danger.

Despite their close similarities, the two legal systems differ in the following ways:

(1) Islamic Shari'a Preceded American Law by Centuries:

A close examination of Islamic law and jurisprudence reveals that Prophet Mohammad created the timetable system of abortion more than fifteen centuries ago. Thus, the Hadith of the Prophet, which determined the framework on abortion, predated the 1973 decision of the U.S. Supreme Court. In other words, it is abundantly clear that the trimester system applied in Roe v. Wade was similarly adopted by Islamic Shari'a hundreds of years ago.

(2) Permissible Abortion Timeframe:

Under Shari'a, the permissible period for abortion is limited to the first 120 days of pregnancy, approximately the first four months from the time of conception.

As for American law, in Roe v. Wade, the U.S. Supreme Court ruled that the duration of a legal abortion was the first trimester of pregnancy. Later, the Supreme Court, in Planned Parenthood v. Casey, revoked Roe's trimester timetable and allowed abortion until fetal viability, roughly twenty-two or twenty-three weeks after conception. These decisions, however, have now been overruled by Dobbs v. Jackson in 2022.

(3) Restrictions during the First Period of Pregnancy:

According to the majority of Muslim scholars, abortion is permissible within the first period of pregnancy for justifiable reasons, such as rape, a health or life-threatening pregnancy, or when the fetus is severely affected by a genetic defect or deformity.[755]

In contrast, under American law, as stated in Roe and Casey, abortion was a constitutional right and a form of reproductive freedom granted to women before fetal viability. In other words, prior to fetal viability, a pregnant woman had an absolute right to have an abortion without any restrictions or limitations.

The central question raised here is whether it is preferable to have a restricted or absolute right to abortion during the early period of pregnancy.

Since the fetus will have a potential life in most cases and will develop into a normal human being after a few months of pregnancy, the author argues that it is better to impose restrictions on a woman's right to abortion rather than giving her an absolute right to have the procedure. Giving a

---

755 In terms of abortion regulation, international law and Islamic Shari'a share certain similarities. In other words, both systems require a valid reason for abortion. In contrast to Shari'a, however, international law treats abortion in a consistent manner throughout the entire pregnancy.

woman the unrestricted right to control her body and have an abortion, even in the early stages of pregnancy for insignificant reasons, strongly violates the potential life of a human being who is about to be born. However, abortion before the fetus is given the spirit of life, based on reasonable foundations, does not cause the same violations. Rather, it saves both the woman and the fetus. Thus, the author argues that Islamic Shari'a, in which abortion is restricted during the first period of pregnancy, has a superior and distinctive system that adequately covers abortion in comparison to prior American law, in which abortion has been an absolute right until fetal viability.

The Most Effective Abortion System

The author concludes, without any prejudice, that Islamic Shari'a is the best system for regulating abortion. The author argues that international law's major flaw, failing to respect the fetus's rights even after viability, does not exist in Shari'a, where the Hadith of Prophet Mohammad restricts abortion after four months of pregnancy, giving the fetus significant consideration.

With regard to Egyptian law's major flaw, failing to respect a woman's right to choose to have an abortion even if the pregnancy is accompanied by abnormalities or is the result of rape, Shari'a addresses this issue fairly by permitting abortion in compelling circumstances during the early stages of pregnancy.

As for prior American law's major flaw, adopted in Roe and Casey, which gave an absolute right to abortion before fetal viability and disregarded the potential life that would develop into a fully functional human being, Shari'a avoids this flaw by permitting abortion under reasonable causes and conditions during the early stages of pregnancy.

From the above-mentioned flaws in each of these legal systems, it is evident that Islamic Shari'a is a unique system. It strikes a fair balance between a woman's right to choose abortion in certain circumstances and the fetus's right to life.

CHAPTER 2

Women's Right to Equality in Employment

The right to work is fundamental for all human beings. According to international human rights standards, gender-based employment equality is indisputable and fully guaranteed.

Many feminists criticize the position of women in Muslim countries, attributing their decline and deterioration to Islam.[1] They argue that because Muslim countries adopt Shari'a in their constitutions and legislation, Muslim women's employment rights are violated.[2] This chapter of the book will examine the validity of such arguments.

First, this chapter will clarify international standards protecting women from employment discrimination. It will also compare these standards to American law and examine whether the U.S. Supreme Court is in agreement with them.

Furthermore, this chapter will address the debate over whether Shari'a promotes equitable employment opportunities for women. Then, it will examine the employment status of women under Egyptian law and assess the current work environment for Egyptian women.

1 Women's Right to Work under International Law

A *The Right to Equal Treatment before the Law*

The right to be equal before the law is protected by an early and influential international instrument of human rights, the U.N. Charter.[3] According to the Charter's preamble, the peoples of the U.N. are determined to "reaffirm faith" in "the equal rights of men and women."[4] "Although there is no universal agreement as to the precise extent of the human rights and fundamental freedoms guaranteed to all by the Charter,"[5] it may be considered an

---

1 Joelle Entelis, *International Human Rights: Islam's Friend or Foe? Algeria as an Example of the Compatibility of International Human Rights Regarding Women's Equality and Islamic Law*, 20 Fordham Int'l L.J. 1251, 54 (1997).

2 *Id.*

3 U.N. Charter.

4 *Id.* at pmbl.

5 Filartiga v. Pena-Irala, 630 F.2d 876, 882 n.9 (2d Cir. 1980).

 | DOI:10.1163/9789004729506_004

actual basis for fundamental human rights when read with other international instruments "to set a threshold of basic human rights."[6] In addition, almost all states adhere to the Charter; "even the few remaining nonmember states have acquiesced to the principles it establishes."[7]

In addition, Article 1 of the UDHR stipulates that "[e]veryone is entitled to all the rights and freedoms set forth in this Declaration, without distinction of any kind, such as ... sex."[8] Although the UDHR is not an obligatory instrument of human rights because it is a declaration and not a binding treaty, it is considered a very significant international human rights instrument that "constitute[s] basic principles of international law"[9] and clarifies "the obligations of member nations under the Charter."[10] Therefore, many commentators consider the UDHR as "part of customary international law."[11]

Similarly, the ICCPR[12] contains general texts prohibiting discrimination. Article 26 of the Covenant stipulates that "the law shall prohibit any discrimination and guarantee to all persons equal and effective protection against discrimination on any ground such as race, colour, sex, language, religion, political or other opinion, national or social origin, property, birth or other status."[13]

Furthermore, CEDAW[14] was mainly created to eradicate discrimination against women. According to the Convention, discrimination against women means "any distinction, exclusion or restriction made on the basis of sex which has the effect or purpose of impairing or nullifying the recognition, enjoyment or exercise by women, irrespective of their marital status, on a basis of equality of men and women, of human rights and fundamental freedoms in the political, economic, social, cultural, civil or any other

6 Marisa Anne Pagnattaro, *Enforcing International Labor Standards: The Potential of the Alien Tort Claims Act*, 37 Vand. J. Transnat'l L. 203, 232 (2004).
7 Restatement (Third) of Foreign Relations Law § 102 cmt. h (Am. Law Inst. 2002).
8 G.A. Res. 217 (III) A, art. 1, Universal Declaration of Human Rights (Dec. 10, 1948) [hereinafter UDHR].
9 Filartiga v. Pena-Irala, 630 F.2d at 882.
10 *Id.* at 883.
11 *Id.*
12 International Covenant on Civil & Political Rights, *opened for signature* Mar. 23, 1976, 999 U.N.T.S. 171 (entered into force Dec. 16, 1966).
13 *Id.* art. 26.
14 Convention on the Elimination of All Forms of Discrimination Against Women, G.A. Res. 34/180, at 193, U.N. GAOR, 34th Sess., Supp. No. 46, U.N. Doc. A/34/46 (Dec. 18, 1979) [hereinafter CEDAW].

field."[15] In addition, CEDAW requires member states to take necessary measures to eradicate all forms of discrimination against women, including embodying the principle of equality in their national legal systems, abolishing discriminatory laws, and establishing public institutions and tribunals to ensure the protection of women against all aspects of discrimination.[16]

B *The Right to Work and Equal Treatment in Employment*

Many international human rights instruments include general texts regarding labor standards. According to the U.N. Charter, member states of the U.N. are required "to employ international machinery for the promotion of the economic and social advancement of all peoples."[17] In addition, Article 55 of the Charter stipulates that "the United Nations shall promote: higher standards of living, full employment, and conditions of economic and social progress and development ... [and] universal respect for, and observance of, human rights and fundamental freedoms for all without distinction as to race, sex, language, or religion."[18]

Similarly, the UDHR uses broad language in stating employment rights. The Declaration stipulates that "everyone has the right to work, to free choice of employment, to just and favorable conditions of work and to protection against unemployment."[19] It also states that "everyone, without any discrimination, has the right to equal pay for equal work."[20] Additionally, the Declaration includes other articles related to one's right to work requiring member states to eradicate slavery,[21] servitude,[22] torture,[23] and "cruel, inhuman, or degrading treatment, or punishment."[24]

In addition, the ICESCR emphasizes one's right to work.[25] Under Article 6 of the Covenant, member states should "recognize the right to work, which includes the right of everyone to the opportunity to gain his living by

15 *Id.* art.1.
16 *Id.* art.2.
17 U.N. Charter, pmbl.
18 *Id.* art. 55.
19 UDHR, *supra* note 8, art. 23.
20 *Id.* art. 23.
21 *Id.* art. 4.
22 *Id.*
23 *Id.* art. 5.
24 *Id.*
25 International Covenant on Economic, Social and Cultural Rights, art. 6, *opened for signature* Dec. 16, 1966, G.A. Res. 2200A, at 49, U.N. GAOR, 21st Sess., Supp. No. 16, U.N. Doc. A/6316 (entered into force Mar. 23, 1976).

work which he freely chooses or accepts," and take appropriate measures to ensure the enjoyment of that right.[26] The second paragraph of this article imposes means of implementing the full realization of the right to work, including "technical and vocational guidance and training programmes, policies and techniques to achieve steady economic, social and cultural development, and full and productive employment under conditions safeguarding fundamental political and economic freedoms to the individual."[27] In addition, Article 7 of the Covenant stipulates guidelines for employment treatment.[28] Under this article, everyone should enjoy "fair wages and equal remuneration for work of equal value without distinction of any kind," "safe and healthy working conditions," equal opportunities for promotion, and "reasonable limitation of working hours and periodic holidays with pay, as well as remuneration for public holidays."[29]

Furthermore, CEDAW stresses the right to gender equality in the workplace. Article 11 of the Convention stipulates that member states should take all appropriate measures to eliminate discrimination against women in the field of employment.[30] According to this article, the right to work is an "inalienable right of all human beings."[31] This article requires member states to grant women, on the basis of equality with men, the same opportunities of employment,[32] "the right to free choice of profession and employment, the right to promotion benefits and conditions of service and the right to receive vocational training and retraining, including apprenticeships, advanced vocational training and recurrent training."[33] In addition, this article requires member states to provide women with "the right to equal remuneration, including benefits, and to equal treatment with respect to work of equal value, as well as equality of treatment in the evaluation of the quality of work remuneration, including benefits, and to equal treatment in respect of work of equal value, as well as equality of treatment in the evaluation of the quality of work."[34]

26 *Id.* art. 6(1).
27 *Id.* art. 6(2).
28 *Id.* art. 7.
29 *Id.*
30 CEDAW, *supra* note 14, art. 11.
31 *Id.* art. 11(a).
32 *Id.* art. 11(b).
33 *Id.* art. 11(c).
34 *Id.* art. 11(d). Although Article 11 of CEDAW, the most important international provision seeking to eradicate discrimination against a woman in employment, does not explicitly define sexual harassment in the workplace, the CEDAW Committee stipulates that this article includes an implicit definition for this issue. In General Recommendation

There is a linguistic difference between equal pay for work of equal value and equal pay for equal work.[35] CEDAW protects the first notion because it has a broader scope that could include more protection for female

19, the Committee defined gender-based violence as "a form of discrimination that seriously inhibits women's ability to enjoy rights and freedoms on a basis of equality with men." Comm. on the Elimination of Discrimination Against Women, General Recommendation 19, art. 11, para. 1, U.N. Doc. HRI/GEN/1/Rev. 9 (vol. II) (May 27, 2008). In addition, the Committee stated that "[e]quality in employment can be seriously impaired when women are subjected to gender-specific violence, such as sexual harassment in the workplace." *Id.* para. 17.

The Committee defined sexual harassment as "unwelcome sexually determined behavior as physical contact and advances, sexually colored remarks, showing pornography and sexual demand, whether by words or actions." *Id.* para. 18. Additionally, the Committee stipulates that harassment is discriminatory if a woman "has reasonable grounds to believe that her objection would disadvantage her in connection with her employment, including recruitment or promotion, or when it creates a hostile working environment." *Id.*

Furthermore, the United Nations Declaration on the Elimination of Violence Against Women (DEVAW) defines violence against a woman as "any act of gender-based violence that results in, or is likely to result in, physical, sexual or psychological harm or suffering to women, including threats of such acts, coercion or arbitrary deprivation of liberty, whether occurring in public or in private life." U.N. Declaration on the Elimination of Violence Against Women, G.A. Res. 48/104, art. 1, U.N. Doc. A/RES/48/104 (Dec. 20, 1993). Article 2 of DEVAW states that sexual harassment is an unacceptable behavior that should be eradicated by member states, even if it is committed by private actors. *Id.* art. 2. In addition, the Declaration requires states to "[d]eveloppenal, civil, labour and administrative sanctions in domestic legislation to punish and redress the wrongs caused to women who are subjected to violence." *Id.* art. 4(2).

Moreover, in its first special report on violence against women, the United Nations Commission on Human Rights (UNCHR) declared that the eradication of sexual harassment requires a proper definition of what constitutes such an issue. The report states that a variety of behaviors could fall under this definition, as some behaviors could be deemed normal in one society but sexual crimes in another. Therefore, the report stipulates that, in determining a definition of the issue of sexual harassment, cultural factors should necessarily be considered. Preliminary Rep. of the Special Rap porteur on Violence Against Women, its Cause and Consequences, 1994/45, U.N. ESCOR, Comm'n on H.R., 50th Sess., Agenda Item 11(a), para. 190, U.N. Doc. E/CN.4/1995/42 (1994).

Sexual harassment is also defined by regional bodies. The European Economic Community defines sexual harassment, in a very broad sense, as verbal or physical conduct that has a sexual nature and causes embarrassment to an employee. Res. of May 29, 1990, O.J. (C 157), available at http://eur-lex.europa.eu/en/index.htm (last visited Aug. 21, 2024).

35 Jessica Riggin, *The Potential Impact of CEDAW Ratification on U.S. Employment Discrimination Law: Lessons from Canada*, 42 Colum. Hum. Rts. L. Rev. 541, 560 (2011).

workers' rights.[36] Therefore, according to CEDAW, pay claims could be based on jobs that are quite different in nature.[37] Regarding the implementation of this protection, the CEDAW's Committee recommended that member states "consider the study, development and adoption of job evaluation systems based on gender-neutral criteria that would facilitate the comparison of the value of those jobs of a different nature, in which women presently predominate, with those jobs in which men presently predominate."[38]

C *ILO Non-discrimination and Equality Standards*

ILO is an international agency of the U.N. that specializes in establishing and formulating principles and legislation to protect and promote labor rights; it creates international standards of employment through issuing and publishing agreements and recommendations.[39] The ILO seeks to stipulate "acceptable levels of working conditions and worker protection," such as occupational safety and health, working time, health insurance and social security pensions.[40] The objectives and purposes of the ILO are enshrined in the Declaration of Philadelphia.[41] Under that Declaration, "all human beings, irrespective of race, creed or sex, have the right to pursue both their material well-being and their spiritual development in conditions of freedom and dignity, of economic security and equal opportunity."[42]

To establish a duty on member states, irrespective of whether they have ratified its conventions, the ILO promulgated the Declaration on Fundamental Principles and Rights at Work.[43] Under that Declaration, all member states of the ILO shall respect, protect and realize the following four basic principles: "freedom of association and the effective recognition of the right to collective bargaining," "the elimination of all forms of forced or compulsory labour," "the effective abolition of child labour," and the elimination of discrimination in respect of employment and occupation.[44]

---

36 *Id.*

37 *Id.*

38 Comm. on the Elimination of Discrimination against Women, Rep. of the Comm. on the Elimination of Discrimination against Women, 76, U.N. Doc. A/44/38 (Feb. 13, 1990).

39 International Labour Organization [ILO], Constitution, ch. 2, art. 19 (1919).

40 ILO, Mandate, available at http://www.ilo.org/public/english/about/index.htm (last visited Aug. 21, 2024).

41 Declaration Concerning the Aims and Purposes of the International Labour Organization, adopted May 10, 1944, 15 U.N.T.S. 35.

42 *Id.*

43 ILO, Declaration on Fundamental Principles and Rights at Work, 86th Sess. (June 1998).

44 *Id.* art. 2.

i Convention No. 100 on Equal Remuneration

The ILO Equal Remuneration Convention (Convention No. 100)[45] protects the principle of equal remuneration for work of equal value.[46] On this basis, this Convention compares not only identical works but also the value of the work as a standard between two works.[47] According to the Convention, the term "remuneration" includes basic salary and other bonuses as mentioned in the first article of the Convention,[48] which defines remuneration as broadly as possible in order to eliminate discrimination in all aspects of a worker's compensation.[49]

ii Convention No. 111 on Discrimination

The Discrimination (Employment and Occupation) Convention (ILO Convention No.111)[50] expands the scope of the preceding Convention to ensure equality of treatment in all aspects of employment.[51] The Convention's objective is to eradicate any type of discrimination that may occur in the workplace.[52] It contains a definition of discrimination in very broad language: "any distinction, exclusion or preference made on the basis of race, colour, sex, religion, political opinion, national extraction or social origin, which has the effect of nullifying or impairing equality of opportunity or treatment in employment or occupation."[53] This Convention uses the same language to define discrimination as other conventions, such as CEDAW and the International Convention on the Elimination of All Forms of Racial Discrimination (CERD).[54] Therefore, according to Convention No. 111, the definition of discrimination "continues to be a sound and up-to-date basis for any international monitoring."[55]

---

45 Convention concerning Equal Remuneration for Men and Women Workers for Equal Value, No. 100, June 29, 1951, 165 U.N.T.S. 303 [hereinafter Convention No. 100].

46 *Id.* art. 1(b).

47 Constance Thomas, *Monitoring International Labor Standards: Article Information, Sources, and Measures of International Labor Standards on Employment Discrimination*, 24 Comp. Lab. L. & Pol'y J. 365, 369 (2003).

48 Convention No. 100, *supra* note 45, art. 1(a).

49 Thomas, *supra* note 47.

50 Convention Concerning Discrimination in Respect of Employment and Occupation, ILO Convention No. 111, adopted June 25, 1958, 362 U.N.T.S. 31 [hereinafter Convention No. 111].

51 *Id.* art. 2.

52 *Id.*

53 *Id.* art.1.

54 International Convention on the Elimination of All Forms of Racial Discrimination (CERD), G.A. Res. 2106 (XX), at 47, U.N. GAOR, 20th Sess., Supp. No. 14, U.N. Doc. A/6014 (Dec. 21, 1965).

55 Thomas, *supra* note 47, at 368.

The ILO Committee of Experts on the Application of Conventions and Recommendations (CEACR), the legal body that monitors member states' compliance with international labor standards, stipulates that the definition of discrimination under Convention No. 111 covers both direct and indirect discrimination.[56] Direct discrimination includes laws, regulations and policies, which "explicitly exclude or disadvantage workers on the basis of characteristics" such as race, sex, or age.[57] On the other hand, indirect discrimination exists when employment regulations or practices appear to be neutral but, in reality, they negatively affect "a disproportionate number of members of a particular group" of workers.[58] In other words, indirect discrimination occurs when the practices and policies of an employer result in unequal treatment of one group of workers over another.[59] Regulations on part-time work could be a good example of this type of discrimination. If these regulations treat part-time workers less favorably than full-time workers, they may indirectly constitute discrimination against women because the majority of part-time workers are often women.[60] Furthermore, the Committee of Experts expanded the interpretation of the prohibition of gender discrimination under the scope of Convention No. 111. According to the Committee, this type of discrimination includes sexual harassment,[61] husband's approval on work and travel,[62] and work opportunities based on negative pregnancy tests.[63]

Article 3 of Convention No. 111 requires member states to undertake the following obligations:

A) Foster cooperation between an employer and its employees so that the Convention's policy can be respected.[64]

---

56 Int'l Labour Conference, *Equality in Employment and Occupation: General Survey by the* Committee *of* Experts *on the Application of Conventions and Recommendations*, para. 26 (1988) [hereinafter Committee of Experts, *General Survey*, 1988].

57 ILO, Director-General, *Time for Equality at Work: Global Report under the Follow-up to the ILO Declaration on Fundamental Principles and Rights at Work*, para. 56, delivered to the 91st Session of the International Labour Conference, Report I (B) (Mar. 2003).

58 *Id.* para. 57.

59 *Id.* para. 58.

60 *Id.*

61 Int'l Labor. Office, Comm. of Experts, *General Survey on Equality in Employment and Occupation* 158 (1986).

62 Rep. of the Comm. of Experts on the Application of Conventions and Recommendations, Rep. III (Part 1A), para. 366 Chad, Congo 372, Int'l Labor Conference, 98th Session (2009).

63 *Id.* at 374 Dominican Republic.

64 Convention No. 111, *supra* note 50, art. 3(a).

B) Enact legislation and develop educational programs to promote the Convention's principles.[65]

C) Abolish any legal act, administrative instruction, or practice that is inconsistent with the convention's policy.[66]

D) Guarantee that the Convention's policy is pursued "under the direct control of a national authority."[67]

E) "Ensure observance of the policy in the activities of vocational guidance, vocational training and placement services under the direction of a national authority."[68]

F) "Indicate in its annual reports on the application of the Convention the action taken in pursuance of the policy and the results secured by such action."[69]

Although Convention No. 111 has a broad definition of discrimination and requires member states to eradicate any kind of discrimination in the field of employment, there are specific exceptions to the scope of this Convention, as follows:

1. Any distinction due to an inherent requirement of a particular job does not constitute discrimination under the Convention.[70]
2. Disparate employment treatment against a person who is engaged in activities detrimental to the security of the state shall not be considered discriminatory if his or her involvement in committing these dangerous actions is confirmed.[71]
3. "Special measures of protection or assistance" that are enshrined in other international labor standards shall not be considered discriminatory.[72]
4. Special measures provided to certain persons to satisfy "particular requirements of persons who, for reasons such as sex, age, disablement, family responsibilities or social or cultural status, are generally recognised to require special protection or assistance, shall not be deemed to be discrimination."[73]

65 *Id.* art. 3(b).
66 *Id.* art. 3(c).
67 *Id.* art. 3(d).
68 *Id.* art. 3(e).
69 *Id.* art. 3(f).
70 *Id.* art. 1.
71 *Id.* art. 4.
72 *Id.* art. 5(1).
73 *Id.* art. 5(2).

Regarding the first exception, the Committee of Experts stipulated that it must be rigorously applicable. Otherwise, it could unreasonably restrict the protection against discrimination provided by the Convention.[74] Therefore, in applying this exception, careful consideration must be given to job descriptions.[75] Similarly, the Committee of Experts stated that the second exception should be firmly applied.[76] Therefore, in order for this exception to be appropriately implemented, special measures should be adopted to protect the state's security and prevent dangerous activities without punishing individuals for their participation in certain groups or communities.[77]

Concerning the third exception, the Committee of Experts did not stipulate an interpretation. However, it provided specific examples for this exception.[78] The Committee of Experts clarified that this exception aims at protecting women, indigenous people, and aged and disabled persons.[79] As regards the fourth exception, the Committee found that Article 5(2) of the Convention permits states to adopt particular measures for the protection of special groups of workers.[80] These measures should be "justified by the aim of protection and assistance which they are to pursue."[81] In addition, they should be "proportional to the nature and scope of the protection needed or of the pre-existent discrimination" and reexamined from time to time to consider whether they are still needed.[82]

Although this Convention sought to eliminate employment discrimination as much as possible, many commentators believe that it is more descriptive than prescriptive.[83] They recognize that the Convention does not specify a certain method for combating employment discrimination; however, it leaves member states to determine the most effective method for eradicating discriminatory practices in the workplace.[84] According to their view, measures to eliminate employment discrimination vary from one country to another because it is a relative process, and therefore drafters of

74 Committee of Experts, *General Survey*, 1988, *supra* note 56, para. 125.
75 *Id.* para. 127.
76 *Id.* para. 134.
77 *Id.* para. 135.
78 *Id.* paras. 141–56.
79 *Id.* paras. 150–56.
80 Convention No. 111, *supra* note 50, art. 5.
81 Committee of Experts, *General Survey*, 1988, *supra* note 56, para. 147.
82 *Id.*
83 Breen Creighton, *The ILO and the Protection of Fundamental Human Rights in Australia*, 22 Melbourne U. L. R. 239, 252–53 (1998).
84 *Id.*

the Convention could have left this point to be determined by each country based on its domestic legal system.[85]

iii Family Responsibilities Convention

In 1981, the ILO promulgated the Family Responsibilities Convention, which prohibits all forms of discrimination against workers based on family responsibilities.[86] This Convention refers to Convention No. 111 in defining employment discrimination,[87] and applies to all workers, who are responsible for dependent children, "where such responsibilities restrict their possibilities of preparing for, entering, participating in or advancing in economic activity."[88] The Family Responsibilities Convention applies to all classes of workers and all fields of economic activity,[89] and its objective is to provide workers, whether men or women, the right to free choice of employment and to prevent the termination of employment based solely on family responsibilities.[90]

Nevertheless, some commentators believe that the Family Responsibilities Convention has two flaws. The first is that it does not address some employment decisions, such as hiring, and therefore fails to provide protection in this sphere.[91] The second flaw relates to the issue of enforcement because few ILO member states have ratified that Convention and are thus not bound by its provisions.[92]

D *Protection against Pregnancy Discrimination in the Workplace and Special Protection during Pregnancy*

CEDAW emphasizes the protection of pregnant female workers. It requires member states to prevent employment discrimination on grounds of pregnancy.[93] Article 11 of the Convention obliges member states to prohibit "dismissal on the grounds of pregnancy or of maternity leave and

---

85 *Id.* at 253.
86 Workers with Family Responsibilities Convention, June 23, 1981, ILONEX, C156.
87 *Id.* art. 3(2). This article stipulates that "the term discrimination means discrimination in employment and occupation as defined by Articles 1 and 5 of the Discrimination (Employment and Occupation) Convention." *Id.*
88 *Id.* art. 1(1).
89 *Id.* art. 2.
90 *Id.* art. 4.
91 E. Abena Antwi, *Women in the World of Work: After Eighty-Six Years, Has the International Labour Organization Done Enough to Promote Equality?* 31 N.C.J. Int'l L. & Com. Reg. 793, 805 (2006).
92 *Id.*
93 CEDAW, *supra* note 14, art. 11(2).

discrimination in dismissals on the basis of marital status."[94] In addition, this article stipulates that member states should "introduce maternity leave with pay or with comparable social benefits without loss of former employment, seniority or social allowances."[95] Furthermore, according to this article, member states are required to "provide special protection to women during pregnancy in types of work proved to be harmful to them."[96]

The International Conference on Population and Development (ICPD) considered mandatory pregnancy testing as a discriminatory practice against female workers. That conference recommended that U.N. member states "empower women and take steps to eliminate inequalities between men and women as soon as possible by … eliminating discriminatory practices by employers against women, such as those based on proof of contraceptive use or pregnancy status."[97]

It seems that the ICPD's recommendation encouraged U.N. treaty bodies to ban pregnancy testing as a required condition of employment.[98] The CEDAW's Committee states that mandatory pregnancy testing as a condition of employment is considered a violation of a female worker's "rights to informed consent and dignity."[99] In addition, in its concluding observations on the reports of member states, the Committee stated that mandatory pregnancy testing constitutes sex-based discrimination.[100] The Committee requires member states to enact domestic legislation to prevent the termination of work based on pregnancy[101] and ensure the enforcement of such legislation.[102] Furthermore, the Committee required states to take measures to raise pregnant workers' awareness in order to recognize discriminatory practices against their employment rights.[103]

---

94 *Id.* art. 11(a).

95 *Id.* art. 11(b).

96 *Id.* art. 11(d).

97 International Conference on Population and Development, ch. 4, action 4.4(f), Cairo, Egypt, Sept. 5–13, 1994, Programme of Action, U.N. DOC. A/CONF.171/13 (1994).

98 Jennifer M. Swedish, *The SETISA Factory: Mandatory Pregnancy Testing Violates the Human Rights of Honduran Maquila Workers*, 4 Nw. U. J. Int'l Hum. Rts. 363, 370 (2005).

99 CEDAW, General Rec. 24, Women and Health (art. 12), 20th Sess., U.N. DOC. A/54/38/Rev.1, ch. I (Feb. 2, 1999).

100 CEDAW, *Concluding Comments: Colombia,* para. 53, 20th Sess., U.N. DOC. A/54/28 (part I) (Feb. 5, 1999).

101 CEDAW, *Concluding Comments: Mexico,* para. 442, (27)(b) (exceptional) Sess., U.N. DOC. A/57/38 (part 3) (Aug. 28, 2002).

102 CEDAW, *Concluding Observations: Guatemala,* para. 187, (27)(b) (exceptional) Sess., U.N. DOC. A/57/38 (part 3) (Aug. 23, 2002).

103 *Id.*

In addition, in General Comment 28, the HRC denounced pregnancy testing as a condition of employment because it "may interfere with a woman's rights to enjoy privacy and other rights protected by Article 17 [of the ICCPR] on the basis of equality with men."[104] Additionally, in its concluding observations to the reports of member states, the HRC considered mandatory pregnancy testing as an example of the absence of sex equality in employment.[105] The Committee stated that pregnancy testing as a condition of employment violates Article 3 of the Covenant, which protects the right to equality, and Article 17, which protects the right to privacy.[106] Furthermore, the HRC required member states to take necessary measures "to counteract these forms of discrimination against women,"[107] ensure that "women whose rights to equality and privacy have been violated in this way have access to remedies," and prevent "such violations from recurring."[108]

Likewise, the ICESCR Committee found that mandatory pregnancy testing as a condition of employment violates the ICESCR. It denounced such a practice and required member states to take legal action against any employer who engages in it.[109]

Furthermore, the CEACR declared that discrimination on grounds of pregnancy constitutes discrimination based on sex, and therefore violates Convention No. 111.[110] The Committee of Experts concluded that the "discriminatory nature of distinctions on the basis of pregnancy, confinement and related medical conditions is demonstrated by the fact that up to the present time they have only affected women."[111] In addition, the Committee of Experts, while monitoring member states' compliance with the Discrimination Convention, criticized mandatory pregnancy testing as a requirement of employment and therefore required states to "eliminate such discriminatory practices."[112] The Committee suggested particular measures

104 Human Rights Comm., General Comment 28, para. 30, U.N. Doc. CCPR/C/21/Rev.1/Add.10 (Mar. 29, 2000).

105 Human Rights Committee, *Concluding Comments: Poland*, para. 12, 66th Sess., U.N. DOC. CCPR/C/79/Add. 110 (July 28, 1999) [hereinafter Poland-HRC].

106 Human Rights Committee, *Concluding Comments: Mexico*, para. 17, 66th Sess., U.N. DOC. CCPR/C/79/Add. 109 (July 23, 1999) [hereinafter Mexico-HRC].

107 Poland-HRC, *supra* note 105.

108 Mexico-HRC, *supra* note 106.

109 Committee on Economic, Social and Cultural Rights, *Concluding Comments: Mexico*, para. 21, 21st Sess., U.N. DOC. E/C.12/1/Add.41 (Dec. 2, 1999).

110 Committee of Experts, *General Survey*, 1988, *supra* note 56, para. 41.

111 *Id.*

112 Committee of Experts on the Application of Conventions and Recommendations, Individual Observation Concerning Convention No. 111, Discrimination (Employment and

for the eradication of such practices. It required states to raise employers' and workers' awareness in order to realize that pregnancy testing constitutes discrimination against a female worker and to impose penalties on employers practicing such a measure as a condition of employment.[113]

In 1919, the ILO adopted the first Maternity Protection Convention (Convention No. 3).[114] This Convention protects female workers in "any public or private industrial or commercial undertaking."[115] Article 3 of the Convention prevents a female worker from working "during the six weeks following her confinement."[116] In addition, this article requires that a female worker, while on leave, be "paid benefits sufficient for the full and healthy maintenance of herself and her child."[117] Moreover, Article 4 of the Convention permits a female worker to remain at home for longer than a period of six weeks due to medically certified reasons based on pregnancy and makes it unlawful to dismiss her during her absence from work.[118]

In 1952, the ILO promulgated another Maternity Protection Convention (Convention No. 103).[119] This Convention "applies to women employed in industrial undertakings and in non-industrial and agricultural occupations."[120] It addresses agricultural occupations and presents a broad definition and protection for commercial occupations.[121] Under the Convention, maternity leave was expanded to a period of twelve weeks and "shall include a period of compulsory leave after confinement."[122] In addition, the Convention addresses medical benefits that should be given to a female

---

Occupation), 1958: Mexico (ratification: 1961), 2000, para. 5, available at http://www.ilo.org/ilolex/english/iloquery.htm (ILOLEX database) (last visited Aug. 21, 2024).

113 *Id.*

114 Maternity Protection Convention, Nov. 28, 1919, ILOLEX C3.

115 *Id.* art. 3.

116 *Id.* art. 3(a).

117 *Id.* art. 3(c).

118 *Id.* art. (4).

119 Maternity Protection Convention, June 28, 1952, ILOLEX C103.

120 *Id.* art. 1(1).

121 *Id.* art. 1.

122 *Id.* art. 3. Under Article 3(3) of the Convention, "[t]he period of compulsory leave after confinement shall be prescribed by national laws or regulations, but shall in no case be less than six weeks; the remainder of the total period of maternity leave may be provided before the presumed date of confinement or following expiration of the compulsory leave period or partly before the presumed date of confinement and partly following the expiration of the compulsory leave period as may be prescribed by national laws or regulations."

worker while on maternity leave[123] and prohibits her dismissal during such a leave.[124]

The ILO's third and most recent Maternity Protection Convention was promulgated in 2000 (Convention No. 183). That Convention protects all employed women, including those who work "in atypical forms of dependent work."[125] It prevents employers from compelling a female worker to perform types of work that may harm her health or her children's health.[126] Additionally, the Convention prolongs the maternity leave to a period of fourteen weeks.[127] According to the Convention, a female worker is given "the right to return to the same position or an equivalent position paid at the same rate at the end of her maternity leave."[128] Additionally, the Convention prohibits the dismissal of a female worker due to pregnancy or childbirth.[129]

Although ILO conventions aim to protect female workers, some commentators argue that they do not discuss gender-based discriminatory practices when applying for a job.[130] In addition, some commentators see that the Committee of Experts failed to provide a proper mechanism for monitoring the implementation of international labor standards. Such a problem does not exist in Europe because the European Court of Justice has issued many decisions clarifying how international labor standards are invoked; however, in other continents, there is no jurisprudence that flows from ILO conventions.[131] The precedents of the ECJ are not binding on states on other continents. The Court's findings, on the other hand, provide a significant interpretation of gender employment equality, clarifying that a female employee should have equal pay and equal treatment with men in employment and occupation.[132] Therefore, this study shall briefly discuss some cases decided by the ECJ, as follows:

123 *Id.* art. 4 ("Medical benefits shall include pre-natal, confinement and post-natal care by qualified midwives or medical practitioners as well as hospitalisation care where necessary; freedom of choice of doctor and freedom of choice between a public and private hospital shall be respected.").

124 *Id.* art. 6.

125 Maternity Protection Convention, art. 1, June 15, 2000, 2181 U.N.T.S. 255 (entered into force Feb. 7, 2002).

126 *Id.* art. 3.

127 *Id.* art. 4.

128 *Id.* art. 8.

129 *Id.*

130 Human Rights Watch, Mexico, No Guarantees: Sex Discrimination in Mexico's Maquiladora Sector 26 (1996).

131 *Id.*

132 *Id.*

E Cases of Equal Pay under EU Gender Equality Law

In several cases, the ECJ banned both direct and indirect sex-based pay discrimination.[133] The case of Defrenne v. Sabena is an example of direct pay discrimination against a female worker.[134] In that case, Defrenne did not receive equal pay in comparison with her male co-workers, who had identical job duties.[135] The ECJ stated that domestic courts are required to ensure the application of the principle of equal pay for equal work between male and female workers "not only [in] the action of public authorities, but also [in] all agreements which were intended to regulate paid labour collectively, as well as [in] contracts between individuals."[136]

On the other hand, in Jenkins v. Kingsgate, the ECJ banned indirect pay discrimination against female employees.[137] Kingsgate, a manufacturer of women's clothes, employed eighty-nine workers, including thirty-five males and fifty-four females. With the exception of one male employee, all male employees worked full-time, whereas a great number of female employees worked part-time.[138] According to the employer's pay policy, for reasons related to encouraging "greater productivity" at the factory, part-time workers were paid 10% less per hour than the full-time workers.[139] Jenkins, who

133 Case 43/75, Defrenne v. Sabena, 1976 E.C.R. 455 (Defrenne II); Case 96/80, Jenkins v. Kingsgate, 1981 E.C.R. 911; Case 96/80, Jenkins v. Kingsgate, 1981 E.C.R. 911. The principle of equal pay in EU employment law is enshrined in Article 119 of the EEC Treaty, which aims to eradicate wage discrimination where a female worker is employed in the same capacity as her male counterpart. Treaty Establishing the European Economic Community, Mar. 25, 1957, 298 U.N.T.S. 11, art. 119 (1958).

Article 119 of the EEC Treaty was replaced with Article 141 of the EC Treaty that was later replaced with Article 157 of the TFEV Treaty. Article 119 requires states to "ensure and subsequently maintain the application of the principle of equal remuneration for equal work as between men and women workers." EEC Treaty, art. 119. It defines "remuneration" as the "ordinary basic or minimum wage or salary and any additional emoluments … whether in cash or in kind, by the employer to the workers and arising out of the workers' employment." *Id.*

The Equal Pay Directive clarified the meaning of Article 119 of the EEC Treaty. Council Directive 75/117, 1975 O.J. (L 45) 19 [hereinafter Equal Pay Directive].

Article 1 of that Directive stipulates that "the principle of equal pay for men and women outlined in Article 119 of the Treaty … means, for the same work or for work to which equal value is attributed, the elimination of all discrimination on grounds of sex with regard to all aspects and conditions of remuneration." *Id.* art. 1.

134 Case 43/75, Defrenne v. Sabena, 1976 E.C.R. 455 (Defrenne II).

135 *Id.* Facts and Procedures, para. 1.

136 *Id.* Judgment of the Court, para. 1.

137 Case 96/80, Jenkins v. Kingsgate, 1981 E.C.R. 911.

138 *Id.* Facts and Procedures, para. 1.

139 *Id.*

worked thirty hours per week as a part-time employee, complained that she was paid less per hour than her male colleague, who was engaged in full-time work, despite the fact that they performed identical duties.[140] The ECJ found the employer's pay policy discriminatory against female workers.[141] The Court clarified that the difference in pay between full-time and part-time workers does not constitute gender-based discrimination unless "it is in reality an indirect way of reducing the pay of part-time workers on the ground that that group of workers is composed exclusively or predominantly of women."[142]

Similarly, in Berlin v. Botel,[143] the ECJ banned an employer's pay policy involving indirect discrimination against female workers.[144] This case started when Berlin attended work-related and essential training courses.[145] The national law stipulates that employees who receive training courses must be compensated at their regular rate for the hours they spend in training.[146] Berlin, who worked part-time, spent more hours training than her regular working hours; however, she was paid the same amount for her part-time hours. She was not compensated for the additional training hours. If she were a full-time worker, she would have been paid for the training hours within the full-time working hours limit.[147] The ECJ noticed that part-time workers were predominantly women, and therefore found that the application of national law indirectly discriminated against female workers.[148] In addition, the Court required member states to pass national legislation providing remuneration to many more female workers based on "objective factors unconnected with any discrimination based on sex."[149]

Another case involving indirect pay discrimination against a female worker is Bilka v. Weber.[150] In that case, the employer's pay policy allowed only employees who spent at least fifteen years in full-time work to receive an occupational pension.[151] Together with a great number of female workers, Weber spent more than fifteen years doing part-time work but was not

140 *Id.* para. 2.
141 *Id.* Judgment of the Court, para. 1.
142 *Id.*
143 Case 360/90, Berlin v. Botel, 1992 E.C.R. I-3589.
144 *Id.* Judgment of the Court, para. 1.
145 *Id.* Facts and Procedures, para. 1.
146 *Id.*
147 *Id.*
148 *Id.* Judgment of the Court, para. 1.
149 *Id.* para. 2.
150 Case 170/84, Bilka-Kaufhaus v. Weber von Hartz, 1986 E.C.R. 1607.
151 *Id.* Facts and Procedures, para. 1.

given an occupational pension.[152] Therefore, she brought an action against the employer claiming that its policy constituted discrimination based on sex.[153] The ECJ noted that "a much lower proportion of female workers than of male workers worked full time," and therefore the Court found the "exclusion of part-time workers from the occupational pension scheme" involved indirect discrimination against a female worker.[154] However, the Court clarified that the employer could avoid liability "if [it] was able to show that its pay practice could be explained by objectively justified factors unrelated to any discrimination on grounds of sex."[155]

The case of Rummler v. Dato-Druck GmbH involves another type of indirect discriminatory pay policy against a female worker.[156] In that case, the plaintiff, a female employee at a German printing firm, was paid in accordance with the degree of her muscular efforts.[157] The ECJ clarified that an employer could depend on its workers' muscular effort regarding pay determination.[158] However, the Court found that the employer's pay policy included some aspects of discrimination against a female worker.[159] The Court held that in order for a job classification system not to be discriminatory, it should take into account "other criteria in relation to which women workers could have a particular aptitude."[160]

152 *Id.* para. 2.
153 *Id.*
154 *Id.* Judgment of the Court, para. 2.
155 *Id.*
156 Case 237/85, Rummler v. Dato-Druck GmbH, 1986 E.C.R. 2101.
157 *Id.* Facts and Procedures, para. 2.
158 *Id.* Judgment of the Court, para. 1.
159 *Id.*
160 *Id.* The Equal Pay Directive does not require an employer to use a job classification system to determine pay. However, if the employer chooses to use that system, the Equal Pay Directive obliges that it "must be based on the same criteria for both men and women and so drawn to exclude any discrimination on grounds of sex." Equal Pay Directive, *supra* note 133, art. 1(2). In Commission of the European Union v. UK, there was a reference in the British national law regarding the principle of equal pay for work of equal value, the Equal Pay Act of 1970. Case 61/81, Comm'n v. UK, 1982 E.C.R. 2601, Facts and Procedures, para. 2. The law considered the job classification system the only method of determining work of equal value. *Id.* The Commission of the European Union deemed the act contradictory to the Equal Pay Directive and therefore referred the matter to the ECJ. *Id.* para. 3. The ECJ upheld the Commission's point of view and found that the UK failed to fulfill its obligation under the Equal Pay Directive, since its national law necessitates that the job classification system be the sole method for evaluating work of equal value. *Id.* Judgment of the Court, para. 2. In other words, the ECJ stated that, according to the Equal Pay Directive, individuals

F *Cases of Equal Treatment under EU Gender Equality Law*

In many rulings, the ECJ has prohibited both direct and indirect sex-based employment discrimination.[161] The case of Johnston v. Chief Constable of the Royal Ulster Constabulary involved direct discriminatory treatment against a female worker.[162] The Chief Constable of the RUC decided, for security reasons, that female police officers, unlike their male counterparts, would not be equipped with firearms while performing their job duties and would not receive training in the use and handling of firearms.[163] Therefore, in a position requiring the carrying of firearms, he started not to offer or renew contracts for female officers.[164] Johnston, who was a full-time worker at the RUC, was disallowed from carrying firearms while performing her work duties, and her contract was not renewed as a result of the new policy.[165] She brought an action claiming that the new policy of the RUC constituted sex-based discrimination against female workers.[166] The ECJ initially clarified that a state has the power to restrict general duties in order to protect its public safety.[167] However, the Court stated that acts of gender discrimination committed for the purpose of protecting public safety "must be examined in the light of the derogations from the principle of equal treatment for men and women" enshrined in Article 2 of the Equal Treatment Directive.[168] According to the Court, the disparate treatment between a male and a female worker, which Article 2 of the Equal Treatment Directive[169] permits for the protection of women, "do[es] not include risks and danger that do not specifically affect women as such."[170] In other words, the Court found that since the risks of being targets of assassination that armed female police officers might face are likely to occur in the case of male officers too, the new policy of the RUC exceeded the boundaries of the exceptions allowed by Article 2.[171]

could rely on other methods apart from the job classification system to bring equal pay claims. *Id.*

161 Case 222/84, Johnston v. Chief Constable of the Royal Ulster Constabulary, 1986 E.C.R. 1651; Case 345/89, Stoeckel v. French Republic, 1991 E.C.R. I-4047; Case 100/95, Kording v. Senator fur Finanzen, 1997 E.C.R. I-5289.

162 Case 222/84, 1986 E.C.R. 1651.

163 *Id.* Facts and Procedures, para. 1.

164 *Id.*

165 *Id.* para. 2.

166 *Id.* para. 3.

167 *Id.* Judgment of the Court, para. 7.

168 *Id.* para. 8.

169 Council Directive 76/207, 1976 O.J. (L 39) 40 [hereinafter Directive 76/207/EEC].

170 Case 222/84, 1986 E.C.R. 1651, Judgment of the Court, para. 10.

171 *Id.* Judgment of the Court, para. 11.

Another significant case involving direct employment treatment discrimination against a woman is the case of Stoeckel v. French Republic.[172] In that case, a national law banned female workers from working at night in workshops, factories and similar places, but certain derogations from such a rule were permitted.[173] As a result, an employer who was charged for having seventy-seven female workers on the night shift challenged the law, claiming that it discriminated against female workers.[174] The ECJ clarified that, in accordance with Article 2 of the Equal Treatment Directive,[175] some measures could be taken by states to protect a woman in cases of maternity and pregnancy.[176] These measures aim to protect "a woman's biological condition and the special relationship which exists between a woman and her child."[177] However, the Court stated that "since that Directive did not allow any general principle excluding women from night work, the derogations could, indeed, be a source of discrimination."[178] Concerning the State's argument that women could face greater risks during their work at night than during the day, the Court found that alternative measures must be adopted to make female workers avoid such dangers without violating the fundamental principle of equal treatment in employment.[179]

---

172 Case 345/89, 1991 E.C.R. I-4047.

173 *Id.* Facts and Procedures, para. 2.

174 *Id.* para. 1.

175 Directive 76/207/EEC, *supra* note 169.

176 Case 345/89, 1991 E.C.R. I-4047, Judgment of the Court, para. 1. In Ulrich Hofmann v. Barmer Ersatzkasse, where a father of a newborn child sought a paid leave to look after his son after the mother's mandatory period of maternity leave expired, the ECJ held that exceptions to the equal treatment principle derived from Article 2(3) of Directive 76/207/EEC are confined to a woman due to the effects of pregnancy and maternity. Case 184/83, 1984 E.C.R. 3047, Judgment of the Court, para. 1. According to the Court, this derogation aims at protecting a woman's "biological condition during pregnancy" and promoting "the special relationship between a woman and her child over the period which follows pregnancy and childbirth, by preventing that relationship from being disturbed by the multiple burdens which would result from the simultaneous pursuit of employment." *Id.* In addition, the ECJ clarified that the Directive does not provide a man with the right to receive a paid leave to care for his newborn child, even if the parents agree that the father will take such a leave instead of the mother. *Id.* para. 3.

177 Case 345/89, 1991 E.C.R. I-4047, Judgment of the Court, para. 1.

178 *Id.*

179 *Id.* Another case clarifying sex-based employment discrimination in France is Commission of the European Community v. French Republic. Case 318/86, 1988 E.C.R. 3559. In that case, a national law allowed sex to be a determining factor in the separate recruitment of certain corps in the French Civil Services. *Id.* Facts and Procedures, para. 1. The Commission of the European Community ruled that the law was contrary to the

On the other hand, in Kording v. Senator fur Finanzen,[180] the ECJ banned indirect sex-based employment discrimination. In that case, according to the employer's promotion policy, an employee had to pass a qualifying examination in order to work as a tax advisor.[181] However, some employees who exceeded a certain number of work hours were exempted from that exam. Thus, in order to obtain a job as a tax advisor, part-time workers, the majority of whom were women, were required to pass such a qualifying exam. On the contrary, full-time workers, the majority of whom were men, were qualified to practice that job without meeting that requirement.[182] The ECJ noted that direct discrimination against a female worker could arise "through the application of different rules to comparable situations or the application of the same rule to different situations."[183] Therefore, the ECJ reasoned that the measures in question did not involve direct discrimination against a female worker because the length of service required for the exemption from passing the qualifying exam was "extended in exactly the same way for men as for women."[184] Nevertheless, the Court stated that "indirect discrimination arises where a national measure, albeit formulated in neutral terms, works to the disadvantage of far more women than men."[185] Thus, the Court found that the measures in question indirectly discriminated against women, as the number of female part-time workers was significantly greater than that of male part-time workers. According to the Court,

---

Equal Treatment Directive and therefore referred the matter to the ECJ. *Id.* para. 2. In turn, the ECJ upheld the Commission's point of view and found that the State failed to meet its obligations under the treaty. *Id.* Judgment of the Court, para. 5. The Court noted that the two parties "agreed that certain activities connected with the duties performed by the corps of the national police force could be performed by men only or, depending on the case, by women only, whereas certain other duties could be performed by any member of the police force, whether male or female." *Id.* para. 4. However, the Court found that the dispute involved the application of Article 2 of the Equal Treatment Directive, which allows derogations from the principle of equal treatment. *Id.* The Court stipulated that the application of this article should be transparent because derogations from the equal treatment principle should be limited only to specific activities. *Id.* Therefore, the Court ruled that the requirement of transparency was not fulfilled in the separate recruitment system because the number of positions allotted to men and women were not "governed by any objective criterion defined in a legislative provision." *Id.*

180 Case 100/95, 1997 E.C.R. I-5289.

181 *Id.* Facts and Procedures, para. 1.

182 *Id.*

183 *Id.* Judgment of the Court, para. 1.

184 *Id.*

185 *Id.*

since the involved measure was substantially applicable to women rather than men, it constituted indirect sex-based discrimination against a female worker.[186]

---

186 *Id.* The ECJ concluded that the required measures were contrary to Article 3(1) of the Equal Treatment Directive, Directive 76/207/EEC, which requires "the implementation of the principle of equal treatment for men and women as regards access to employment, vocational training and promotion, and working conditions." *Id.* para. 5. In Kalanke v. Freie Hansestadt Bremen, the ECJ banned employment discrimination against a man. Case 450/93, 1995 E.C.R. I-3051. In that case, Mr. Kalanke applied for a job for which a woman also applied. *Id.* Facts and Procedures, para. 1. After they both were considered equally qualified candidates; job priority was given to the female applicant because the national law specified a quota for women that must be adhered to. *Id.* The ECJ clarified that Article 2(4) of Directive 76/207/EEC aims at authorizing measures that, "although discriminatory in appearance, are in fact intended to eliminate or reduce actual instances of inequality which may exist in the reality of social life." *Id.* Judgment of the Court, para. 2. On the other hand, the Court stated that "as a derogation from an individual right laid down in the Directive." such an article should be strictly interpreted. *Id.* Therefore, the Court held that national laws that automatically give priority to female candidates if they are equally qualified with male candidates are incompatible with the Directive and should be revised. *Id.* paras. 1, 3.

Even though the facts of Marschall v. Land Nordrhein-westfalen are similar to those in Kalanke, the ECJ held that a national law giving preference to female candidates was not in violation of the Equal Treatment Directive. Case 409/95, 1997 E.C.R. I-6363, Judgment of the Court, para. 5. The events of this case started when Mr. Marschall, who worked as a teacher, applied for promotion at the same time as one of his female coworkers. *Id.* Facts and Procedures, para. 2. Although both candidates were deemed equally qualified, only the female teacher was promoted, and Marschall's application was denied. *Id.* The employer justified its decision on legal grounds. it argued that, under national law, in cases of equally qualified candidates for appointment or promotion, priority should be given to a woman, unless there are reasons that "tip the balance" in favor of a man. *Id.* para. 1. The ECJ ruled against Marschall, clarifying that the actions taken by the employer were not contrary to the Equal Treatment Directive. *Id.* Judgment of the Court, para. 6. The Court distinguished this case from Kalanke; it stated that the procedures for giving a woman precedence over a man were distinct in each instance. *Id.* para. 1. As for Kalanke, the Court explained that the national law automatically gave priority to a woman who was equally qualified with a man, and therefore the Court deemed the law to be discriminatory. *Id.* In contrast, the law of the present case did not automatically give priority to a woman; rather, a man could have preference if certain factors "tipped the balance" in his favor. *Id.* The Court reasoned that "where male and female candidates are equally qualified, male candidates tend to be promoted ... because of prejudices and stereotypes concerning the role and capacities of women in working life and the fear ... that owing to household and family duties they will be less flexible in their working hours." *Id.* para. 2. In other words, the Court found that "the mere fact that a male candidate and a female candidate are equally qualified does not mean that they have the same chances" and that the man has a larger chance owing to preconceptions and prejudices. *Id.*

In Dekker v. VJV-Centrum, the ECJ protected a female applicant from being denied recruitment based on pregnancy.[187] The case started when Dekker applied to work as an instructor at a training center for young adults (VJV Centrum).[188] In the interview, she informed the interview committee that she was three months pregnant; however, the committee considered her the most qualified candidate for the position.[189] Nevertheless, the board of VJV Centrum refused to appoint Dekker because of her pregnancy. The board argued that the refusal was based on the employer's potential financial loss during a woman's absence on maternity leave.[190] The ECJ reasoned that since only a woman would be denied employment due to pregnancy, "such a refusal therefore constituted direct discrimination on grounds of sex."[191] Furthermore, the Court explicitly stated that "discrimination could not be justified on grounds relating to the financial loss" an employer would incur for the duration of a female worker's maternity leave.[192]

In Webb v. Emo Air Cargo, the ECJ considered the dismissal of a female employee due to pregnancy as discrimination based on sex.[193] In that case, Mrs. Webb was appointed in Mrs. Stewart's place during her absence on maternity leave. However, she was informed that she would have to pursue different work after Stewart returned from leave.[194] Later, Webb discovered she was pregnant and informed the employer. In turn, she was dismissed because she would not be able to work during the period for which she was mainly recruited.[195] The ECJ held that the Equal Treatment Directive[196] bans dismissal of a female employee if she is hired for an indefinite period "with a view, initially, to replacing another employee during the latter's maternity leave and who cannot do so because, shortly after her recruitment, she is herself found to be pregnant."[197] In addition, the Court reasoned that "pregnancy is not in any way comparable with a pathological condition" or the incapability of working due to non-medical causes through which an employer could justify the dismissal of a female employee on grounds

187 Case 177/88, Dekker v. VJV Centrum, 1990 E.C.R. I-3941.
188 *Id.* Facts and Procedures, para. 1.
189 *Id.*
190 *Id.*
191 *Id.* Judgment of the Court, para. 1.
192 *Id.*
193 Case 32/93, Webb v. EMO Air Cargo Limited, 1994 E.C.R. I-3567, Judgment of the Court, para. 2.
194 *Id.* Facts and Procedures, para. 1.
195 *Id.*
196 Directive 76/207/EEC, *supra* note 169.
197 Case 32/93, 1994 E.C.R. I-3567, Judgment of the Court, para. 3.

unrelated to her gender.[198] Nevertheless, in other cases, the ECJ has clarified that dismissing a female employee due to illnesses attributable to pregnancy or confinement does not constitute sex-based discrimination.[199]

In Danmark v. Dansk Arbejdsgiverforening, Hertz began working as a salesperson and cashier at Aldi Market in July 1982.[200] Later, in June 1983, she gave birth and received a 24-week maternity leave in accordance with national law. At the end of her leave, she returned to work in the last days of 1983.[201] For more than one year, Hertz enjoyed good health, but later she started to suffer from certain diseases as a result of pregnancy. Because of her recurrent sick leaves, she was dismissed from work in June 1985.[202] The ECJ noted that dismissing a female employee because of pregnancy constitutes discrimination on the basis of sex.[203] However, the Court considered that dismissing a female employee because of her absence on sick leave is not discrimination against women since a male worker could also be dismissed for the same reason.[204] The Court stated that according to the Equal Treatment Directive,[205] an employer should not dismiss a female employee because of her absence on maternity leave; rather, the Directive "does not preclude dismissals which are the result of absences due to an illness [even if such an illness is] attributable to pregnancy or confinement."[206]

In summary, the ECJ followed the International Labor Standards of the ILO and provided women with comprehensive protection against direct and indirect sex-based employment discrimination. In addition, the

---

198 *Id.* para. 2. Similarly, in Beltermann v. Arbeiterwohlfahrt, the plaintiff worked as a nurse with the elderly. Case 421/92, 1994 E.C.R. I-1657, Facts and Procedures para. 1. Owing to special family conditions, she signed a contract with the employer allowing her to work solely at night. *Id.* Later, due to her pregnancy, she was dismissed. *Id.* The employer justified her dismissal on a legal basis, citing a national law that protects pregnant female employees by prohibiting their nighttime employment. *Id.* The ECJ held that the plaintiff's dismissal constituted sex-based discrimination. *Id.* Judgment of the Court, para. 2. The Court stated that the prohibition on nighttime work due to pregnancy "takes effect only for a limited period in relation to the total length of the contract," and therefore a contract for an indefinite duration could not be dissolved due to the temporary infirmity of a pregnant employee. *Id.*

199 Case 179/88, Danmark v. Dansk Arbejdsgiverforening, 1990 E.C.R. I-3979.

200 *Id.* Facts and Procedures, para. 1.

201 *Id.*

202 *Id.*

203 *Id.* Judgment of the Court, para. 1.

204 *Id.*

205 Directive 76/207/EEC, *supra* note 169.

206 Case 179/88, 1990 E.C.R. I-3979, Judgment of the Court, para. 3.

ECJ granted women well-grounded protection against pregnancy discrimination in the workplace.

2 Women's Right to Work under American Law

A *Equal Pay in American Law*

In the 1960s, the history of legal solutions for sex discrimination in the U.S. started with the Equal Pay Act that banned sex discrimination in employees' wages.[207] This Act was passed in 1963. It aimed to require courts to investigate whether the pay disparity between the sexes – male and female workers – was based on discriminatory grounds or was justified.[208]

The Equal Pay Act had a limited scope; it only protected the principle of "equal pay for equal work."[209] It could apply if a plaintiff and a comparator had "substantially equal" jobs.[210] According to the Equal Pay Act, female workers could bring claims if they did not receive equal pay in comparison with their male counterparts who performed "substantially equal" work duties in the same business institution.[211] Therefore, the Equal Pay Act merely sought to eradicate the clearest type of pay discrimination, where female

207 29 U.S.C. § 206(d) (1963).

208 Leora F. Eisenstadt, *Privileged but Equal? A Comparison of U.S. and Israeli Notions of Sex Equality in Employment Law*, 40 Vand. J. Transnat'l L. 357, 391–92 (2007).

209 County of Washington v. Gunther, 452 U.S. 161, 184–88 (1981) (Rehnquist, J., dissenting). The related part of the Equal Pay Act states:

> No employer having employees subject to any provisions of this section shall discriminate, within any establishment in which such employees are employed, between employees on the basis of sex by paying wages to employees in such establishment at a rate less than the rate at which he pays wages to employees of the opposite sex in such establishment for equal work on jobs the performance of which requires equal skill, effort, and responsibility, and which are performed under similar working conditions, except where such payment is made pursuant to (i) a seniority system; (ii) a merit system; (iii) a system which measures earnings by quantity or quality of production; or (iv) a differential based on any other factor other than sex: Provided, that an employer who is paying a wage rate differential in violation of this subsection shall not, in order to comply with the provisions of this subsection, reduce the wage rate of any employee.

29 U.S.C. 206(d)(1).

210 Hodgson v. American Bank of Commerce, 447 F.2d 416 (5th Cir. 1971).

211 Ursula R. Kubal, *Comment: U.S. Multinational Corporations Abroad: A Comparative Perspective on Sex Discrimination Law in the United States and the European Union*, 25 N.C.J. Int'l L. & Com. Reg. 207, 218 (1999).

workers' job duties were "substantially equal" to those of male workers but they were compensated at a different rate.[212]

Laffey v. Northwest Airlines is a good example of how the Equal Pay Act could be used to clarify potential claims.[213] In that case, a group of female workers, who were "employed as stewardesses," had work duties equal to those of their male colleagues, "serving as pursers," but were paid lower wages.[214] The United States Court of Appeals for the District of Columbia Circuit held that the employer's pay policy violated the Equal Pay Act.[215] The Court stated that "the contrast in pay is a consequence of the historical willingness of women to accept inferior financial rewards for equivalent work – precisely the outmoded practice which the Equal Pay Act sought to eradicate."[216]

In a similar case, the United States Court of Appeals for the Fifth Circuit overturned a ruling that allowed a wage disparity between male and female bank tellers due to the male tellers' superior professional role in "supervising the cashing of checks, helping the other tellers balance out, and generally acting as troubleshooters when unusual or difficult problems arose."[217] The Court found it was "doubtful at best that such small, insignificant additional duties [could] ever serve as a justification for the differential evidenced in the Bank's wage figures."[218]

Later on, the Equal Pay Act was eventually superseded by the Civil Rights Act of 1964, under which discrimination in employment, voting, education, public accommodation facilities, and federal programs is prohibited.[219] Employment discrimination was specifically prohibited under Title VII of the Civil Rights Act that bans discrimination on grounds of sex, religion, ethnicity, race, and national origin in all employment aspects such as compensation, privileges and conditions.[220]

In County of Washington v. Gunther,[221] the Supreme Court clarified the differences between Title VII of the Civil Rights Act and the Equal Pay Act, noting that a claim of wage discrimination based on sex could be brought

212 *Id.*

213 Laffey v. Northwest Airlines, Inc., 567 F.2d 429 (D.C. Cir. 1976).

214 *Id.* at 429.

215 *Id.* at 452.

216 *Id.* at 451.

217 Hodgson, 447 F.2d. at 422.

218 *Id.*

219 Hope Landrine & Elizabeth A. Klonoff, Discrimination Against Women: Prevalence, Consequences, and Remedies 177 (1997).

220 42 U.S.C. §2000e-2(a) (1964).

221 County of Wash. v. Gunther, 452 U.S. 161 (1981).

under Title VII even if it did not meet the equal work requirement of the Equal Pay Act.[222] The Court held that workers could not be "precluded from suing under Title VII to protest ... discriminatory compensation practices merely because their jobs were not equal to higher paying jobs held by members of the opposite sex."[223] In addition, the Court declared that the prohibition of employment discrimination under Title VII was intended to be largely inclusive.[224] According to the Court, Title VII did not ban only overt discrimination, but also prohibited "practices that are fair in form, but discriminatory in operation,"[225] and "the structure of Title VII litigation" was "designed to reflect this approach."[226] On the other hand, the Court affirmed that the Equal Pay Act was structured in a different way, "to confine the application of the Act to wage differentials attributable to sex discrimination." Besides, the Court clarified that the Equal Pay Act's structure of litigation was designed to allow employers to "defend against charges of discrimination where their pay differentials are based on a bona fide use of other factors other than sex."[227] Therefore, according to the Court, under the Equal Pay Act, courts were not allowed to "substitute their judgment for the judgment of the employer ... who has established and applied a bona fide job rating system, so long as it does not discriminate on the basis of sex."[228]

In addition, the Supreme Court in Gunther granted lower courts discretionary power to determine what a plaintiff should submit to demonstrate a sex-based pay discrimination claim under Title VII.[229] For example, the United States Courts of Appeal for the Fifth and Seventh Circuits decided that, in order for plaintiffs to demonstrate disparate treatment claims of sex-based wage discrimination under Title VII, they could either satisfy the equal pay standard of the Equal Pay Act or produce direct evidence of intentional discrimination.[230] On the other hand, the United States Court of Appeals for the Eleventh Circuit decided that plaintiffs could use indirect evidence to demonstrate disparate treatment of sex-based pay claims under Title VII.[231]

---

222 *Id.* at 165.
223 *Id.*
224 *Id.* at 170.
225 *Id.* (quoting *Griggs* v. *Duke Power Co.*, 401 U.S. 424, 431 (1971)).
226 *Id.*
227 *Id.*
228 *Id.* at 170–71.
229 Kubal, *supra* note 211, at 220–21.
230 Plemer v. Parsons-Gilbane, 713 F.2d 1127 (5th Cir. 1983).
231 Miranda v. B & B Cash Grocery Store, Inc., 975 F.2d 1518, 1526 (11th Cir. 1992).

B Equal Treatment in American Law

In addition to its significant role in combating sex-based wage discrimination, Title VII of the Civil Rights Act is considered the foundation of federal anti-discrimination law because it provides broad protection for the principle of non-discrimination based on numerous protected classes.[232] All employment relationships are covered by Title VII.[233] It bans pre-employment discriminatory practices, during-employment discriminatory practices, and post-employment discriminatory practices.[234]

Under Title VII, it is an unlawful practice "to fail or refuse to hire or to discharge any individual, or otherwise to discriminate against any individual with respect to his [or her] compensation, terms, conditions, or privileges of employment, because of such individual's race, color, religion, sex, or national origin."[235] In addition, according to the Statute, an employer is prohibited from limiting, segregating, or classifying "his employees or applicants for employment in any way which would deprive or tend to deprive any individual of employment opportunities or otherwise adversely affect his status as an employee" due to the mentioned grounds of discrimination.[236] Furthermore, Title VII prohibits employment agencies from failing or refusing to refer for employment, or otherwise discriminating against, any individual on the basis of race, color, religion, sex, or national origin, or classifying or referring for employment on such discriminatory grounds.[237]

Title VII applies to all private employers who engage in commerce and have at least fifteen employees, individual workers in their capacity as employer agents,[238] and all paid employees who do not have independent contracts, with the exception of those in military services and state and local governments.[239] In addition, the federal government, as an employer, is covered by a related amendment that is not mentioned in the main body of the Act.[240]

The Civil Rights Act contains exceptions to employment discrimination for a few qualities or characteristics that employers may consider when

232 Kubal, *supra* note 211, at 236.
233 Rogers v. EEOC, 454 F.2d 234, 238 (5th Cir. 1971).
234 Veprinsky v. Fluor Daniel, Inc., 87 F.3d 881, 888 (7th Cir. 1996); Durham Life Ins. Co. v. Evans, 166 F.3d 139, 157 (3d Cir. 1999).
235 42 U.S.C. § 2000e -2(a)(1) (1964).
236 *Id.* § 2000 2(a)(2).
237 *Id.* § 2000e (b).
238 *Id.*
239 *Id.* § 2000e(f)-16(a).
240 *Id.* § 2000e(b).

hiring or retaining employees; however, such exceptions should be "reasonably necessary to the normal operation of that particular business or enterprise."[241]

Regarding sex-based employment discrimination, courts in the U.S. have applied Title VII of the Civil Rights Act to eradicate both disparate treatment discrimination where a policy of an employer obviously discriminates against a female worker, and disparate impact discrimination where a policy of an employer seems to be neutral but in practice constitutes discrimination against a female worker.[242] The study will discuss both types of discrimination as follows:

C *Disparate Treatment Discrimination*

Disparate treatment discrimination is "the most easily understood type of discrimination."[243] Under such discrimination, a female employee has to prove that her employer deliberately treated her in a different way because of her sex.[244] In addition, disparate treatment discrimination may occur when an employer circumscribes employment opportunities for certain classes of female workers, including a woman having "pre-school-age children."[245]

The Supreme Court has clarified that an employer's policy that is based on different treatment between male and female employees could lead to liability under Title VII. In Phillips v. Martin Marietta Corp., Ida Phillips was denied employment due to her gender.[246] She brought an action alleging the violation of Title VII and complained against the employer's policy that rejected "job applications from women with pre-school-age children" while accepting applications from their male counterparts.[247]

The Supreme Court held that the employer's policy constituted discrimination against women. The Court's finding was based on the violation of Title VII requiring "persons of like qualifications be given employment opportunities irrespective of their sex."[248] The Court reasoned that the employer's policy treated women with very young children differently than their male counterparts. In addition, it found that the condition in question

241 *Id.* § 2000e-2(e).
242 F. Eisenstadt, *supra* note 208, at 392.
243 Int'l Bhd. of Teamsters v. United States, 431 U.S. 324, 335 n.15 (1977).
244 Phillips v. Martin Marietta Corp., 400 U.S. 542, 544 (1971).
245 *Id.*
246 *Id.* at 543.
247 *Id.*
248 *Id.* at 544.

was not "a bona fide occupational qualification reasonably necessary to the normal operation of that particular business or enterprise."[249]

In International Union v. Johnson Controls,[250] fertile female employees were excluded from specific lead-exposed jobs due to the employer's fetal protection policy.[251] That policy was created because exposure to high levels of lead poses health risks and may increase the risk of birth defects in infants born to female workers.[252]

In that case, the Supreme Court held that the employer's "fetal-protection policy" constituted gender-based discrimination against a female worker.[253] The Court clarified that the discrimination of the employer's policy was clear because "fertile men, but not fertile women, are given a choice as to whether they wish to risk their reproductive health for a particular job."[254] In addition, the Court affirmed that Title VII bans classifications based on sex "in terms and conditions of employment, in hiring and discharging decisions, and in other employment decisions" that could negatively affect the status of a female worker.[255]

The Court further noted that the facts of this case were similar to those in Phillips,[256] in which the Court found that the employer's policy was discriminatory because it established "one hiring policy for women and another for men – each having pre-school-age children."[257] Likewise, the Court in Johnson determined that the employer's policy discriminated against a female worker since it required her, but not a male worker, "to produce proof that she is not capable of reproducing."[258]

Furthermore, the Court explained that the employer's policy was biased because it did not apply to the company's female workers' reproductive capacity equally as it did to male workers. It clarified that the "absence of a malevolent motive" did not change a "facially discriminatory policy into a neutral policy with a discriminatory effect."[259] In addition, according to the Court, discriminatory practices in employment, if they involve unequal "treatment through explicit facial discrimination,

249 *Id.*
250 Int'l Union v. Johnson Controls, 499 U.S. 187 (1991).
251 *Id.* at 192.
252 *Id.* at 191.
253 *Id.* at 200.
254 *Id.* at 197.
255 *Id.*
256 Phillips v. Martin Marietta Corp., 400 U.S. 542 (1971).
257 *Id.* at 544.
258 Johnson, 499 U.S. at 198.
259 *Id.* at 199.

do not depend on why the employer discriminates but rather on the explicit terms of the discrimination."[260] In other words, the Court determined that an employer's good intentions do not negate the notion that the employer's "explicit gender-based policy" constitutes sex discrimination under Title VII, unless the employer demonstrates that sex is a "bona fide occupational qualification."[261]

D *The Supreme Court's Mixed-Motives Analysis under Title VII (Price Waterhouse v. Hopkins)*

A challenged decision about employment could be based on both legitimate and illegitimate reasons.[262] In Price Waterhouse v. Hopkins, the contested decision was the result of a number of interrelated factors.[263] Therefore, the Supreme Court used different analyses to review cases with mixed-motives.[264]

Price Waterhouse was the first case in which the Supreme Court explicitly addressed mixed-motive analyses in the context of Title VII of the Civil Rights Act.[265] Prior to this case, the Supreme Court had applied the First Amendment of the Constitution[266] and the National Labor Relations Act ("NLRA")[267] to mixed-motive cases.[268] Therefore, to deduce gender-based mixed-motive discrimination in Price Waterhouse, the Supreme Court relied on its judgments in Mt. Healthy City School District Board of Education v. Doyle, where the Court applied mixed-motive analysis to a case involving a violation of the First Amendment of the Constitution,[269] and NLRB v. Transportation Management Corporation, in which the Court

260 *Id.*
261 *Id.* at 199–200.
262 Price Waterhouse v. Hopkins, 490 U.S. 228, 260 (1989) (White, J., concurring).
263 *Id.*
264 Kelley E. Dowd, *The Correct Application of the Evidentiary Standard in Title VII Mixed-Motive Cases: Stacks v. Southwestern Bell Yellow Pages, Inc.*, 28 Creighton L. Rev. 1095, 1105 (1995).
265 *Id.*
266 U.S. Const. amend. I. Under the First Amendment of the U.S. Constitution, "Congress shall make no law respecting an establishment of religion, or prohibiting the free exercise thereof; or abridging the freedom of speech, or of the press; or the right of the people peaceably to assemble, and to petition the Government for a redress of grievance." *Id.*
267 29 U. S. C. §§ 158(a) (1).
268 Mt. Healthy City School Dist. Bd. of Educ. v. Doyle, 429 U.S. 274, 284 (1977) (addressing the First Amendment); NLRB v. Transp. Mgmt. Corp., 462 U.S. 393, 404 (1983) (applying the National Labor Relations Act).
269 *Id.*

applied mixed-motive analysis to a case involving a violation of the National Labor Relations Act (NLRA).[270]

In Mt. Healthy, a teacher whose contract was not renewed by a school board filed a complaint alleging the violation of his constitutional rights under the First Amendment.[271] The school board refused to renew the contract due to three reasons: the teacher's "notable lack of tact in handling professional matters," his use of "obscene gestures to correct students in a situation in the cafeteria causing considerable concern among those students present," and his disclosure to a national radio station concerning "the suggestion of the Board of Education that teachers establish an appropriate dress code for professional people."[272]

In reviewing these reasons, the Supreme Court found that the dismissal decision was based on both legitimate and illegitimate grounds and therefore applied a mixed-motive analysis.[273] The Court first placed the burden of proof on the teacher to demonstrate that his conduct was based on permissible foundations and that this conduct played a "substantial" or "motivating factor" in making the challenged decision.[274] The Court noted that the First Amendment of the Constitution protected the teacher's disclosure to the local radio station, and therefore it found that such conduct was permissible under the Constitution. The Court reasoned that because this permissible conduct was a substantial factor in not renewing the teacher's employment contract, an illegitimate reason was a substantial factor in making the challenged decision.[275] According to the Court, "there [was] no suggestion by the Board that [the teacher] violated any established policy, or that its reaction to his communication to the radio station was anything more than an ad hoc response to [the teacher's] action in making the memorandum public."[276] The Court then shifted the burden of proof to the board to show "by a preponderance of the evidence that it would have reached the same decision ... in the absence of the protected conduct."[277] According to the Court, although the employee showed that an illegitimate reason was a substantial or motivating factor in the dismissal decision, the

270 Transp. Mgmt., 462 U.S. 393.
271 Mt. Healthy, 429 U.S. at 276.
272 *Id.* at 283 n.1.
273 *Id.* at 287.
274 *Id.* at 284.
275 *Id.*
276 *Id.*
277 *Id.* at 287.

employer could avoid liability by demonstrating that it would have made the same decision regardless of the employee's legal conduct.[278]

Similarly, in Transportation Management, the Supreme Court applied the same mixed-motive analysis of Mt. Healthy.[279] That case started when a bus driver challenged the biased practices of his employer, claiming that it dismissed him because of his union activities.[280] The worker's main argument was based on the National Labor Relations Act (NLRA) which prohibits the discharge of a worker due to his participation in union activities.[281] In reviewing the case, the Supreme Court clarified that the employer could avoid liability if it shows that the dismissal decision was based solely on legitimate grounds.[282] In other words, the Court stated that in order to avoid liability, the employer must demonstrate "by a preponderance of the evidence that the worker would have been fired even if he had not been involved [in] ... the [activities of the] union."[283]

Back to the Price Waterhouse Decision:

In Price Waterhouse, although Hopkins had generated an outstanding track record of securing successful major contracts for the partnership, Price Waterhouse, one of the nation's largest accounting firms, denied her admission as a partner.[284] When Hopkins inquired about the reasons for her rejection, she was told that she was denied admission due to the difficulties she had with some "inter-personal skills," particularly her tough, aggressive and "macho" behavior.[285] Although her achievements were praised by all partners and she was described as "an outstanding professional," there were obvious signs that a number of the partners reacted in a negative way to Hopkins' personality because she was a woman. "One partner described her as macho ... another suggested that she overcompensated for being a woman ... a third advised her to take a course at charm school."[286] Additionally, many partners "criticized her use of profanity; in response, one partner suggested that those partners objected to her swearing only because it's a

278 *Id.*

279 Transp. Mgmt., 462 U.S. at 403.

280 *Id.* at 396.

281 *Id.* at 394. Under the National Labor Relations Act (NLRA), an employer is prohibited from dismissing a worker for involvement in union activities. 29 U. S. C. § 158 (a)(1), (3).

282 Transp. Mgmt., 462 U.S. at 395.

283 *Id.*

284 Price Waterhouse, 490 U.S. at 231–34.

285 *Id.* at 234–35. According to all partners, "she was sometimes overly aggressive, unduly harsh, difficult to work with and impatient with staff." *Id.*

286 *Id.*

lady using foul language."[287] Furthermore, in order not to lose chances for partnership, she was advised to "walk more femininely, talk more femininely, dress more femininely, wear make-up, have her hair styled, and wear jewelry."[288]

The Supreme Court found that the denial of admission to partnership was based on both nondiscriminatory permissible and discriminatory impermissible reasons. Therefore, the Court investigated the case using a mixed motive analysis.[289] The difficulty with interpersonal skills was the nondiscriminatory reason for denying her partnership; however, the consideration of sex stereotypes was the discriminatory reason for the denial.[290]

The Court placed the burden of proof on the plaintiff to show that a discriminatory factor was part of the employer's decision.[291] After the plaintiff satisfied this requirement, the Court stipulated that the employer, "if it wishes to prevail," could avoid liability by proving that the same decision could have been reached in the absence of discriminatory factors.[292] The Court stated that "when a plaintiff in a Title VII case proves that her gender played a motivating part in an employment decision, the [employer] may avoid a finding of liability only by proving by a preponderance of the evidence that it would have made the same decision even if it had not taken the plaintiff's gender into account."[293]

In that case, the employer argued that the plaintiff failed to demonstrate that gender considerations were the true reasons for not promoting her.[294] However, the Court rejected that argument, declaring that in mixed-motive cases where a contested employment decision is "a product of a mixture of legitimate and illegitimate motives," it "makes no sense to ask [about] the true reason for the decision."[295]

E *The Civil Rights Act of 1991*

Title VII was amended by the Civil Rights Act of 1991. This Act stipulates that, "except as otherwise provided in this subchapter, an unlawful employment practice is established when the complaining party demonstrates

287 *Id.* at 235.
288 *Id.*
289 *Id.* at 252.
290 *Id.*
291 *Id.* at 246.
292 *Id.*
293 *Id.* at 285.
294 *Id.* at 246–47.
295 *Id.*

that race, color, religion, sex, or national origin was a motivating factor for any employment practice, even though other factors also motivated the practice."[296]

The Civil Rights Act of 1991 overturned a part of the Price Waterhouse decision.[297] According to the Act, once an employee proves that discriminatory considerations are a motivating factor in the adverse treatment, he or she is entitled to relief because an employer cannot avoid liability under any circumstance.[298] On the other hand, according to the Price Waterhouse decision, if an employee shows that a sex-based factor played a part in the employment decision-making process, the employer may avoid liability by demonstrating that in the absence of this factor, it would have made the same decision.[299]

Under the 1991 Civil Rights Act, if an employee demonstrates that a discriminatory factor played a role in making a challenged employment decision and the employer shows that the same decision could have been made in the absence of that factor, the employer is not exempt from liability, but the type of remedy granted to the employee may vary.[300] In this case, courts "shall not award damages or issue an order requiring any admission, reinstatement, hiring, promotion, or payment"[301]; however, they "may grant declaratory relief, injunctive relief and attorney's fees."[302]

F *Disparate Impact Discrimination*

Because only one case of gender-based disparate impact discrimination has been decided by the Supreme Court,[303] this study will discuss other cases involving racial employment discrimination in order to clarify how the Supreme Court arrived at the disparate impact theory of discrimination.

Griggs v. Duke Power Co.[304] was the first case in which the Supreme Court adopted the disparate impact theory of discrimination.[305] In that

296 42 U.S.C. 2000e-2(m).
297 E. Dowd., *supra* note 264, at 1110.
298 *Id.* at 1110–11.
299 Price Waterhouse, 490 U.S. at 246.
300 E. Dowd., *supra* note 264, at 1110–11.
301 42 U.S.C. § 2000e-5g(2)(B)(ii) (Supp. v. 1993).
302 *Id.*
303 Dothard v. Rawlinson, 433 U.S. 321 (1977).
304 Griggs v. Duke Power Co., 401 U.S. 424 (1971).
305 Robert Belton, *The 40th Anniversary of Title VII of the Civil Rights Act of 1964 Symposium, Title VII at Forty: A Brief Look at the Birth, Death, and Resurrection of the Disparate Impact Theory of Discrimination* [*phi*], 22 Hofstra Lab. & Emp. L.J. 431, 34 (2005).

case, a group of African American employees brought an action under Title VII challenging the employment requirements of a high school diploma or passing intelligence tests as a condition for hiring and promotion[306]; they were able to prove that such requirements had an unduly negative impact on them.[307]

The Supreme Court noted that the plaintiffs were African Americans, who "have long received inferior education in segregated schools."[308] Therefore, the Court found that although the measure in question was facially neutral, it had a disparate impact on African American employees and was not justified as a business necessity.[309] According to the Court, the "absence of discriminatory intent does not redeem employment procedures or testing mechanisms that operate as built-in headwinds for minority groups and are unrelated to measuring job capability."[310] In other words, since the employer could not demonstrate a connection between its selection procedures and business necessity, the Court held that the measure in question violated Title VII.[311]

Based on its reasoning in Griggs, the Supreme Court decided a number of disparate impact discrimination cases involving violations of Title VII.[312] In Albemarle Paper Company v. Moody, the Court held that in order for an employer to avoid liability under Title VII, it has to show by "professionally acceptable methods" that prejudiced tests are "predictive of or significantly correlated with important elements of work behavior which comprise or are relevant to the job."[313] However, the Court determined that the employer's business necessity argument could be reversed if the employee demonstrates "that other tests or selection devices, without a similarly undesirable racial effect, would also serve the employer's legitimate interest."[314]

306 Griggs, 401 U.S. at 427–28.

307 *Id.* at 436.

308 *Id.* at 430. The Court reached this conclusion based on its reasoning in Gaston County v. United States. 395 U.S. 285 (1969). In that case, the Supreme Court noted the inferior education provided to African Americans in North Carolina; therefore, the Court "barred the institution of a literacy test for voter registration." Griggs, 401 U.S. at 430–31. In addition, the Court clarified that this test constituted indirect racial discrimination against voters. *Id.*

309 *Id.* at 429–31.

310 *Id.* at 432.

311 *Id.* at 431.

312 Yiyang Wu, *Scaling the Wall and Running the Mile: The Role of Physical-selection Procedures in the Disparate Impact Narrative*, 160 U. Pa. L. Rev. 1195, 1200 (2012).

313 Albemarle Paper Co. v. Moody, 422 U.S. 405, 431 (1975).

314 *Id.* at 425. The Supreme Court in Wards Cove Packing Co. v. Atonio tried to change this standard when it held that "the judiciary should proceed with care before

Another significant case that updates the disparate impact theory of discrimination is Ricci v. DeStefano.[315] In that case, a group of firefighters, who were white and Hispanic, took legal action against their employer because it refused to officially state the results of a promotion exam; they argued that the refusal to certify such results violated the Equal Protection Clause of the Constitution.[316] On the other hand, the employer argued that it refused to certify the result to avoid liability under Title VII because it would have a disparate impact on black firefighters.[317]

The Supreme Court noted that an employer would not be found liable under Title VII for invalidating promotion test results that would amount to racial discrimination.[318] However, the Court stated that "doing so, absent a strong basis in evidence of an impermissible disparate impact, amounts to the sort of racial preference that Congress has disclaimed, … and is antithetical to the notion of a workplace where individuals are guaranteed equal opportunity regardless of race."[319] According to the Court, "the employer must have a strong basis in evidence to believe it will be subject to disparate-impact liability if it fails to take the race-conscious, discriminatory action."[320] However, the Court found that the employer did not present sufficient evidence that it would be liable for disparate impact discrimination if it certified the test results, and thus ruled in favor of the plaintiffs.[321]

G *The Gender-Based Disparate Impact Case* (*Dothard v. Rawlinson*)

The only gender-based disparate impact case decided by the Supreme Court is Dothard v. Rawlinson.[322] The case started when an employer refused to hire Rawlinson as a prison guard because she did not satisfy the 120-pound minimum weight requirement imposed by the Alabama Statute.[323]

---

mandating that an employer must adopt a plaintiff's alternative selection or hiring practice in response to a Title VII suit." 490 U.S. 642, 661 (1989). However, Congress disagreed with the Wards Cove approach and passed the Civil Rights Act of 1991, which established a defense available to employers based on "business necessity" that had been used in cases prior to Wards Cove. Civil Rights Act of 1991, § 3(2).

315 Ricci v. DeStefano, 129 S. Ct. 2658 (2009).

316 *Id.* at 2664.

317 *Id.*

318 *Id.* at 2676–77.

319 *Id.* at 2677.

320 *Id.*

321 *Id.*

322 Dothard v. Rawlinson, 433 U.S. 321 (1977).

323 *Id.* at 323–24.

However, Rawlinson proved that the minimum weight and height restrictions of the Alabama Statute would eliminate less than 1% of the nationwide male population, whereas they would exclude more than 40% of the female population.[324] The Supreme Court found that this evidence was sufficient to demonstrate that the statutory height and requirements standards had a disparate impact on female applicants.[325]

In that case, the defendant argued that the measures in question were job-related and "essential to effective job performance as a correctional counselor." However, the Supreme Court rejected that argument because the defendant did not deliver proper evidentiary support regarding the "amount of strength thought essential to good job performance."[326] The Court found that the defendant "failed to offer evidence of any kind in specific justification of the statutory standards," and therefore it rejected the defendant's argument of business necessity.[327]

H *Pregnancy Discrimination Act* (PDA)

The cause for enacting the PDA was the case of General Electric Company v. Gilbert.[328] In that case, a group of female employees complained against an employer's benefit policy that excluded pregnancy-related disabilities from the otherwise comprehensive temporary disability policy.[329] Their argument was based on Title VII's prohibitions against both disparate treatment and disparate impact discrimination.[330]

The Supreme Court's majority opinion decided that such an exclusion did not constitute unlawful sex discrimination under Title VII.[331] In its

---

324 *Id.* at 329–30. The Supreme Court noted that "the District Court found that the [minimum height] requirement would operate to exclude 33.29% of the women in the United States between the ages of 18–79, while excluding only 1.28% of men between the same ages. The 120-pound weight restriction would exclude 22.29% of the women and 2.35% of the men in this age group." *Id.*

325 *Id.* at 331. The Court stated:

> We cannot say that the District Court was wrong in holding that the statutory height and weight standards had a discriminatory impact on women applicants. The plaintiffs in a case such as this are not required to exhaust every possible source of evidence, if the evidence actually presented on its face conspicuously demonstrates a job requirement's grossly discriminatory impact.
>
> *Id.*

326 *Id.*

327 *Id.*

328 Gen. Elec. Co. v. Gilbert, 429 U.S. 125 (1976).

329 *Id.* at 127–28.

330 *Id.*

331 *Id.* at 145–46.

reasoning, the Supreme Court focused on the plaintiffs' argument of disparate treatment discrimination.[332] However, the Court rejected this argument because it did not find a connection between gender and the excluded disability, and also because the employer treated male and female employees equally in other categories of benefits covered by the employer's comprehensive temporary disability policy.[333] Regardless of the fact that only women can become pregnant, the Supreme Court held that discrimination based on pregnancy did not constitute unlawful gender discrimination because non-pregnant female employees were fully enjoying the employer's benefit plan. In other words, the Court reasoned that there was a "lack of identity between the excluded disability and gender" because not all female workers were negatively affected by the exclusion.[334]

The Court further noted that the employer's policy divided workers into two groups: "pregnant women and non-pregnant persons."[335] It reasoned that although "the first group is exclusively females, the second includes members of both sexes."[336] Therefore, the Court found that the employer's policy treated non-pregnant female employees the same as male employees.[337] In other words, the Court found facial parity between female and male employees because the employer's policy did not indicate that disability benefits were confined to male employees and unavailable to females.[338]

In addition, the Court stated that "[p]regnancy is, of course, confined to women, but it is in other ways significantly different from the typical covered disease or disability."[339] According to the Court, because pregnancy "is often a voluntarily undertaken and desired," it could be treated differently than other disabilities or diseases under the employer's policy.[340]

The Court clarified that the employer did not deliberately discriminate against pregnant female workers; instead, it explained that female workers could suffer from the risks of uncovered pregnancy-related disabilities only because of the biological fact that only women become pregnant.[341] According to the Court, "gender-based discrimination does not result simply

332 *Id.* at 132–36.
333 *Id.*
334 *Id.* at 135.
335 *Id.*
336 *Id.*
337 *Id.* at 137–40.
338 *Id.*
339 *Id.* at 136.
340 *Id.*
341 *Id.* at 138–39.

because an employer's disability-benefits plan is less than all-inclusive."[342] In addition, the Court stated that "pregnancy-related disabilities constitute an additional risk, unique to women, and the failure to compensate them for this risk does not destroy the presumed parity of the benefits, accruing to men and women alike, which results from the facially evenhanded inclusion of risks."[343] The Court stipulated that requiring inclusion of pregnancy in existing disability plans "would endanger the commonsense notion that an employer who has no disability benefits program at all does not violate Title VII even though the under inclusion of risks impacts, as a result of pregnancy-related disabilities, [impacts] more heavily upon one gender than upon the other."[344] According to the Court, because "there is no facial gender based discrimination in that case, so, too, there is none here."[345]

In short, the Supreme Court declared that "the exclusion of pregnancy disability benefits from petitioner's plan [was not] a simple pretext for discriminating against women."[346] Therefore, the Court concluded that the employer's "disability-benefits plan [did] not violate Title VII because of its failure to cover pregnancy-related disabilities."[347]

Nevertheless, the Court's decision was followed by a vigorous dissent that harshly criticized the majority opinion for failing to recognize the pregnancy exclusion as "sex-linked."[348] According to the dissent, because only women would suffer from the risks of the uncovered disability, the majority opinion should have considered the exclusion discriminatory against a female worker.[349] The dissent found that the majority opinion did not examine the nature of the excluded disability; however, it employed a formal equality analysis to compare two categories of employees: pregnant female employees and non-pregnant employees of both sexes.[350]

The dissent clarified that the majority opinion should have taken into account the sex-linked benefits that were confined to male workers instead of concentrating on the mutual coverage of risks that were equally assigned to both sexes.[351] The dissent found that according to the employer's policy, "all

342 *Id.*
343 *Id.* at 139.
344 *Id.* at 139–40.
345 *Id.*
346 *Id.* at 136.
347 *Id.* at 146.
348 *Id.* at 148–49. (Brennan, J., dissenting).
349 *Id.* (Brennan, J., dissenting).
350 *Id.* (Brennan, J., dissenting).
351 *Id.* at 152–53. (Brennan, J., dissenting).

mutually contractible risks are covered irrespective of gender, [but the policy] also insures risks such as prostatectomies, vasectomies, and circumcisions that are specific to the reproductive system of men and for which there exist no female counterparts covered by the plan."[352] Therefore, the dissent decided that the employer's temporary disability policy was discriminatory on its face since "pregnancy affords the only disability, sex-specific or otherwise, that is excluded from coverage."[353]

In 1978, the dissent prevailed, as Congress amended Title VII by enacting the Pregnancy Discrimination Act (PDA) of 1978, which prohibits sex discrimination based on pregnancy.[354] The PDA modified the definition of discrimination as follows: "the terms because of sex or on the basis of sex include, but are not limited to, because of or on the basis of pregnancy, childbirth, or related medical conditions; and women affected by pregnancy, childbirth, or related medical conditions shall be treated the same for all employment-related purposes, including receipt of benefits under fringe benefit programs, as other persons not so affected but similar in their ability or inability to work."[355]

I *Challenges under Title VII after the PDA*

The PDA revoked Gilbert because "it makes clear that it is discriminatory to treat pregnancy-related conditions less favorably than other medical conditions," as stated by the Supreme Court in Newport News Dock Company v. EEOC.[356] In that case, a plaintiff complained against an employer's medical policy, which offered identical "hospitalization and medical-surgical coverage" for a female and a male employee, but differed in terms of the medical treatment provided to her or his spouse. The employer's medical policy covered all illnesses and other medical conditions for female employees' spouses; however, it restricted the "pregnancy-related benefits" for male employees' spouses. In other words, the employer's medical policy covered all medical conditions for all employees, irrespective of gender, but differentiated between female employees and male employees' spouses in terms of pregnancy-related hospitalization insurance coverage. The medical insurance covered pregnancy hospitalization for female employees but did

352 *Id.* (Brennan, J., dissenting).
353 *Id.* (Brennan, J., dissenting).
354 P.D.A. 1978§ 2, 92 Stat at 2076. The PDA was enacted and went into force on October 31, 1978; its application to employee benefit plans took effect on April 29, 1979.
355 42 U.S.C. § 2000e(k) (2000).
356 Newport News Dock Co. v. EEOC, 462 U.S. 669, 684 (1983).

not include coverage for pregnancy hospitalization for spouses of male employees.[357]

The Court clarified that "[h]ealth insurance and other fringe benefits" are types of "compensation, terms, conditions, or privileges of employment" that should be provided equally to male and female workers under Title VII.[358] Therefore, according to the Court, "if a private employer were to provide complete health insurance coverage for the dependents of its female employees, and no coverage at all for the dependents of its male employees, it would violate Title VII."[359] Thus, the Court found that the employer's plan unlawfully provided the spouses of male employees with less comprehensive medical coverage than the coverage given to the spouses of female employees.[360]

In addition, the Court reasoned that while Gilbert decided that an "otherwise inclusive plan that singled out pregnancy-related benefits for exclusion was nondiscriminatory on its face, because only women can become pregnant, Congress has unequivocally rejected that reasoning" by enacting the PDA of 1978.[361] The Court clarified that by enacting the PDA, Congress did not revoke the prohibition of the "original" type of discrimination, the discrimination based on an employee's sex; however, as stated by the Court, Congress just affirmed that it is an unlawful practice for an employer to discriminate based on an employee's pregnancy.[362] In other words, according to the Court, Congress enacted the PDA to affirm that pregnancy-based employment discrimination is merely a type of employment discrimination based on sex, which is prohibited under Title VII.[363]

The Court went further to note that "since the sex of the spouse is always the opposite of the sex of the employee, it follows inexorably that discrimination against female spouses in the provision of fringe benefits is also discrimination against male employees."[364] Thus, the Court determined that

---

357 *Id.* at 671–72.

358 *Id.* at 682. The Court initially clarified that Title VII makes it an unlawful practice of employment to "discriminate against any individual with respect to his compensation, terms, conditions, or privileges of employment, because of such individual's race, color, religion, sex, or national origin." *Id.*

359 Newport News, 462 U.S. at 682.

360 *Id.* at 683–84.

361 *Id.* at 684.

362 *Id.* at 684–85.

363 *Id.*

364 *Id.* at 684.

the employer's medical plan constituted discrimination based on sex.[365] It considered such a plan "the mirror image of the plan at issue in Gilbert," and as a result, the Court determined that it violated Title VII because it discriminates against male employees.[366]

In summary, the U.S. Supreme Court applied Title VII of the Civil Rights Act in a manner that provided full protection for women against employment discrimination, whether in treatment or pay. Like the ECJ, the U.S. Supreme Court protected a woman from disparate treatment and impact discrimination. However, the ECJ and the U.S. Supreme Court may differ in terms of the number of cases they have considered. In other words, in comparison to the U.S. Supreme Court, the ECJ heard a greater number of cases involving indirect sex-based discrimination against female workers. In addition, following the enactment of the PDA, both the U.S. Supreme Court and the ECJ protected pregnant women from pregnancy-related employment discrimination, as evidenced in the Newport News Dock Company case.

3 Women's Right to Work under Shari'a

The section will discuss this topic from two different Islamic perspectives.

A *The First Perspective: Restricting Women's Right to Work*

According to Shari'a, there is a perspective that imposes numerous restrictions on Muslim women's right to work. Under this perspective, in order for Muslim women to work, the following conditions must be met:

i Legitimacy of Work

According to this requirement, Muslim women cannot practice haram jobs, which are forbidden under the primary sources of Shari'a, the Qur'an and Sunna.[367] For example, a Muslim woman cannot work as a prostitute, a bartender, or in the field of usury. Instead, she can work in the fields of trade, medicine, teaching or any other field permitted by Islamic law.[368]

---

365 *Id.* at 685.

366 *Id.*

367 Gamal El-Deen Mahmoud, Hekook Al-Mar'a Fe Al-Mogtama'a Al-Islamy Wa Al-Tashre'e Al-Masry (Women's Rights between Islamic Societies and Egyptian Law) 50 (Vol. 2, 2006) (trans. by author).

368 Youssef El-Azazi, Amal El-Mara'a Fe Mezan Al- Shari'a Al-Islamia (Woman's Right to Work Under Islamic Law) 114 (2007) (trans. by author).

ii Strict Compliance with the Rules of Shari'a

Under this concept, a Muslim woman must adhere to Islamic teachings during her working hours, such as by wearing a hijab and modest clothing,[369] acting with restraint, dealing gingerly with foreign men, and lowering her gaze.[370]

iii No Tough Tasks

A Muslim woman's work must be compatible with her physiological, physical, and spiritual nature as a female.[371] Therefore, under Shari'a, tough work, such as building, working at coal mines or joining the military, is confined to men.[372]

iv Guardian's Permission

A Muslim woman's guardian under Shari'a is her closest male relative, who is morally and financially responsible for her. The guardian could be a husband, a father, a brother or an uncle.[373] With regard to a married woman, her guardian is her husband; if she is unmarried, her father is her guardian. However, in the event that her father passes away, one of her brothers or uncles could serve as her male guardian.[374]

Under that requirement, a woman must obtain her husband's or guardian's permission before starting work.[375] Nevertheless, such permission is not exclusive to a woman's work, as certain conservative Muslim scholars argue that a Muslim woman cannot leave her home without the consent of her husband or guardian.[376]

---

369 Abu El-A'ala El-Mawdoodi, Al-Hijab (The Hijab) 168 (Dar El-Ketab, 1995) (trans. by author).

370 Youssef El-Karadawy, Hayat Al-Mara'a Al-Muslema Fe Etar El-Hedood El-Shar'aia (The Life of a Muslim Woman within the Framework of Legitimate Limits) 41 (Dar El-Kotob Wa Al-Watha'ek Al- Kawmia, 2011) (trans. by author).

371 Khawala Abd-El-Lateef El-A'tiki, Wazeeft Al-Mar'a Al-Muslema Fe A'lam El-Youm (Muslim Women's Mission in the Present Time) 24 (1991) (trans. by author).

372 El-Azazi, *supra* note 368, at 118 (trans. by author).

373 *Id.* at 112.

374 *Id.*

375 Marawan Ibrahim El-Kesy, Akhlakyat Al-Ta'amol Al-Osary Fe Al-Islam (The Ethics of Family Dealings in Islam) 58–59 (Dar El-Kotob El-Elmia, 2019) (trans. by author).

376 *Id.*

v Top Priority for Marital Duties

According to the requirement of top priority for marital duties, a Muslim woman's primary roles are as a mother and a wife.[377] Therefore, her major and principal responsibility is to perform her daily activities and household chores at home, such as cooking, cleaning, caring for her children, etc.[378] On the other hand, a Muslim woman's work outside the home is not obligatory and is regarded as a secondary matter. Therefore, a woman cannot work outside the home or engage in public activities unless she balances her professional obligations with marital duties.[379]

vi Urgent Need for Work

This condition ensures that a Muslim woman cannot work unless she is in dire financial need.[380] Under that perspective, a woman can only work if she has no other means of income and has to earn her living. In other words, if a woman lacks living expenses due to her husband's death or inability to work, she can work to support herself and her family members.[381]

B *Arguments of the Strict View*

Conservative Muslim scholars adopt some arguments to support their point of view, as follows:

i Al-Qawamah (Men Are in Charge of Women)

Under the Qur'an, "Men are in charge of women."[382] Some Muslim scholars use this verse to give men superiority over women; they argue that because a man is in charge of a woman, he is in a higher rank than she is.[383] They believe that a man is better than a woman and can perform all work and

377 Samir Bomadian, Al-Mara'a Al-Muslema Bain Al-Sharq Wa Al-Gharb, Bain Takreem Al-Islam Wa Zolm Al-Insan (A Muslim Woman Between the East and the West, Islam's Honor and Human Oppression) 121 (Dar El-Kotob El-Elmia, 2011) (trans. by author).

378 Mohammad Abd-El- Kader Abu-Fares, Hekook Al-Mar'a Al-Madania Wa Al-Seyasia Fe Al-Islam (Women's Civil and Political Rights in Islam) 19–20 (2000) (trans. by author).

379 *Id.*

380 Mohammad Metwalli Ash-Sha'rawi, Al-Mara'a fe Al-Qur'an (Women in the Qur'an) 121 (1998) (trans. by author).

381 *Id.*

382 Qur'an, *Surat An-Nisa'* 4:34. This verse states that "Men are in charge of women, because Allah hath made the one of them to excel the other, and because they spend of their property (for the support of women)." *Id.* This verse is misinterpreted by some Muslim scholars to legitimize discrimination against women.

383 Abu-Fares, *supra* note 378, at 154–55 (trans. by author).

activities better than she can.[384] A woman is considered a submissive creature and a tool for reproduction; her role in life is to stay at home, bear children, nurture them and serve her husband.[385] In addition, according to their view, a woman is entirely different from a man, who is a strong, tough, smart and clever creature, and therefore a woman could not have a chance to compete with him in workplaces since her work product and outcome are always inferior to those of a man.[386]

ii Husband's Obligation of Expenditure

One of the well-known principles of Islam is that a Muslim husband is financially responsible for his family members.[387] Therefore, he is required to provide his wife and minor children with three main types of responsibilities: food, clothing and housing at an adequate level.[388] In addition, a Muslim husband is responsible for his family's medical and educational expenses.[389] In other words, under Shari'a, a man is required to provide proper everyday meals, suitable clothing, appropriate housing and other basic needs for his wife and children.[390] This principle is derived from

384 *Id.*
385 *Id.* at 19.
386 *Id.* at 161.
387 Abd-El-Rahman El-Barzangy, Feqh Al-Osra Almuslema wa Nawazelha fe Al-Gharb (Jurisprudence of a Muslim Family in Comparison with the West) 216–17 (Dar-Almohdatheen, 2008) (trans. by author).
388 Ashraf Mostafa Kamal, Kwaneen Al-Ahwal Al-Shakhseya Moalakn A'la Nesosaha (Comments on Family Law in Egypt) 19 (1, 2014) (trans. by author).
389 *Id.*
390 *Id.* The amount of expenditure that a husband has to spend on his wife, according to scholars of Shafi'a and Hanafia, is determined only in line with a husband's financial status, whether he is wealthy or poor. El-Barzangy, *supra* note 387, at 219 (trans. by author). This view is based on the Qur'an, because it says: "Let a man of wealth spend from his wealth, and he whose provision is restricted - let him spend from what Allah has given him. Allah does not charge a soul except [according to] what He has given it." Qur'an, *Surat At-Talaq* 65:7. Under this opinion, a husband's financial status is the only criterion for determining the amount of expenditure, regardless of a wife's financial or social status. El-Barzangy, *supra* note 387, at 219 (trans. by author).

On the other hand, according to scholars of Malikia and Hanabila, the amount of expenditure is based on both the financial status of a wife and a husband. *Id.* at 219. Therefore, the pre-marriage financial status of a wife should be taken into account. *Id.* In other words, if a wife belongs to a wealthy family and is used to a high standard of living, her husband has to provide her with enough funds to enable her to continue her pre-marriage lifestyle. *Id.* This perspective is based on Sunna, as it is narrated that Prophet Mohammad addressed one of his companions' wives saying: "Take [from your

the Qur'an, as it says: "Mothers may breastfeed their children two complete years for whoever wishes to complete the nursing [period]. Upon the father is the mothers' provision and their clothing according to what is acceptable."[391]

Some Muslim scholars use this well-known principle to circumscribe a woman's right to work.[392] They argue that because a woman's husband is required to provide her with food, clothing, housing and other related

husband's wealth] what is sufficient for you and your children, and the amount should be just and reasonable." Sahih Al-Bukhari (Vol. 7, Book 64, Hadith 277). Besides, scholars supporting this view believe that a husband's financial status is also an important criterion in determining the amount of expenditure since the Qur'an states: "Allah does not charge a soul except [with that within] its capacity." Qur'an, *Surat Al-Baqarah* 2:28.

Under Shari'a, a husband has two religious duties towards his wife: moral and financial duties. El-Barzangy, *supra* note 387, at 212 (trans. by author).

With regard to the financial duties, they consist of expenditures and dowry. *Id.* The dowry is a gift given to a bride when a contract of marriage is finalized or consummated; it is regarded as an expression of closeness and love. *Id.* In addition, according to Shari'a, dowry is necessary since the Qur'an says: "And give the women [upon marriage] their [bridal] gifts graciously." Qur'an, *Surat An-Nisa'* 4:4. Regarding the expenditures, as the study mentioned above, they include food, clothing, housing and other related items. El-Barzangy, *supra* note 387, at 218 (trans. by author).

Regarding the moral obligations, a husband should be concerned about his wife and treat her with respect. *Id.* at 220. This duty is derived from the Qur'an as it says: "And live with them in kindness for if you dislike them - perhaps you dislike a thing and Allah makes therein much good." Qur'an, *Surat An-Nisa'* 4:19.

Besides, Sunna is full of Hadiths urging a husband to deal properly with his wife. For example, Prophet Mohammad said: "The best amongst you is the one who acts best with his family and I act best towards my family." Ibn Majah, Sunan, Kitab an Nikah, 1/636. In another Hadith, he said: "Treat women well, for they have been created from a rib. The rib is most curved in its upper part, so that if you try to straighten it out, it will break, but if you leave it as it is, it will remain intact. Therefore, follow my advice on giving women fair treatment." Al-Bukhari, Sahih, Kitab an-Nikah (Fath al-Bari, 9/206–207). Furthermore, the Prophet said: "Women are the other half of men…Fear Allah in respect of women…. Heaven lies beneath the feet of mother." Jalaluddin Al-Suyuti, Al-Jami' As-Saghir Fe Ahadith Al-Bashir An-Nadhir, 1/536.

The second moral duty is to have intercourse with a wife. Such a duty is derived from the Qur'an, as it says: "And do not approach them until they are pure. And when they have purified themselves, then come to them from where Allah has ordained for you." Qur'an, *Surat Al-Baqarah* 2:222. The purpose of this obligation is to gratify a wife's sexual desire and protect her from illegal sexual relationships. El-Barzangy, *supra* note 387, at 221 (trans. by author).

391 Qur'an, *Surat Al-Baqarah* 2:233.

392 El-Azazi, *supra* note 368, at 115 (trans. by author).

expenses, she has no need to work and must therefore stay at home and take care of her children.[393]

iii Wife's Obligation of Obedience

Islam is concerned with maintaining good marital relations between a wife and a husband. Therefore, a Muslim wife is required to obey her husband,[394] whereas a Muslim husband is obligated to care for his wife and minor children and treat them with kindness.[395] The obligation of a wife's obedience to her husband is derived from the Sunna. It is narrated that Prophet Mohammad said: "If I were to command anyone to prostrate to anything other than Allah, I would have commanded women to prostrate to their husbands. By the One in whose hand is the soul of Mohammad, no woman will fulfill her duty towards her Lord unless she fulfills her duty towards her husband."[396]

Some Muslim scholars use this obligation as a pretext to circumscribe a woman's right to work.[397] They argue that a wife must obtain her husband's approval to work, and if he refuses, she should submit to his decision.[398]

iv Women's Deficiencies in Intelligence and Religion

The argument that women are deficient in intelligence and religion is also derived from the Sunna. It is narrated that when Prophet Mohammad went out to the Musalla to offer Al-Fitr prayer, he passed by the women and said: "I have not seen anyone more deficient in intelligence and religion than you." The women asked, "O Allah's Apostle! What is deficient in our intelligence and religion?" He said: "Is not the evidence of two women equal to the witness of one man?"[399] They replied in the affirmative. He said: "This is the deficiency in her intelligence." Then the Prophet said: "Isn't it true that a

393 *Id.*

394 Al-Hafez Gamal-Al-Deen Abe-Farag Abd-El-Rahman, Ahkam Al-Nesa' (Rules for Muslim Women) 74 (2013) (trans. by author).

395 El-Barzangy, *supra* note 387, at 220 (trans. by author). In this respect, the Qur'an says: "And live with them in kindness. For if you dislike them - perhaps you dislike a thing and Allah makes therein much good." Qur'an, *Surat An-Nesa'* 4:19.

396 Sunan Tirmidhi (Vol. 1, Book 7, Hadith 1159).

397 El-Kesy, *supra* note 375, at 58 (trans. by author).

398 Abu-Fares, *supra* note 378, at 95 (trans. by author).

399 Qur'an says: "And bring to witness two witnesses from among your men. And if there are not two men [available], then a man and two women from those whom you accept as witnesses - so that if one of the women errs, then the other can remind her." Qur'an, *Surat Al-Baqarah* 2:282. Some Muslim scholars interpret this verse as establishing that a woman's testimony is equivalent to half that of a man's. Mohammad Emara,

woman can neither pray nor fast during her menses?" The women replied in the affirmative. He said: "This is the deficiency in her religion."[400]

Some Muslim scholars use this narration to justify depriving women of the right to work. According to their view, women are inherently less intelligent and, as a result, are unable to perform work as effectively as men.[401] They consider men to be superior, while women are regarded as deficient and driven by emotion.[402]

Altahreer Al-Islami Le-Almar'a, Al-Rad a'la Shobhat Al'gholah (Women's Liberty in Islam against Some Wrongful Perceptions) 71 (2002) (trans. by author).

However, other scholars believe that this is an incorrect interpretation owing to the great linguistic differences between testimony and the notion of bearing witness. *Id.* at 71–72.

Under Islam, the notion of bearing witness is applied to financial transactions, whereas testimony is required before a judge. *Id.* at 72. The above-mentioned verse neither imposes a general rule that could be adopted in judicial disputes nor does it handle testimony before a judge. It only refers to bearing witness in debt transactions and guiding debtors to ensure the maintenance of their financial rights. *Id.*

Regarding judicial disputes, Shari'a established other rules derived from a Prophetic Hadith saying: "The positive evidence lies on the accuser and an oath is required of one who denies." Al-Baihaqi Sunan (10/252). According to this Hadith, the evidence is regarded as the basis on which a claim is built. The evidence could be the testimony of a man or a woman. In other words, the testimony of one woman could be adopted as evidence of a crime, right or violation. Emara, *supra* note 399, at 73–74 (trans. by author). If there was a contradiction between a man's and a woman's testimony, the judge has discretionary power to endorse the woman's testimony and reject the man's. *Id.* On the other hand, if a judge, based on all the evidence presented, has a reasonable doubt of guilt, he must rule in the defendant's favor. This principle is derived from Sunna, as it is narrated that the Prophet said: "Prevent a punishment in case of doubt. Release the accused if possible, for it is better that the ruler be wrong in forgiving than wrong in punishing." Mohammad Abu-Zahrah, Al-Jarimah wa Al-'Uqubah Fe Al-Fiqh Al-Islami (Crime and Punishment in Islamic Jurisprudence) 218 (1974).

Under Shari'a, the rationale for considering a woman's bearing witness in financial transactions as equivalent to half of a man's is not based on her intelligence deficiency or anticipated economic shortcomings. Rather, this practice stems from the historical background, in which men typically had a higher level of experience in economics and financial transactions. Emara, *supra* note 399, at 81 (trans. by author).

In accordance with the perspective of Ibn Taymiyyah, who is a well-known Muslim scholar, philosopher, theologian and logician, if a woman is experienced in debts and sales, her bearing witness shall be equal to that of a man in all disputes, including financial ones. *Id.* at 79.

400 Sahih Al-Bukhari (Vol. 1, Book 6, Hadith 301).

401 Abu-Fares, *supra* note 378, at 161 (trans. by author).

402 *Id.*

In addition, some other Muslim scholars use this belief as a pretext to prohibit women from holding certain public positions or serving as judges.[403] They argue that, because women are considered to have lower intellectual capabilities than men, roles that require intelligence and critical thinking should be reserved exclusively for men.[404]

v Never Will Succeed a Nation That Makes a Woman Their Ruler

Similarly, the argument that no nation with a woman ruler will succeed is based on the Sunna. It is narrated that when Prophet Mohammad heard that the people of Persia made the daughter of Khosrau their queen (ruler), he said: "Never will succeed such a nation as makes a woman their ruler."[405]

Some Muslim scholars use this narration as an argument to prevent women from taking high-profile public positions, such as being president or prime minister of a state.[406] In addition, other stricter Muslim scholars have expanded this argument to ban women from working in any leadership roles, such as being a minister or a manager of a company, claiming that such positions should only be confined to men.[407]

C *The Second Perspective: Supporting Women's Right to Work*

In accordance with this view, Muslim husbands and wives have to maintain a balance between their home and work obligations.

i Regarding Home Obligations

Islam determined a general scope of responsibilities for each spouse, whether a husband or a wife, in the sense that both of them have duties towards the other and towards his or her children.[408] This scope of responsibilities is necessary to keep peace, affection and intimacy within the family.[409] These interpretations are supported by the Qur'an, which states: "And of His signs is that He created for you from yourselves mates that you may find tranquility in them; and He placed between you affection and mercy. Indeed, in that are signs for a people who give thought?"[410] The Qur'an also states: "They are clothing for you and you are clothing for them."[411]

---

403 El-Azazi, *supra* note 368, at 119 (trans. by author).
404 *Id.*
405 Sahih Al-Bukhari (Vol. 9, Book 88, Hadith 219).
406 Abu-Fares, *supra* note 378, at 157–58.
407 *Id.* at 173–74.
408 Mohammad El-Sadek Afifi, Al-Mogtama'a Al-Islami wa Bena'a Al-Osra (Families in Muslim Communities), 34–35 (1981) (trans. by author).
409 El-Mawdoodi, *supra* note 369, at 150 (trans. by author).
410 Qur'an, *Surat Ar-Rum* 30:21.
411 Qur'an, *Surat Al-Baqarah* 2:187.

Inside the Muslim family, each spouse, whether a husband or a wife, has his or her own responsibilities.[412] A Muslim wife is burdened by pregnancy, childbirth, and raising her children until they reach maturity.[413] During that period, children are taught ethics, morals and etiquette.[414] In addition, children are provided with their mothers' affection and friendly treatment so that they will become upright citizens serving their society and nation.[415] A Muslim husband's role is to be financially responsible for his wife and minor children.[416] That responsibility includes providing everyday food, clothes and appropriate housing.[417] In addition, he has to afford his family members' education, medical care and other necessary needs.[418] In short, a wife's responsibility towards her family is moral, whereas a husband's duty is of a financial and material nature. That scope of responsibilities is derived mainly from the Sunna. Prophet Mohammad said: "Every one of you is a guardian and is responsible for his charge; the ruler is a guardian and is responsible for his subjects; the man is a guardian in his family and responsible for his charges; a woman is a guardian of her husband's house and responsible for her charges."[419]

Furthermore, both a Muslim husband and a Muslim wife should assist the other in fulfilling his or her own responsibilities, meaning that they must not place obstacles in the way of one another. Therefore, a Muslim wife has to take into consideration her husband's financial status and refrain from purchasing luxuries and accessories if her husband is impoverished.[420] Nevertheless, if a husband is wealthy, a Muslim wife could ask for financial assistance in light of her husband's income.[421] As for a Muslim husband, he should not disturb the moral atmosphere created by the wife for their children, either by causing trivial difficulties or instilling undesirable behaviors in them.[422]

Islam stipulates this scope of family responsibilities in the case of a progressive marriage and in the case of divorce. Therefore, if a couple is separated or divorced, the man or husband continues to be financially

412 Afifi, *supra* note 408, at 34–35 (trans. by author).
413 El-Barzangy, *supra* note 387, at 228 (trans. by author).
414 *Id.*
415 *Id.*
416 Kamal, *supra* note 388, at 18–19 (trans. by author).
417 *Id.*
418 *Id.*
419 Sahih Al-Bukhari (Vol. 3, Book 46, Hadith 733).
420 Emara, *supra* note 399, at 32.
421 *Id.*
422 *Id.*

responsible for their children,[423] although the woman is the legitimate custodian of the children.[424] In other words, children live under the custody of their mother after divorce,[425] whereas their father remains financially responsible for them.[426]

Nevertheless, this role distribution is not an unchangeable Islamic rule; rather, it is a general framework suiting the physical, moral and mental potentialities of each couple.[427] That is, if a Muslim wife had better employment opportunities than her husband, she would assume his role and become financially responsible for the family.[428] The husband would be in charge of family matters, including raising children. In addition, a wife who is involved in several hours of work has the right to hire a maid to take care of her children and perform household tasks.[429]

ii Regarding Work Duties

Liberal Muslim scholars believe that Muslim women can work outside their homes and participate in social and political activities on an equal basis with men.[430] According to their point of view, restricting a woman's right to work is clear discrimination.[431] Therefore, they liberate Muslim women from the majority of the aforementioned restrictions while adopting only three conditions, which are enumerated below.

1. Women's work must be legal.
2. Women must adhere to Islamic teachings during work.
3. They should not be involved in very tough work.[432]

Under this view, if a Muslim woman fulfills these requirements, her work shall be halal in Islam.[433] The first and second requirements are not confined to women since men are also committed to them.[434] In other words, neither a Muslim man nor a Muslim woman can violate his or her religious duties by working haram jobs, such as working in wine sales or drug

423 Kamal, *supra* note 388, at 723 (trans. by author).
424 *Id.* at 860.
425 *Id.*
426 *Id.* at 723.
427 Emara, *supra* note 399, at 28 (trans. by author).
428 *Id.*
429 Kamal, *supra* note 388, at 725–26 (trans. by author).
430 Mohammad Abd-El-Aleem Morsi, Al-Islam Wa Makanat Al-Mar'a (Islam and Women's Status) 230–31 (Maktabat Al-Abikan, 1997) (trans. by author).
431 *Id.*
432 Mahmoud, *supra* note 367, at 50–51 (trans. by author).
433 *Id.*
434 Emara, *supra* note 399, at 31 (trans. by author).

smuggling, because they both are equally prohibited from working impermissible jobs.[435]

On the other hand, the third requirement, prohibiting Muslim women from working in tough fields, is intended to favor women in order to preserve their instinctive nature as females.[436] In other words, Shari'a requires a man to perform tough tasks; however, from a merciful and affectionate perspective, Shari'a prohibits a woman from these works and gives her other responsibilities related to her marital duties and household responsibilities.[437]

According to liberal Muslim scholars, Islam grants a woman full employment rights.[438] They believe that a woman's right to work is enshrined in the Qur'an since it requires both a man and a woman to participate in public and social activities, as it equally requires both of them to do what is right and forbid what is wrong.[439] Qur'an says: "The believing men and believing women are allies of one another. They enjoin what is right and forbid what is wrong and establish prayer and give zakah and obey Allah and His Messenger."[440] Thus, the Qur'an paved the way for a woman, on the basis of equality with a man, to work and provide her society with positive activities that help others keep on the straight path.[441] In addition, the

---

435 *Id.*

436 Mahmoud, *supra* note 367, at 64 (trans. by author). This requirement is derived from the primary sources of Islam, the Qur'an and Sunna. The Qur'an says: "So We said, O Adam, indeed this is an enemy to you and to your wife. Then let him not remove you from Paradise so you would suffer." Qur'an, *Surat Taha* 20:117. From a linguistic interpretation, Allah said, addressing both Adam and Eve, "Then let him not remove you [both Adam and Eve] from Paradise so you [Adam alone] would suffer." The verb "suffer" was adopted to address the singular second person, not the dual second person. Thus, suffering was confined to Adam alone, and that reveals that only men are commanded to perform tough tasks.

Regarding the Sunna, it is narrated that when female companions asked Prophet Mohammad what kind of work a Muslim woman could perform, he said: "In what they can and bear to carry out." Emara, *supra* note 399, at 33 (trans. by author). Under this Sunna, a Muslim woman is not obliged to perform hard tasks that she cannot bear. *Id.*

437 *Id.*

438 Morsi, *supra* note 430, at 231 (trans. by author).

439 *Id.*

440 Qur'an, *Surat At-Tawbah* 9:71.

441 A close overview of the Qur'an reveals that all general commands are equally directed at both a man and a woman. Mohammad Ramadan, Kholaset Al-Tahkeekat Fe El-Rad A'la Al-Shobohat Wa Al-Tasawrat (Summary of Investigations in Response to Suspicions and Perceptions) 161 (Dar El-Kotob El-Elmia, 2008) (trans. by author). However, the phrase "[t]he believing men and believing women are allies of one another" assures that there is a diversity of work obligations between both sexes. These

Qur'an says: "Men have a share in what they earn, and women have theirs in what they earn."[442] This text makes it quite obvious that women are equally qualified as men to engage in financial transactions and to own property. In other words, this verse does not imply or refer to any prejudice towards women concerning property ownership and the free disposal of their money. Therefore, according to the Qur'an, women are fully entitled, on the basis of equality with men, to work, own, sell, purchase, or engage in any financial dealings without any barriers or limitations. Moreover, the Sunna encourages women to work outside the home and participate actively in the social life of their communities.[443] It is narrated that when a group of women asked the Prophet what kind of work they could participate in, he answered, "In what they can and bear to carry out."[444] According to this Hadith, a woman can be involved in any type of work that does not harm her nature as a female.[445]

D Refuting the Arguments of the Strict View

i Al-Qawamah

In line with the correct interpretation of Shari'a, the word "Qawamah" (being in charge of someone) does not refer to any kind of superiority over a woman. Rather, it refers to care, responsibility and generosity.[446] The literal text of the verse reads, "Men are in charge of women, because Allah

---

obligations are based on his or her capabilities and qualifications; however, they must cooperate with each other to perform their roles properly. Emara, *supra* note 399, at 32 (trans. by author).

In addition, Islam recognizes that a woman's pledge is separate from a man's, so that both a man and a woman can freely embrace Islam. Mohammad Anas Ga'afar, Mabad'e Nezam Al-Hokm Fe Al-Islam wa Mada Ta'athor Al-Dostoor Al-Masry Beha (Principles of the Islamic Regime and the Extent to Which They Influence the Egyptian Constitution) 127 (2010) (trans. by author). This fact is derived from the Qur'an, which states:

> O Prophet, when the believing women come to you pledging to you that they will not associate anything with Allah, nor will they steal, nor will they commit unlawful sexual intercourse, nor will they kill their children, nor will they bring forth a slander they have invented between their arms and legs, nor will they disobey you in what is right - then accept their pledge and ask forgiveness for them of Allah. Indeed, Allah is Forgiving and Merciful.

Qur'an, *Surat Al-Mumtahanah* 60:12.

442 Qur'an, *Surat An-Nisa'* 4:32.

443 Morsi, *supra* note 430, at 231 (trans. by author).

444 Emara, *supra* note 399, at 33 (trans. by author).

445 *Id.*

446 Abbas El-Akad, Al-Mara' Fe Al-Qura'n (Women in the Qura'n) 9–10 (Dar Hindawi, 2014) (trans. by author).

hath made the one of them to excel the other, and because they spend of their property (for the support of women)."[447] Therefore, the term "Qawamah" is closely linked with money spending and giving and does not imply any form of superiority, humiliation or servitude towards women.[448]

Notably, the Sunna of Prophet Mohammad supports this view since it is narrated that the Prophet said: "Women are but shaqa'iq (sisters or twin halves) of men."[449] In addition, it is narrated that when the Prophet's wife, Aisha, was asked about her husband, she replied: "He always helped with the housework and would at times mend his clothes, repair his shoes and sweep the floor. He would milk, protect and feed his animals, as well as perform housework."[450] Moreover, the Prophet encouraged his companions to follow his example and said in another Hadith: "The best among you is he who treats his woman best."[451]

ii Husband's Obligation of Expenditure

Some Muslim scholars argue that if a wife had the right to work and earn money, Islam would have required her to share financial responsibilities with her husband.[452] To refute such an argument, it is necessary to clarify that, according to Shari'a, a husband's obligation of expenditure towards his family members is not based on his wife's financial situation.[453] Rather, a wife is financially dependent on her husband, who has to provide her with food, clothes, a house, medicine and other necessary needs regardless of her other sources of income.[454] Thus, in all cases, a husband is obligated to provide his wife with all necessary expenses, regardless of her wealth or employment status.[455]

iii Wife's Obligation of Obedience

The obligation of a Muslim wife's obedience to her husband is disputed under Shari'a. Some Muslim scholars believe that there is no Islamic source

447 Qur'an, *Surat An-Nisa'* 4:34.
448 El-Akad, *supra* note 446, at 10 (trans. by author).
449 Abu-Dawd, Sunan, Kitab at-Tahara, 1/61.
450 Sahih Al-Bukhari (Vol. 3, Hadith 1409). It is narrated that Aisha also said that Prophet Mohammad "used to keep himself busy serving his family and when it was time for prayer, he would get up for prayer." Sahih Al-Bukhari (Vol. 73, Book 8, Hadith 65).
451 At-Tirmidhi, Sahih, Abwab ar-Rada, 2/1091.
452 El-Azazi, *supra* note 368, at 115 (trans. by author).
453 El-Barzangy, *supra* note 387, at 219 (trans. by author).
454 *Id.*
455 *Id.*

compelling a wife to strictly obey her husband without any discussion or consultation.[456] They argue that the obligation of obedience is based on a misunderstanding of the term "Qawamah" (being in charge of someone).[457] As the study clarified earlier, "Qawamah" refers to a husband's financial responsibility and generosity toward his wife, but it never pertains to his authority over her.[458] Since "Qawamah" as men's superiority over women is misinterpreted, a woman's strict obedience to her husband has no Islamic basis.

Nevertheless, consultation (Shura) is a well-known principle in Islam, enshrined in many verses of the Qur'an and Hadiths of the Prophet. The Qur'an describes the inhabitants of paradise as follows: "And those who have responded to their Lord and established the prayers and whose affairs are determined by consultation among themselves, and from what We have provided them, they spend."[459] The Qur'an also recommended that Prophet Mohammad consult with his companions.[460]

As for the Sunna, Prophet Mohammad said: "There is no failure to the one who consulted others in a matter and no regret for the one who sought the guidance of God in a matter and no deviation from the right path for the one who adopted moderation and balance in their affairs."[461] Thus, sources of Islam emphasize that Shura is a fundamental Islamic behavior that should be implemented in all Muslim community affairs.[462] In other words, Shura should be regarded as a methodology of the Muslim community that includes the family.[463] Therefore, a husband should discuss with his wife all family-related decisions and refrain from pressuring her to cease her employment.[464]

---

456 Bassam Ali El-Amoush, Moraga'at Fe Al-Fekr Al-Islamy (Reviews of Islamic Thoughts) 75 (Dar El-Akademioun, 2015) (trans. by author).

457 Emara, *supra* note 399, at 30 (trans. by author).

458 El-Akad, *supra* note 446, at 10 (trans. by author).

459 Qur'an, *Surat Ash-Shura* 42:38.

460 The Qur'an says:

> So by mercy from Allah, [Mohammad], you were lenient with them. And if you had been rude [in speech] and harsh in heart, they would have disbanded from about you. So pardon them and ask forgiveness for them and consult them in the matter. And when you have decided, then rely upon Allah. Indeed, Allah loves those who rely [upon Him].

Qur'an, *Surat Al-Imran* 3:159.

461 Emara, *supra* note 399, at 105 (trans. by author).

462 Ramadan, *supra* note 441, at 168 (trans. by author).

463 *Id.*

464 Emara, *supra* note 399, at 28 (trans. by author).

On the other hand, a large number of Muslim scholars emphasize that a wife's obligation of obedience is mandated by Shari'a; however, such an obligation is not absolute.[465] According to their point of view, in order for a wife to obey her husband, certain requirements should be fulfilled.[466] In other words, the duty of obedience is closely related to a husband's protection of his wife in the sense that he must preserve her life, dignity, honor and reputation.[467] Under this view, it could be argued that forcing a wife not to work violates a husband's moral obligation to protect his wife. If a husband forbids his wife from working, this may lead to her unhappiness and psychological strain; hence, the wife may choose to work despite her husband's wishes.

iv Women's Deficiencies in Intelligence and Religion

Muslim scholars advocating women's right to work acknowledge that the Hadith that "women are deficient in intelligence and religion" is misunderstood and misinterpreted.[468] According to the narration of this Hadith, it was uttered on the day of Eid Al-Fitr,[469] a day of gladness and joy, and therefore the Prophet did not intend to irritate or bother Muslim women.[470] Instead, he was attempting to communicate compliments and appreciation.[471] Therefore, the term "deficiency in intelligence" was meant to refer to the supremacy of a woman's behavior in terms of passion and feelings over intelligence and thought. In other words, Prophet Mohammad did not intend to disparage or demean women's intelligence; rather, he said this hadith to clarify that women's emotions and passions must not outweigh or surpass their intellect, intelligence and competence.[472] In this regard, it is crucial to note that some of the hadiths ascribed to Prophet Mohammad were not actually said by him. In addition, some other hadiths attributed to

465 El-Barzangy, *supra* note 387, at 226 (trans. by author).
466 *Id.* at 433–34.
467 *Id.* at 434.
468 Ra'ed Mahmoud Telozy, Defa'a An Karamat Al-Mara'a Al-Muslima, Dafa' Al-Shobhat Alaty Tothar Hawla Al-Mara'a Al-Muslima Wa Nakdeha Mn Al-Hadith Al-Nabawy Al-Sharif (Defending the Dignity of a Muslim Woman: Repelling Suspicions Raised about Them and Criticizing Them in Light of the Prophet's Noble Hadith) 213 (Dar El-Kotob El-Elmia, 2015) (trans. by author).
469 Eid Al-Fitr is the celebration that marks the end of the fasting month of Ramadan.
470 Telozy, *supra* note 468 (trans. by author).
471 Emara, *supra* note 399, at 92 (trans. by author).
472 *Id.* at 90–91.

Prophet Mohammad should not be taken at face value or in their literal sense.

Under Shari'a, a person's mental health is the cause of responsibility.[473] Since men and women are treated equally in Islam (in terms of worship, rewards and punishments), this fact acknowledges that women have fully functional minds that are on par with men's.[474] Assuming otherwise would lead to either males being held solely accountable for their actions while women are exempt from responsibility owing to their lower IQs, or to unequal rewards and penalties being handed out to men and women on the basis of their sexes.[475]

According to the Qur'an, women have an outstanding status alongside men. The Qur'an states: "For men and women who have surrendered believing men and women; obedient men and women; truthful men and women, patient men and women, humble men and women, men and women who give charity, men and women who fast, men and women who guard their privates, men and women who remember Allah in abundance, for them Allah has prepared forgiveness and a mighty wage."[476] Although it is grammatically correct in Arabic to use the plural male noun to refer to both males and females, in this verse women are referred to on an equal basis with men. This strongly affirms that, under the Qur'an, women and men are equally treated concerning all acts of worship. In another interesting verse, the Qur'an upholds that both men and women have equal rewards and punishments. The Qur'an says: "And whosoever does a righteous deed, be it male or female, believing, we shall assuredly give him to live a goodly life; and We shall recompense them their wage, according to the best of what they did."[477] This verse refers to both males and females in order to confirm that all religious obligations, rewards and punishments are equally imposed on them.[478]

473 Ramadan, *supra* note 441, at 161–64 (trans. by author).

474 *Id.*

475 Emara, *supra* note 399, at 92 (trans. by author).

476 Qur'an, *Surat Al-Ahzaab* 33:35.

477 Qur'an, *Surat An-Nahl* 16:97.

478 In addition, the Qur'an says: "Whoever has done the smallest particle of good will see it; and whosoever has done an atom's weight of evil shall see it." Qur'an, *Surat Az-Zalzalah* 99:7–8. Similarly, the Qur'an says: "whoever hopes to meet Allah, he should do good deeds." Qur'an, *Surat AL-Kahf* 18:110. These verses are obviously applicable to both men and women, and that strongly clarifies that all rewards and punishments are equally imposed upon all Muslims without any distinction based on sex.

On the other hand, the vast majority of Muslim scholars believe that a woman's deficiency in religion does not undervalue her status in Islam; rather, it indicates that a woman, due to her instinctive nature as a female, has more legal flexibility than a man has.[479] For example, although a man and a woman may not fast in Ramadan in the case of severe travel or sickness, a woman alone is exempt from repeating missed prayers during menstruation, childbirth, and other circumstances.[480] These legal permissions are motivated by kindness and concern and are ultimately beneficial to women.[481]

v Never Will Succeed a Nation That Makes a Woman Their Ruler

Liberal Muslim scholars acknowledge a woman's right to hold positions of leadership, even the presidency.[482] They recognize that this Hadith is regarded as a prophecy rather than a piece of legislation.[483] Their point of view is based on the historical context in which this Hadith was uttered.[484] Prophet Mohammad was reportedly informed by two men, who had recently returned from Persia, that the Persian Empire was ruled by a woman; he predicted by inspiration that the Persian Empire under the rule of this woman would collapse soon. Thus, this Hadith is specifically applicable to the Persian Empire at that time and should not be applied to other nations ruled by women.[485] In other words, the interpretation of this Hadith must not be broadened to prohibit women from running for president or holding leadership roles.[486] Furthermore, it is necessary in this context to reiterate that a number of the sayings reported to Prophet Mohammad were not his own. The erroneously alleged proverbs and sayings of Prophet Mohammad must not be attributed to him.

In summary, after reviewing the previous arguments, including the strict point of view opposing women's right to work as well as the flexible view advocating women's right to work, it is affirmed that there is no source in Shari'a preventing women from occupying high-ranking positions within the state, whether as a leading figure, president, judge or other highly elevated position. In other words, all the arguments used to ban women's work

479 Telozy, *supra* note 468, at 213 (trans. by author).
480 Ramadan, *supra* note 441, at 161–62 (trans. by author).
481 Emara, *supra* note 399, at 93 (trans. by author).
482 El-Amoush, *supra* note 456, at 85 (trans. by author).
483 *Id.*
484 Ramadan, *supra* note 441, at 168–69 (trans. by author).
485 *Id.*
486 El-Amoush, *supra* note 456, at 85–86 (trans. by author).

are without merit and invalid under Shari'a. However, some Muslim scholars, who identify themselves as guardians of Islam, hold erroneous religious viewpoints under misleading slogans. They intentionally conceal clear facts about Islam and replace them with unfounded ideas that undermine the apparent evidence in the Qur'an. They are primarily concerned with enhancing their own views, regardless of any other opposing opinions. In addition, they fabricate some traditions about Prophet Mohammad. As a result, some Muslims elevate the views of those scholars to sacred status without confirming their close agreement with the Qur'an and Sunna. This fact is asserted in the Qur'an: "With clear signs and Books (We sent the Messengers). And We have also sent down unto you (Mohammad) the reminder and the advice (the Qur'an), that you may explain clearly to people what is sent down to them, and that they may give thought."[487] According to this verse, it is evident that the Qur'an urges Muslims to contemplate and consider the meanings and implications of its words rather than blindly adopting the interpretations provided by specific Muslim scholars.

4 Women's Right to Work under Egyptian Law

A *Women's Right to Employment Equality under the Law*

The Egyptian Constitution has been amended several times in recent years due to ongoing political changes in Egypt. This section of the book is concerned mainly with articles of the 1971 Constitution[488] because of their several applications in rulings issued by high courts. This section will discuss these articles and their applications by high courts, as follows:

Article 11 of the 1971 Constitution stipulates that the State shall ensure harmonization between a woman's obligations towards her family and work and guarantee her equal status with a man in economic, political, social and cultural spheres without violating rules of Shari'a.[489] In addition, Article 40

487 Qur'an, *Surat An-Nahl* 16:44.

488 Constitution of the Arab Republic of Egypt, Sept. 11, 1971 [hereinafter 1971 Constitution]. The right to work is enshrined in Article 13 of the 1971 Constitution. *Id.* art. 13. This article stipulates that work is a state-guaranteed right, an obligation and a privilege for all citizens, and that outstanding workers shall be properly appreciated by the State and society. In addition, under this article, no person shall be compelled to perform labor unless required by law to perform a national or public service for adequate remuneration. *Id.*

489 *Id.* art. 11. This article corresponds to the second paragraph of Article 10 of the 2012 Constitution, stating that the State shall ensure reconciliation between a woman's

of the 1971 Constitution states that citizens are equal before the law; they should have the same rights and duties without discrimination on the basis of sex, race, language, religion or faith.[490]

---

duties towards her family and work. Constitution of the Arab Republic of Egypt, art. 10, Dec. 26, 2012 [hereinafter 2012 Constitution]. In addition, this article is similar to Article 11 of the 2014 Constitution, stipulating that the State shall guarantee a woman's equality with a man in civil, political, economic and social fields according to the Constitution. Constitution of the Arab Republic of Egypt, Jan. 18, 2014, art. 11 [hereinafter 2014 Constitution].

Notably, Article 11 of the 2014 Constitution is considered to have a more secular nature since it ensures women's equality with men on the basis of the Constitution, whereas Article 11 of the 1971 Constitution protects women's equality on the basis of Shari'a. In contrast, the 2012 Constitution, which was promulgated in the era of President Mohammad Morsi, the Muslim Brothers' regime, did not include an explicit article referring to women's equality with men. 2012 Constitution, *supra* note 489.

490 1971 Constitution, *supra* note 488, at art. 40. This article was replaced by the first paragraph of Article 11 of the 2014 Constitution; however, it has no alternatives in the 2012 Constitution that was promulgated in the era of President Morsi.

Article 35 of the Labor Law prohibits wage discrimination based on sex, origin, language, religion, faith, or any other grounds of discrimination. Law No. 12 of 2003, art. 35, April 7, 2003 (Egypt) (trans. by author).

Article 88 of the Labor Law eliminates any kind of employment discrimination against a woman and ensures gender equality in the workplace. *Id.* art. 88.

Article 91 of the Labor Law states that a female worker, who is employed for more than ten months in the private sector, is entitled to two 90-day periods of paid maternity leave during the course of her entire service tenure. *Id.* art. 91.

Article 92 of the Labor Law stipulates that a female worker cannot be dismissed during her maternity leave. *Id.* art. 92.

Regarding breastfeeding rights for an employed woman, Article 93 of the Labor Law states that a female worker, during her daily working hours, with no deduction from wages, is entitled to have two rest periods, each of which is not less than thirty minutes, to breastfeed her child. *Id.* art. 93.

Under Article 94 of that law, a female worker is entitled to unpaid childcare leave for a period of two years. *Id.* art. 94. This leave is applicable only two times during a female worker's entire service period if she works in a private sector establishment employing fifty or more workers. *Id.*

Concerning the Civil Servants Law, Article 70 stipulates that a female worker has the right to take unpaid childcare leave for a period of two years. Law No. 47 of 1978, art. 70, July 20, 1978 (Egypt) (trans. by author). This leave is available for a maximum of three occasions throughout her entire service period. *Id.*

It should be noted that the Labor Law is applicable to all private sector employees. Law No. 12 of 2003, *supra* note 490, art. 4 (trans. by author). On the other hand, the Law of Civil Servants is applicable for public sector employees. Law No. 47 of 1978, *supra* note 490, art. 1 (trans. by author). In other words, employees working in the private sector can bring claims against an employer based on the Labor Law. Law No. 12 of 2003, *supra* note 490, art. 4 (trans. by author). However, public sector employees

In a very interesting case, the Supreme Constitutional Court (SCC)[491] declared that a woman's right to work does not undermine the fundamental

can sue their employers based on the Civil Servants Law. Law No. 47 of 1978, *supra* note 490, art. 1 (trans. by author).

As for the Child Law, Article 70 states that a female worker, whether in the public or private sector, is entitled to a fully paid leave for three months after childbirth. Law No. 12 of 1996, art. 70, March 29, 1996 (Egypt) (trans. by author). However, she does not receive this leave more than three times during her entire service period. *Id.* Additionally, this article stipulates that a pregnant woman's daily working hours shall be reduced by at least one hour starting from the sixth month of pregnancy and until delivery. *Id.* In addition, under this article, it is forbidden to employ a pregnant woman for any overtime work during pregnancy and until the end of the first six months following the newborn child's birth. *Id.*

Article 71 of the Child Law is similar to Article 93 of the Labor Law stipulating that, during the first two years following the child's birth, a nursing mother is entitled to two sessions of at least half an hour to breastfeed her child every day. *Id.* art. 71. These two intervals are considered part of her working hours, and no pay deductions are made for them. *Id.*

Furthermore, under Article 72 of the Child Law, a female worker in the public sector or in a private sector establishment that employs fifty or more employees is entitled to up to three unpaid childcare leaves throughout her entire service tenure, each of which is valid for two years. *Id.* art. 72.

491 In the 1971 Constitution, the Supreme Constitutional Court (SCC) was established for the first time. According to this Constitution, the SCC shall be "an independent" and "self-standing judiciary body" having an exclusive specialization to monitor "the constitutionality of the laws and regulations" and interpret the "legislative texts." 1971 Constitution, *supra* note 488, art. 174–75. In accordance with Article 175 of the 1971 Constitution, Law 48/1979 was enacted to clarify the authority of the SCC. *Id.* art. 175.

Article 3 of that law stated that the SCC consists of a president and an adequate number of members; however, seven members must issue its rulings. Law No. 48 of 1979, art. 3, September 6, 1979 (Egypt) (trans. by author).

Article 25 of that law determined the authority of the SCC to "(1) issue binding interpretations of existing legislation should there be inconsistent interpretation by the lower courts; (2) resolve jurisdictional conflicts between judicial bodies, typically from the civil and administrative branches; and (3) perform judicial review, through constitutional interpretation, of existing legislation." Luna Droubi, *The Constitutionality of the Niqab Ban in Egypt: A Symbol of Egypt's Struggle for a Legal Identity*, 56 N.Y.L. Sch. L. Rev. 687, 694 (2012).

Regarding Article 26, it stated that the SCC shall interpret legislative acts issued by legislative bodies and resolutions issued by the President of the Republic. Law 48/1979, *supra* note 491, art. 26 (trans. by author).

Article 27 gave the Court the power to decide the unconstitutionality of any law or regulation falling within its jurisdiction in relation to the given dispute. *Id.* art. 27 (trans. by author).

Islamic principle of a husband's financial obligation to his wife.[492] The SCC decided that, regardless of a husband's consent, a wife has the full right to work and, in addition, is entitled to her husband's financial support.[493] That case started when a woman got married and became a housewife. Later, she found an excellent job opportunity, but her husband tried to prevent her from working and required her to focus only on family duties.[494] However, she ignored her husband's disapproval and went to work. As a result, the husband stopped spending on his wife because she defied him.[495] In response to her husband's action, the wife brought a claim before the family court in order to compel him to provide financial assistance.[496] Her argument was based on Article 1 of Law No. 25 of 1920.[497] This article requires a husband to financially support his wife after marriage. According to this article, a husband's financial support shall be forfeited if a wife refuses to submit herself to him or leaves home without his permission, unless she leaves home to perform lawful work.[498]

On the other hand, the husband initially argued that his wife no longer needed his financial support because she worked and had a stable income.[499] His second argument was based on an opinion of Shari'a stipulating that a husband's financial support for his wife is closely linked with a wife's commitment to obey him. He argued that since his wife defied him and began working without his consent, she violated the obligation of obedience to which she should have been bound, and therefore he was no longer obligated to financially support her.[500] Thus, the husband challenged the constitutionality of the above-mentioned article, which gives a wife the right to join the workforce regardless of her husband's permission. He claimed that this article violated Article 2 and Article 9 of the Constitution.[501] Article 2 states that the Islamic Shari'a is the major source of

492 Case No. 18/Judicial Year 14/ Supreme Constitutional Court of Egypt (May 3, 1997) (trans. by author).

493 *Id.*

494 *Id.*

495 *Id.* In this case, the husband largely relied on a viewpoint of Shari'a suggesting that a wife's commitment to obey her husband is directly proportional to her husband's financial support for her.

496 Case No. 18/14, *supra* note 492 (trans. by author).

497 Law No. 25 of 1920, art. 1, July 15, 1920, as amended, July 4, 1985 (Egypt) (trans. by author).

498 *Id.*

499 Case No. 18/14, *supra* note 492 (trans. by author).

500 *Id.*

501 *Id.*

legislation.[502] Article 9 stipulates that a family is the basic unit of society and is built on religion, ethics and patriotism; the State should provide families with traditions, values and customs while stressing and developing this feature within Egyptian society's connections.[503] The husband alleged that the contested article violated a husband's right to his wife's obedience, and this may negatively affect family relationships and ties.[504] The family court deemed the unconstitutionality claim plausible, and therefore it referred the case to the SCC.[505]

The SCC ruled in favor of the wife, finding that the contested law did not violate the Constitution; its decision was based mainly on Shari'a provisions.[506] First, the Court rejected the husband's first argument, reasoning that, under Shari'a, a husband's financial obligations towards his wife are not based on her financial status. Therefore, according to the Court, a working wife who is able to earn an income is nonetheless entitled to her husband's financial support. Secondly, the Court affirmed that Islam encourages a woman to work as long as she balances work obligations with marital duties. In addition, the Court discussed religious issues, emphasizing that women used to work in commerce and other fields in the era of the Prophet.[507] Furthermore, the Court addressed social issues, stressing that both a man and a woman have to co-build society, so a man cannot violate his wife's right to work.[508] Moreover, the Court turned to other articles of the 1971 Constitution, stating that a husband could violate Article 40 of the Constitution, which requires the State to respect equality between a man and a woman in all spheres of life,[509] if he prevents his wife from working.[510] In addition, the Court noted that Article 11 of the Constitution requires the State to enable a wife to balance marital responsibilities and work obligations.[511] Therefore, according to the Court, a husband can

502 1971 Constitution, *supra* note 488, art. 2.

503 *Id.* art. 9.

504 Case No. 18/14, *supra* note 492 (trans. by author).

505 *Id.*

506 *Id.* Rules of Shari'a are considered mandatory laws and are given superior rank under the Constitution. 1971 Constitution, *supra* note 488, art. 2. Thus, courts can discuss and apply such rules to the facts of cases. In addition, any law that contradicts Shari'a shall be considered unconstitutional for violating Article 2 of the Constitution stipulating that the principles of Shari'a are the main source of legislation in Egypt. *Id.*

507 Case No. 18/14, *supra* note 492 (trans. by author).

508 *Id.*

509 1971 Constitution, *supra* note 488, art. 40.

510 Case No. 18/14, *supra* note 492 (trans. by author).

511 1971 Constitution, *supra* note 488, art. 40.

neither violate his wife's right to work protected by the Constitution nor restrict this constitutional right by dismissing his financial obligation towards her if she works without his consent.[512]

In another interesting case, the SCC declared the unconstitutionality of an article involving discrimination against mothers working as teaching staff members.[513] In that case, a female professor challenged the constitutionality of Article 91 of Law No. 49 of 1972.[514] Under this article, a teaching staff member was entitled to take leaves for scientific missions, tasks, and childcare; however, the total period of such leaves should not exceed ten years during his or her entire service period.[515] The SCC found that this article made a distinction between mothers working as teaching staff members and other female employees working at governmental entities.[516] According to the Civil Servants Law, all female employees are entitled to childcare leave at any time.[517] On the other hand, mothers working as teaching staff members were prohibited from taking that leave if they had exceeded ten years' leave in scientific missions or tasks.[518] The Court stated that the challenged article constituted sex-based employment discrimination because it provided male staff members with the opportunity to fully utilize the allowed ten-year leave in scientific missions or tasks, whereas women's allowed ten-year leave included childcare leave.[519]

Likewise, in a similar case, the SCC declared the unconstitutionality of a governmental resolution that included discrimination against a female worker.[520] In that case, the Minister of Agriculture issued a resolution under which each worker in the Ministry of Agriculture would be granted ownership of agricultural land.[521] According to that resolution, the share of each

---

512 Case No. 18/14, *supra* note 492 (trans. by author).

513 Case No. 81/Judicial Year 25/ Supreme Constitutional Court of Egypt (February 13, 2005) (trans. by author).

514 Law No. 49 of 1972, art. 91, October 5, 1972 (Egypt) (trans. by author).

515 *Id.*

516 Case No. 81/25, *supra* note 513 (trans. by author).

517 *Id.* Under Article 70 of the Civil Servants Law, a female worker has the right to take unpaid childcare leave for a period of two years; this leave is available three times during her entire service period. Law No. 47 of 1978, *supra* note 490, art. 70 (trans. by author).

518 Case No. 81/25, *supra* note 492 (trans. by author).

519 *Id.*

520 Case No. 163/Judicial Year 20/ Supreme Constitutional Court of Egypt (November 4, 2000) (trans. by author).

521 *Id.*

male worker was double that of a female worker's share.[522] The SCC found that the resolution violated several articles of the 1971 Constitution.[523] These articles are Article 8[524] stipulating that the State must ensure equal opportunities for all citizens, and Article 11[525] requiring equality between a man and a woman in all fields of life.[526] In addition, the Court affirmed that the resolution constituted discrimination based on sex, and therefore violated Article 40[527] of the Constitution banning any kind of discrimination between citizens.[528]

In another case involving a challenge to a female worker's right to equality in the workplace, the High Administrative Court (HAC)[529] revoked another ministerial decision constituting gender-based discrimination against a female worker.[530] In that case, the Egyptian Ministry of Education decided to provide employees working in remote governorates with travel allowances.[531] According to that decision, every six months, a married male employee would receive three train tickets: one for himself and two for members of his family. In addition, this ministerial decision stipulated that a male employee, who does not travel and remains at work, would be entitled to substitute allowances.[532] The HAC declared that the contested

---

522 Resolution No. 324 of 1991, Minister of Agriculture and Land Reclamation, April 28, 1991 (Egypt) (trans. by author).
523 Case No. 163/20, *supra* note 520 (trans. by author).
524 1971 Constitution, *supra* note 488, art. 8.
525 *Id.* art. 11.
526 Case No. 163/20, *supra* note 520 (trans. by author).
527 1971 Constitution, *supra* note 488, art. 40.
528 Case No. 163/20, *supra* note 520 (trans. by author).
529 The administrative judicial body is separate from the regular judiciary under Egyptian law, which is developed from French law. Droubi, *supra* note 491, at 688. In other words, administrative courts are part of a larger judicial body known as the Council of the State, which was founded by Law 112/1946. These courts settle administrative conflicts. Law No. 112/1946 (Egypt) (trans. by author). The highest court in the Egyptian administrative judiciary is the High Administrative Court (HAC), whose president is the head of the Council of the State. The law of the Council of the State was amended many times. Law 112/1946 was replaced with Law 9/1949 that was replaced with Law 165/1955 that was replaced with Law 55/1959 that was replaced with Law 47/1972. All these laws grant the Council of the State the authority to consider all administrative disputes. In the 2012 and 2014 Constitutions, neither the specifications nor the formation of the Council of the State were amended. 2012 Constitution, *supra* note 489; 2014 Constitution, *supra* note 489.
530 Case No. 2185/Judicial Year 44/High Administrative Court of Egypt (March 10, 2005) (trans. by author).
531 *Id.*
532 *Id.*

decision constituted discrimination based on sex.[533] In addition, the Court asserted that female employees should be given financial allowances on the basis of equality with their male counterparts.[534] Nevertheless, the Ministry of Education argued that some female employees might not be eligible for financial allowances if their husbands, who work at the same location, are also eligible.[535] The Court rejected that argument, clarifying that a female employee should be entitled to financial allowances for herself and two of her family members, even if her husband was given the same allowances.[536]

In another exciting case, the HAC protected a pregnant woman's right to be promoted in the workplace.[537] In that case, a female administrative prosecutor's work was reviewed while she was pregnant, since administrative prosecutors' work is typically evaluated every two years by the inspection department for promotion purposes.[538] Due to the plaintiff's below-average grade, she was not promoted to a higher position like her counterparts.[539] As a result, she challenged the inspection findings, arguing that she should not have been inspected during the period of pregnancy.[540] She asserted that she was suffering from abnormal conditions during her pregnancy, and this negatively affected her work output and achievements. In addition, she asked the Court to nullify that report and compel the administrative authority to re-inspect her work within a new time frame.[541] The HAC noted that a pregnant woman might be subject to a variety of complications arising from the physical alterations that could occur during the period of pregnancy.[542] Therefore, the Court considered pregnancy as kind of a pathological condition and criticized the administrative authority for inspecting the

533 *Id.* The Court relied on Article 40 of the 1971 Constitution, which stipulates equality between a man and a woman in all spheres of life. 1971 Constitution, supra note 488, art. 40.

534 Case No. 2185/44, *supra* note 540 (trans. by author).

535 *Id.*

536 *Id.*

537 Case No. 1325/Judicial Year 51/High Administrative Court of Egypt (June 22, 2008) (trans. by author).

538 *Id.*

539 *Id.* Commonly, the work of members of judicial bodies is evaluated as part of the promotion process. Everyone who receives a passing grade or higher is anticipated to be promoted to the next level.

540 Case No. 1325/51, *supra* note 537 (trans. by author).

541 *Id.* A member of the administrative prosecution who disagrees with the findings of an inspection may appeal to the Supreme Council of the Administrative Prosecution; if that body decides against them, they may file a petition with the administrative judiciary.

542 Case No. 1325/51, *supra* note 537 (trans. by author).

plaintiff's work during the pregnancy period. In addition, the Court found that the inspection order was based on an abuse of power.[543] Therefore, the Court annulled the plaintiff's inspection order and its subsequent impacts, and required the administrative authority to re-inspect the plaintiff's work during a different period than the term of her pregnancy.[544]

B Restrictions on Women's Right to Travel and Work Abroad

In 1959, the Egyptian Minister of Interior issued a resolution giving an Egyptian husband the right to prevent his wife from leaving the country.[545] According to the resolution, a wife was required to obtain prior consent from her husband before passport issuance or renewal. In addition, a husband was entitled to revoke his wife's passport in order to prevent her from traveling outside the country.[546] Due to the resolution, a great number of

543 *Id.*

544 *Id.* In 2009, the HAC issued a decision in a case involving a challenge to a female worker's right to take unpaid childcare leave. Case No. 17355/Judicial Year 50/High Administrative Court of Egypt (June 6, 2009) (trans. by author). The case started when the plaintiff, who was recently appointed as a permanent employee at the Ministry of the Interior, requested an unpaid childcare leave. *Id.* However, her manager refused because she applied for the leave within a short time after being permanently appointed, and therefore she was dismissed from work. *Id.* She brought a case to challenge the dismissal decision. The HAC declared that a temporary female employee might be denied unpaid childcare leave, but once she becomes permanently appointed, she has an absolute right to take it, even if she applies for it shortly after being permanently appointed. *Id.* In another case decided by the Court of Cassation, an employer refused to allow a female worker, who was on an approved unpaid childcare leave for two years, to return to work before the end of her leave. Case No. 2124/Judicial Year 53/ Egyptian Court of Cassation (April 13, 1993) (trans. by author). She filed a lawsuit against her employer, requesting to have her leave canceled and to be refunded her basic salary, bonuses, rewards and promotions starting from the date she submitted her return request. *Id.* The Court of Cassation emphasized a female employee's entitlement to unpaid childcare leave and to have it revoked at any time. *Id.* As for the financial issue, the Court differentiated between the basic salary and the variable remuneration. *Id.* The Court decided to reimburse the plaintiff's basic salary, commencing from her return request date. *Id.* However, the Court determined that the plaintiff was not entitled to any variable compensation above her normal wage because such compensation is not payable in successive months and is only given to employees who deserve recognition for their accomplishments. *Id.*

545 Resolution No. 63 of 1959, Minister of Interior, June 23, 1959 (Egypt) (trans. by author). Article 3 of the Minister of Interior's resolution states that a wife's passport shall be issued or renewed with a written consent of her husband before she travels abroad..., and in addition, the husband is entitled to revoke his approval by submitting a request to the Egyptian Passport Authority. *Id.* art. 3.

546 *Id.*

women were prevented from working and traveling abroad. This study will discuss two cases dealing with this resolution, as follows:

i The Case of the EgyptAir Hostess

In 1984, while working as an airhostess for Egypt Air Company, the plaintiff married her Egyptian husband, had two children, and continued her career for ten years.[547] Once disagreements arose between the couple, she sued her husband for divorce, and the court ruled in her favor.[548] In response, her husband filed an appeal. In addition, in order to take revenge, he submitted a request to the Egyptian Passport Authority to place his wife's name on a travel ban list.[549] Because the wife was prevented from traveling abroad and practicing her profession, she brought a lawsuit to challenge the Egyptian Passport Authority's decision.[550]

The trial court reversed the contested decision; its ruling was based on the termination of the marriage between the spouses.[551] The court noted that although the ruling that divorced the spouses was not final and was still on appeal, marital life has ended between them. Therefore, the court found that the plaintiff was not compelled to obey her husband and get his prior consent before traveling abroad.[552]

The husband appealed this ruling before the HAC.[553] He argued that the trial court misapplied the law by adopting the ruling of divorce, which was not final and was still under appeal, so that it could be overturned and marital life would be resumed.[554] Therefore, the wife should have been compelled to obey her husband and get his prior consent before traveling abroad in accordance with the Minister of Interior's resolution. The HAC upheld the decision of the trial court and dismissed the appeal; however, it reversed the trial court's reasoning. In other words, the HAC based its ruling

547 Case No. 5234/Judicial Year 42/High Administrative Court of Egypt (October 31, 1999) (trans. by author).

548 Case No. 2479/Judicial Year 50/Cairo Administrative Court (May 14, 1996) (trans. by author).

549 *Id.* If a husband wants to prevent his wife from leaving Egypt, he must first submit a request to the Egyptian Passport Authority requesting that her name be placed on the travel ban lists, as per Minister of Interior Resolution No. 63 of 1959. Resolution No. 63 of 1959, *supra* note 545.

550 Case No. 2479/50, *supra* note 548 (trans. by author).

551 *Id.*

552 *Id.* In Egypt, all Muslim family-related domestic laws are derived from Islamic law. All Muslim scholars agree that a divorced woman has no obligation to obey her ex-husband.

553 Case No. 5234/42, *supra* note 587 (trans. by author).

554 *Id.*

on the husband's abusive use of his wife's obligation of obedience.[555] The HAC noted that before marital life started between the couple, the husband was fully aware of his wife's work nature and allowed her to work for a decade, but once they had a dispute, he decided to prevent her from working and going abroad.[556] Moreover, the Court stipulated that the husband had no logical reason to violate his wife's right to work and travel. It added that even though the husband had a legal capacity to prevent his wife from traveling abroad, he had already relinquished such a capacity for more than ten years. Thus, according to the Court, the husband could not withdraw his waiver after the passing of this long term.[557] The Court concluded that the husband sought to prevent his wife from traveling abroad out of disagreement and not to safeguard the family's best interests.[558]

ii The Case of the British Airways Hostess

In this case, a husband, whose wife was an air hostess working at British airways, submitted a written request to the Egyptian Passports Authority to prevent his wife from traveling abroad.[559] In response, a decision was taken to place the wife's name on a travel ban list. As a result, the wife was prevented from work, and therefore she brought an action to challenge the Egyptian Passport Authority's decision.[560]

The contested decision was upheld by the trial court, which based its reasoning on the argument of a wife's obligation to obey her husband.[561] The court declared that the husband had absolute power to permit or disapprove his wife's traveling abroad, if desired. Despite all of the plaintiff's financial and psychological losses, the court ruled against her, giving the husband full capacity to restrict her freedom to travel abroad and force her dismissal from her job.[562] However, the wife did not accept the trial court's ruling, and therefore she appealed it before the HAC, which reversed the ruling and revoked the contested decision.[563]

---

555 *Id.* Abusive use of rights with the intent to harm others is prohibited by Egyptian law. Civil Law, Egypt, 15 Oct. 1949.
556 Case No. 5234/42, *supra* note 547 (trans. by author).
557 *Id.*
558 *Id.*
559 Case No. 6734/Judicial Year 44/High Administrative Court of Egypt (April 4, 1999) (trans. by author).
560 *Id.*
561 Case No. 2573/Judicial Year 52/Cairo Administrative Court (June 2, 1998) (trans. by author).
562 *Id.*
563 Case No. 6734/44, *supra* note 559 (trans. by author).

The HAC's decision was based on the principles of Islamic Shari'a, adopted as the major source of legislation under Article 2 of the Egyptian Constitution.[564] It stated that Shari'a provides a woman with the full right to work on condition of the work's legitimacy and compatibility with her feminine nature and duties towards her family.[565] In addition, the Court emphasized that once a husband marries a working wife, he implicitly permits her to work, and therefore he cannot withdraw his approval later. The Court adopted the Hadith of Prophet Mohammad, in which he said believers must abide by their conditions unless they make what is unlawful lawful, or vice versa.[566]

iii The Case of the Wife Employed in Dubai

In 2000, the SCC confirmed the unconstitutionality of the Minister of Interior's resolution.[567] In that case, the plaintiff had a valid Egyptian passport and worked in the Emirate of Dubai. She was surprised to learn that her husband had placed her name on a travel ban list.[568] Therefore, she brought a case before a court with appropriate jurisdiction to challenge the constitutionality of the Minister of Interior's resolution.[569] Since the court found the unconstitutionality claim valid, it referred the case to the SCC.[570]

The SCC ruled in favor of the plaintiff, stipulating that the Minister of Interior's resolution was unconstitutional because it violated Article 41 of the Constitution ensuring the right to freedom of movement.[571] In addition, the SCC found that the resolution violated Article 50 of the Constitution, stipulating that no citizen should be forced to live in a particular place,[572] and Article 52 of the Constitution, which guarantees individuals' right to temporary or permanent immigration.[573]

---

564 1971 Constitution, *supra* note 488, art. 2.

565 Case No. 6734/44, *supra* note 559 (trans. by author).

566 *Id.*

567 Case No. 243/Judicial Year 21/ Supreme Constitutional Court of Egypt (November 4, 2000) (trans. by author).

568 *Id.*

569 Resolution No. 63 of 1959, *supra* note 545.

570 Case No. 243/21, *supra* note 567 (trans. by author).

571 1971 Constitution, *supra* note 488, at art. 41. This article states that "individual freedom is a natural right that must be protected and ensured. Save for the case of being caught red-handed, no person may be arrested, inspected, detained or his freedom restricted or prevented from free movement except under an order necessitated by investigations and preservation of the security of the society." *Id.*

572 *Id.* art. 50. This article states that no citizen shall be "resid[ing] in place nor forced to reside in a particular place, except in the cases defined by the law." *Id.*

573 *Id.* art. 52. This article stipulates that "citizens shall have the right to permanent or temporary immigration. The law shall regulate this right and the measures and conditions for immigration and leaving the country." *Id.*

In line with the SCC's decision, a wife no longer requires a husband's permission to obtain a passport or depart the Country.[574] Nevertheless, domestic authorities did not apply this ruling without a court order for a considerable period of time.[575] An Egyptian wife could not travel abroad if her husband disapproved, unless she obtained a judicial ruling allowing her to travel.[576] As a result, several cases were brought before the Egyptian courts subsequent to the SCC's decision.[577]

---

574 Case No. 243/21, *supra* note 567 (trans. by author). Since Egyptian law is based on the French legal system, Egyptian lower courts are not compliant with the rulings of high courts, such as the HAC and the Court of Cassation. However, according to the Egyptian legal system, the SCC is the highest judicial power in the Country that determines the constitutionality of domestic laws and regulations, and its decisions are binding on all Egyptian courts. Law No. 48 /1979, art. 49 (Egypt) (trans. by author). Therefore, the HAC and other courts are bound to follow and apply the SCC's decisions. *Id.*

In 2001, the HAC reversed a trial court's decision and revoked the contested decision of the Egyptian Passport Authority. Case No. 3975/Judicial Year 45/High Administrative Court of Egypt (February 17, 2001) (trans. by author). In that case, the HAC relied on the SCC's ruling declaring the unconstitutionality of the Minister of Interior's resolution. *Id.* The case started when a married woman was admitted to work as an airhostess for Egypt Air Company. *Id.* Before she started her new job, her husband submitted a written consent to the Egyptian Passports Authority allowing her to work and travel abroad. *Id.* She proceeded to work until she was promoted to a higher position. *Id.* On September 10, 1998, she was surprised to find her name placed on the travel ban list. *Id.* Later, she knew that the Egyptian Passports Authority took that action in response to her husband's request in his capacity under the Minister of Interior's resolution. Resolution No. 63 of 1959, *supra* note 545 (trans. by author). In turn, she brought an action to challenge the Egyptian Passport Authority's decision. Case No. 3975/45, *supra* note 574 (trans. by author). However, the trial court upheld the contested decision. *Id.* The court's ruling was based on the husband's absolute control over his wife's right to travel internationally under the Minister of Interior's resolution. *Id.* The court declared that the husband, according to the resolution, has the full power to allow or deny his wife's international travel, and he can cancel his earlier approval if he changes his mind later. Furthermore, it added that no restrictions should be imposed on the husband's decision. *Id.* It should be noted that the HAC's ruling was issued on February 17, 2001, whereas the trial court's ruling was issued on February 16, 1999. On November 4, 2000, the SCC declared the unconstitutionality of the Minister of Interior's resolution. Case No. 243/21, *supra* note 567 (trans. by author). In other words, the SCC's decision was issued in the period between the trial court's ruling and the HAC's ruling. Therefore, the trial court's ruling was not based on the SCC's ruling, while the HAC was required to comply with the SCC's decision.

575 Case No. 13567/Judicial Year 53/ Administrative Court of Egypt (May 26, 2009) (trans. by author).

576 *Id.*

577 In 2009, after ten years of the SCC's ruling, another Egyptian wife was prevented from traveling abroad owing to her husband's disapproval. *Id.* She worked with her husband

C *Women's Exclusion from Major Positions in Egypt*

A close review of Egypt's recent history reveals that Egyptian women have been excluded from high-level government positions. In other words, no Egyptian woman has ever served as president or even run in a presidential election.[578] Furthermore, no Egyptian woman has ever held the positions of vice-president, prime minister, minister of foreign affairs, justice, interior or defense in modern Egyptian history. In addition, successive ministerial changes have witnessed the appointment of only a small number of female ministers, who often hold ministerial positions in non-sovereign ministries such as the ministry of manpower and the ministry of social solidarity, etc.

With regard to the employment of women in judicial work, this study will discuss this point in detail because of several cases challenging the exclusion of female law graduates from judicial appointments.

Egyptian female law graduates suffered greatly because they were barred from pursuing judicial careers that had formerly been restricted to male law graduates.[579] Although the exclusion of women was not stated in the constitution or statutory laws, the absence of female judges revealed a normatively biased practice by government officials.[580]

A female law graduate with honors applied for a judicial position in the administrative judiciary, but was not selected.[581] She believed that she was

in the United Arab Emirates. *Id.* On her return from Egypt, she found her name placed on the travel ban list upon her husband's request. *Id.* She brought a case before an administrative court with appropriate jurisdiction and waited for the court's decision. *Id.* The court ruled in the wife's favor, citing the SCC's decision that confirmed the unconstitutionality of the Minister of Interior's resolution. *Id.*

578 From a historical perspective, until the current time, seven male presidents followed King Farouq II, who was compelled to step down in 1952. After the 1952 revolution, Egyptian presidents were elected through a public referendum. For example, President Anwar Al-Sadat succeeded President Gamal Abdel-Nasser after a public referendum. Alison Elizabeth Chase, *The Politics of Lending and Reform: The International Monetary Fund and the Nation of Egypt, 42 Stan. J. Int'l L. 193, 208* (2006). The same thing occurred with President Sadat, as Hosni Mubarak, who was Sadat's vice president, became the Egyptian president in a public referendum after Sadat's assassination. *Id.* Later, in 2005, the Egyptian Constitution was amended to impose multiple-candidate presidential elections. Law No. 174 of 2005, July 2, 2005 (Egypt) (trans. by author). In addition, the number of terms a president may serve has been restricted to two, as opposed to an infinite number. *Id.*

579 Engy Abdelkader, *To Judge or Not to Judge: A Comparative Analysis of Islamic Jurisprudential Approaches to Female Judges in the Muslim Community World (Indonesia, Egypt, and Iran)*, 37 Fordham Int'l L. J. 309, 352 (2014).

580 *Id.*

581 Case No. 317/Judicial Year 20/High Administrative Court of Egypt (June 2, 1979) (trans. by author).

being discriminated against because she was a woman, and therefore she filed a complaint about the denial of her application.[582] Her main argument was based on Article 11 of the Constitution prohibiting discrimination on the basis of sex.[583]

The HAC noted two reasons for such exclusion.[584] The first reason was based on Egyptian customs and traditions that deemed the appointment of women to the judiciary inappropriate. As for the second reason, the Court noted that the exclusion might have been based on a view of Shari'a that bans appointing a woman as a judge. Nevertheless, the Court asserted that Shari'a has no explicit rule banning the appointment of a woman as a judge, nor does it contain a provision granting her this right.[585] In a similar vein, the Court clarified that while no domestic law bans appointing women to judicial careers, no legal provision explicitly supports such an issue either. Thus, the Court declared that the discretionary power of the administrative authority was permissible since it did not violate provisions of Shari'a or domestic laws, and therefore the Court upheld the exclusion decision.[586]

Later, several female law graduates battled for their rights by filing lawsuits.[587] However, courts upheld decisions excluding women from the judiciary because they chose to close the door on such appointments.[588]

Nevertheless, in 2000, the first female judge, Tahany El-Gebaly, was appointed to the Supreme Constitutional Court.[589] Several factors contributed to this accomplishment, including Shari'a references that permit the practice and secular feminist movements that strongly argued that the Constitution ensures gender equality and cited women's service in the government and parliament as evidence of their capacity to be appointed to the bench.[590]

Furthermore, from 2007 to 2015, three presidential resolutions were issued to appoint sixty-eight women as judges.[591] These resolutions could be

582 *Id.*
583 1971 Constitution, *supra* note 488, art. 11.
584 Case No. 317/20, *supra* note 581.
585 *Id.*
586 *Id.*
587 Abdelkader, *supra* note 579, at 353.
588 *Id.*
589 *Id.* at 354. Justice Tahany El-Gebaly was dismissed later in 2012 after amending the Egyptian Constitution and reducing the SCC's judges from 18 to only 11. 2012 Constitution, *supra* note 489, art. 176.
590 Abdelkader, *supra* note 579, at 354.
591 Resolution No. 95 of 2007, President of the Republic, April 12, 2007 (Egypt) (trans. by author); Resolution No. 119 of 2008, President of the Republic, May 3, 2008 (Egypt) (trans. by author); Resolution No. 235 of 2015, President of the Republic, June 18, 2015 (Egypt) (trans. by author). In 2007, President Mubarak issued a resolution appointing thirty women, who had previously served as administrative prosecutors, to be judges

considered a positive step towards achieving equality between men and women and a move in the right direction towards reducing gender discrimination in Egypt.[592] Despite their advantages, the resolutions were flawed to some degree because most female judges were not given the seniority they deserved.[593]

Nevertheless, Egypt has recently made substantial progress in terms of women's right to work, particularly concerning their appointment to judicial positions. Women have been appointed as prosecutors in the Egyptian General Prosecutor's Office[594] and as judges in the Council of the State for the very first time.[595] In addition, 73 women have been appointed as judges in a number of other courts.[596] This is a major victory for women's rights and a step toward eradicating sexism and prejudice in Egypt, where discrimination against women has long been the norm for decades and centuries. Despite these improvements, men continue to dominate the judiciary system. The overwhelming majority of judges are men, while the number of female judges is negligible in comparison.

In short, it is clear that Egypt still lacks gender employment equality, despite some courts' decisions and the recent progress in the field. Egypt still has a long way to go in order to eliminate discrimination against women and achieve gender parity with men in the workplace.

5 Concluding Analysis of Women's Right to Equality in Employment

Equality in employment is strongly protected under international law. Various international human rights conventions, such as the UDHR, the ICESCR, and CEDAW, set out labor standards to protect women's right to equality in employment. In addition, there are more specialized ILO conventions, such as Conventions No. 100 and No. 111, that emphasize equality

in courts. In addition, in 2008, another presidential resolution was issued to appoint twelve female administrative prosecutors as judges, and in 2015, twenty-six female administrative prosecutors were appointed as judges.

592 Abdelkader, *supra* note 579, at 354.

593 Case No. 135/Judicial Year 31/ Supreme Constitutional Court of Egypt (June 6, 2010) (trans. by author). Every Egyptian judge has a position of seniority depending on the year of graduation. This seniority determines salaries, promotions and incentives. *Id.*

594 Decision of the Supreme Judiciary Council, September 25, 2022 (Egypt) (trans. by author).

595 Resolution No. 247 of 2022, President of the Republic, June 5, 2022 (Egypt) (trans. by author).

596 Resolution No. 338 of 2022, President of the Republic, July 31, 2022 (Egypt) (trans. by author).

between men and women in employment, including remuneration and treatment. Furthermore, in accordance with the international human rights conventions, pregnant women are protected from any discrimination based on pregnancy. This is clearly manifested in Article 11 of CEDAW banning the dismissal of any female worker based on pregnancy, some of the recommendations issued by the U.N. treaty bodies that ban pregnancy testing as a requirement of employment, and the ILO's Maternity Protection Conventions.

With regard to the ECJ, it applied international standards and managed to protect a female worker from direct and indirect pay and treatment discrimination, as well as discrimination based on pregnancy. Therefore, the Court succeeded in providing significant decisions for gender employment equality and clarified that female employees must enjoy the same employment and occupational opportunities as male employees.

This chapter of the book concludes that American law is consistent with international human rights standards with regard to providing protection from any kind of discrimination against a woman in employment. Title VII of the Civil Rights Act and the Supreme Court's interpretation of it emphasize this issue.

Furthermore, this chapter tackled a woman's right to work under Shari'a by discussing two different points of view: advocating and opposing. It addressed arguments of those who oppose women's right to work and refuted them with the arguments of proponent scholars. Moreover, this chapter confirmed that Shari'a has no sacred texts prohibiting a woman from taking high positions within the state. In other words, all arguments adopted by those opposing a woman's right to work are proven to be baseless and invalid.

Although Shari'a is regarded as the main source of legislation in Egypt, Egyptian female workers have suffered a lot from several kinds of discrimination by official authorities. Until recently, an Egyptian woman did not have the right to travel abroad without the prior consent of her husband; thus, she was deprived of several positions, such as airline hostess. This reflects that Egyptian law not only discriminated against female workers but also put them in an inferior rank to Egyptian men. In addition, this chapter shed light on certain positions that were confined to men in the past, such as the position of judge. Before 2007, a woman was excluded from this position, and only about 30 female judges were appointed in that year. Furthermore, certain sovereign positions, including the presidency, vice-presidency, and important ministries, were never held by Egyptian women.

Such discrimination against women in Egypt has no relation to Islamic Shari'a. Rather, it may be attributed to governing regimes or long-established social patterns and cultural stereotypes that dominated in Egypt several generations ago.

It could be argued that the situation for Egyptian women appears to be improving as a result of recent court judgments and resolutions promoting gender equality in judicial positions. However, much more progress should be made in terms of women's employment equality in order for Egyptian women to have the same rights as men in the workplace and be free from all forms of discrimination.

CHAPTER 3

Women's Right to Wear Islamic Clothing

Many women around the world wear a certain kind of clothing, through which they are manifested as Muslims. Some of them wear a headscarf,[1] while others cover their whole bodies, including their faces, and wear a veil.[2] These women wear such clothing at all times, in streets, shops, educational institutions and works; however, they may not care about the reactions of others, who may feel surprised or bothered by such Islamic clothing.

Some countries impose restrictions on a woman's right to wear Islamic clothing, considering such dress a type of religious symbol that expresses religious faith.[3] These countries raise several lines of argument for restricting the manifestation of religious symbols. One of their arguments is the need to control certain environments for specific official purposes, such as the judiciary system, the parliament, and prisons. In these places, according to their argument, religious symbols may have negative effects on a state's ability to perform its missions.[4]

In addition, it could be argued that religious apparel or symbols might have a negative impact on states' public health, safety, or order.[5] For example, if a religious scholar drives a motorcycle while wearing a turban and refuses to wear a motorcycle helmet, he may injure himself. Therefore, states may intervene to protect the public health.[6] Another example is that if a woman wears a veil and refuses to remove it to be photographed for a driver's license, states could intervene to protect the public safety of the entire society.[7] Other countries ban religious symbols in order to protect the

---

1 Shaira Nanwani, *The Burqa Ban: An Unreasonable Limitation on Religious Freedom or a Justifiable Restriction?* 25 Emory Int'l L. Rev. 1431, 1436 (2011).

2 Chidi Emmanuel, *Hijab Is Not a Ticket to Heaven*, Kuwait Times, Jan. 29, 2010, at 33, available at http://issuu.com/kuwaitnews/docs/kt20100129 (last visited Jul. 10, 2024).

3 Peter G. Danchin, *Suspect Symbols: Value Pluralism as a Theory of Religious Freedom in International Law*, 33 Yale J. Int'l L . 1, 5 (2008).

4 *Id.*

5 International Covenant on Civil & Political Rights, art. 18(3), *opened for signature* Mar. 23, 1976, 999 U.N.T.S. 171 (entered into force Dec. 16, 1966) [hereinafter ICCPR].

6 G. Danchin, *supra* note 3.

7 *Id.*

 | DOI:10.1163/9789004729506_005

public order of their societies, claiming that such symbols are closely connected with violence and a lack of tolerance.[8]

There is another reason why states restrict the manifestation of religion.[9] This argument might be made in the event of a violation of a state's public principles, such as secularism and neutrality.[10] For example, the existence of religious attire or symbols at police stations, courts, and public schools could impair the principle of secularism and give states a particular religious identity. As a result, countries may circumscribe the use of these clothes or symbols in order to prevent a certain religion from having an advantage or precedence over secular concepts and democratic values dominating the society.[11]

Similarly, some countries claim that the freedoms and rights of others can be protected by banning religious manifestations.[12] These countries may enact laws preventing students and teachers from wearing religious garments or symbols at educational institutions, claiming that such symbols constitute a kind of provocation or proselytization.[13]

Lastly, other countries seek to restrict the wearing of religious attire in order to protect a woman's right to equality.[14] They consider pressuring or compelling a woman to wear religious dresses as a kind of gender discrimination and a repression of feminine sexuality.[15]

Since a woman's Islamic clothing is a duty under Islam, this chapter of the book will explore Islamic Shari'a's perspective on imposing certain attire on women. It will clarify whether Shari'a imposes the hijab or niqab and discuss the reasons why Muslim women choose to wear such Islamic clothing. In addition, this chapter will examine the legal status of the hijab and niqab in Egypt, a prominent Muslim country. It will explain whether a Muslim woman is required to wear specific Islamic clothing under Egyptian law, whose major source of legislation is Shari'a. Furthermore, this chapter will determine whether a woman has an absolute or restricted right under

8 *Id.* at 6.

9 Dominique Custos, *Secularism in French Public Schools: Back to War? The French Statute of March 15, 2004*, 54 Am. J. Comp. L. 337, 368–69 (2006).

10 *Id.*

11 *Id.*

12 L. Elizabeth Chamblee, *Note: Rhetoric or Rights? When Culture and Religion Bar Girls' Right to Education*, 44 Va. J. Int'l L. 1073, 1111 (2004).

13 *Id.*

14 G. Danchin, *supra* note 3, at 8.

15 Hera Hashmi, *Comment: Too Much to Bare? A Comparative Analysis of the Headscarf in France, Turkey, and the United States*, 10 RRGC 409, 416 (2010).

international and American law to wear Islamic clothing in order to fulfill her religious obligations.

1 The Duty of Islamic Clothing under Shari'a

A *The Controversy between Hijab and Niqab*

According to Islam, there are certain attire standards for women; this fact is the subject of serious and numerous debates.[16] Women's Islamic dress became obligatory on the basis of verse 31 of chapter 24 of the Qur'an: "And they should not display their beauty and ornaments except what (ordinarily) appear …."[17]

The meaning of this verse is implicit since it does not obviously enjoin a woman to wear a particular Islamic dress; rather, it simply requires a woman to be modest, and this requirement is interpreted to describe specific styles of scarves and veils.[18] Requiring a woman to be modest is of great controversy among Muslim scholars because they differ on what parts of a woman's body may appear. In other words, Muslim scholars vary on what parts of a Muslim woman's body should be covered to seem modest.[19] This controversy led to several Islamic ways of dressing for women in Muslim societies, such as the sitar, burqa', niqab, chador, and hijab.[20] The sitar is a long cloak covering all of the woman's body, face and eyes. The burqa' is a full-body veil with a mesh concealing the face. The niqab is a full-face veil that only reveals the eyes. The chador is a long cloak that does not cover the face. The hijab, or headscarf, is a tied scarf around a woman's neck and head.[21]

The aforementioned verse gives a woman the full right to freely determine which parts of her body can be seen; however, she often decides to wear a hijab or niqab.[22] Muslim women who follow the majority of Shari'a's scholars are in favor of the hijab, whereas women who adhere to other conservative religious scholars prefer to wear the niqab.[23]

---

16 Nanwani, *supra* note 1, *at* 1436–37.

17 Qur'an, *Surat Al-Nūr* 24:31.

18 Nanwani, *supra* note 1, at 1435.

19 *Id.* at 1437.

20 *Id.* at 1436.

21 *Id.*

22 *Id.* at 1437.

23 Nathan J. Brown & Clark B. Lombardi, *The Supreme Constitutional Court of Egypt on Islamic Law, Veiling and Civil Rights: An Annotated Translation of Supreme*

Supporters of the hijab, the majority of Shari'a scholars, confirm that the hijab is the mandatory Islamic garment.[24] They believe that sources of Shari'a do not impose the wearing of the niqab on a Muslim woman.[25] Their point of view is based on the following arguments:

- It is narrated that Jabir Ibn Abdullah[26] recounted a story he witnessed during the life of Prophet Mohammad in which a woman with spots and bruises on her cheeks approached the Prophet when he was giving a speech (khutbah) and spoke to him. In line with that narration, supporters of hijab argue that hijab, not niqab, is the mandatory Islamic garment, as Jabir was able to accurately observe the bruises and spots on a woman's face, and that she talked with the Prophet, who did not mandate her to wear a niqab.[27]
- It is attributed to Aisha, the wife of Prophet Mohammad, that she said: The believing women used to pray Fajr (the Dawn Prayer) wearing their cloaks and return home in the darkness without being identified by others.[28] Anti-niqab Muslim scholars argue that the dark night was the reason for not recognizing women in this narration. According to their viewpoint, if women had been concealing their faces, they would not have been identifiable regardless of the darkness.[29]

On the other hand, some of Shafi'a's and Malikia's scholars adopt the niqab as a religious duty. They raise the following two lines of argument to support their view.

- It is attributed to Aisha that she said: May Allah be pleased with the wives of Ansar. When the verse of the veil was revealed, they immediately ripped their cloaks and covered their faces.[30]
- It is attributed to Asma' Bint Abi Bakr, one of the Prophet's companions, that she said: We used to cover our faces from men, and we usually comb our hair before starting the Hajj or Umra, major or minor pilgrimage.[31]

Constitutional Court of Egypt Case No. 8 of Judicial Year 17 (May 18, 1996), 21 am. U. int'l L. rev. 137, 156 (2005–06).

24 Kamal El-Sayed Abu-Malik, Sahih Fiqh el Sunna (Sunna Understanding) 385 (2005) (trans. by author).

25 *Id.*

26 Jabir Ibn Abdullah is one of the well-known companions of Prophet Mohammad.

27 Abu-Malik, *supra* note 24 (trans. by author).

28 Sahih Al-Bukhari (Vol. 1, Book 8, Hadith 368).

29 Abu-Malik, *supra* note 24 (trans. by author).

30 Hashmi, *supra* note 15, at 413 (quoting Anne Sofie Roald, Women in Islam: The Western Experience, 266 (2001)).

31 Abu-Malik, *supra* note 24 (trans. by author).

B *Hijab Is the Mandatory Islamic Clothing*

This study shall expose certain arguments affirming that the hijab is mandatory, whereas the niqab is neither banned nor obligatory. By raising the following two arguments, the debate over the hijab and niqab shall be resolved. These two arguments are based on logical reasoning, as follows:

i No Sources Command Women to Cover Their Faces

The primary sources of Shari'a, the Qur'an and the Sunna, did not clearly determine the requirements of a Muslim woman's dress.[32] Reading verse 31 of chapter 24 of the Qur'an, which states "they should not display their beauty and ornaments except what ordinarily appears," may help one recognize that a woman should be modest, but this verse does not impose specific requirements on a woman's clothing.[33] The phrase "except what ordinarily appears" suggests that certain parts of a woman's body shall remain uncovered. Muslim scholars who support the hijab as the mandatory Islamic clothing agree that the face, hands and feet are the parts of a woman's body that could "ordinarily appear."[34] On the other hand, this phrase and the entire verse do not necessitate or mandate that a woman wear a niqab.[35]

Nevertheless, the majority of Muslim scholars agree that some requirements of a woman's clothing should be fulfilled.[36] According to their view, it is inappropriate for a woman to wear garments that are either transparent or too tight. In such cases, a woman would be unable to adhere to Islamic clothing requirements, violating the principle of modesty.[37]

It is worth noting that imposing modesty is more inclusive and logical than mandating that a woman wear specific apparel. An example would be illustrated by considering two women, one of whom wore a headscarf without displaying modesty, while the other was modest but did not wear a headscarf. Although neither of them is dedicated to the Shari'a's requirements, the latter could be considered more favorable from an Islamic perspective. The first woman obviously breaches the need for modesty imposed by the Qur'an; however, the second violates the interpretation of the Qur'an that is accepted by the majority of Muslim scholars, which mandates that a

32 Nanwani, *supra* note 1, at 1436–37.

33 Gamal El-Deen Mahmoud, Hekook Al-Mar'a Fe Al-Mogtama'a Al-Islamy Wa Al-Tashre'e Al-Masry (Women's Rights between Islamic Societies and Egyptian Law) 18 (Vol. 2, 2006) (trans. by author).

34 *Id.*

35 *Id.* at 21.

36 Hamed Ahmad Taher, Kaifa Tosbeheen Asa'd Emra'a (The Way to Become the Happiest Woman) 191 (2007) (trans. by author).

37 *Id.*

woman wear a hijab. In other words, the former clearly violates the Qur'anic text, while the latter violates the interpretation of that text.

ii Islam Imposes Lowering the Gaze on Both Men and Women

Lowering the gaze refers to the act of avoiding prolonged eye contact between a man and a woman, which can potentially lead to temptation, and is considered forbidden.[38] The verse that precedes the one addressing women's modesty pertains to men's obligation to lower their gaze.[39] The requirement for males to lower their gaze implies that niqab is not mandatory. In other words, if a woman's face is covered, the male will have no visual access to her; hence, there is no need to expect him to lower his gaze.

This part of the Qur'an consists of three phases: 1- The first requires men to lower their gaze: "Say to the believing men that they should lower their gaze". 2- The second necessitates that women lower their gaze: "And tell the believing women to lower their gaze". 3- The third entails that women maintain modesty in their attire.[40] The order of these obligations highlights the priority given to men lowering their gaze before addressing women's modesty. This sequence implies that the niqab is not a mandatory dress code for women; if it were, the gaze-lowering requirement would be superfluous.

---

38 Abu El-A'ala El-Mawdoodi, Al-Hijab (The Hijab) 182–83 (Dar El-Ketab, 1995) (trans. by author). The renowned Egyptian scholar, Sheikh Mohammad Mottwalli Ash-Sha'rawi, one of the most famous interpreters of the Qur'an, notes that Islam bans prolonged eye contact between a man and a woman, as it may lead to temptation. Mohammad Metwalli Ash-Sha'rawi, Al-Mara'a fe Al-Qur'an (Women in the Qur'an) 109 (1998) (trans. by author). He argues that Islam attempts to overcome adultery by encouraging a man and a woman to lower their gaze. To support his argument, Ash-Sha'rawi cites the narration of Adam and Eve mentioned in the Qur'an as an example. *Id.* According to the Qur'an, Allah did not instruct Adam and Eve to refrain from eating the fruit of the tree. If this were the case, Adam and Eve could inhale its fragrance and be deceived by its attractiveness. *Id.* Rather, the Qur'an stated that Allah forbade them from approaching the tree, so they could not be fascinated by its beauty. Qur'an, *Surat Al-A'raf* 7:19. The subsequent events are well known, since both Adam and Eve failed the test by consuming the forbidden fruit from the tree, resulting in their expulsion from paradise and relocation to earth. Similarly, according to the interpretation of Ash-Sha'rawi, the Qur'an addresses the issue of adultery by urging men and women to lower their gazes. This is because the extended eye contact between a man and a woman could potentially generate a sexual desire that eventually leads to sexual harassment or an illegitimate sexual relationship. Ash-Sha'rawi, *supra* note 38, (trans. by author). Accordingly, Islam not only prohibited adultery or sexual harassment but also mandated that men and women lower their gaze. *Id.*

39 Qur'an, *Surat Al-Nūr* 24:30.

40 *Id.* at 30–31.

The argument that the niqab is not mandatory due to men's commandment to lower their gaze is comparable to the argument presented in Aisha's narration. According to her, women used to attend the Fajr prayer without being identifiable by others due to the darkness.[41] In other words, if women had been covering their faces, Aisha would not have cited darkness as the primary reason for their anonymity. Similarly, the requirement for men to lower their gaze would be redundant if women were required to wear the niqab. This argument supports the view that the niqab is not mandatory and that the hijab is the required attire in Islam.

C *Why Do Many Muslim Women Wear Islamic Clothing? Is This a Choice of Their Free Will?*

The motivations for wearing Islamic clothing are diverse. It is a well-known fact that religious and political leaders in certain countries force women to wear full-face veils in all public spaces.[42] This is an explicit example of gender discrimination against women. However, women in many other countries willingly opt to wear hijab without any similar directives.

In addition, in some other cases, family members may force or pressure a woman to wear Islamic clothing, such as a hijab or niqab.[43] Compelling a woman to wear such apparel undoubtedly constitutes oppression and discrimination against her. This represents a clear violation of the principles of gender equality and human dignity.[44] However, it is important to differentiate between coercion and parental encouragement. Some Muslim parents encourage their children to participate in Islamic traditions and follow Islamic teachings.[45] They may advise their daughters to dress modestly and wear Islamic garments, such as the hijab. This form of guidance is similar to practices in other religions, where parents may advise their children to wear religious attire or symbols like the kirpan, yarmulke, or a pendant of St. Joseph.[46] In such contexts, parental influence is generally not

---

41 Sahih Al-Bukhari, *supra* note 28.

42 Karima Bennoune, *Secularism and Human Rights: A Contextual Analysis of Headscarves, Religious Expression, and Women's Equality Under International Law*, 45 Colum. J. Transnat'l L. 367, 390 (2006).

43 Bridgette Dunlap, *Protecting the Space to be Unveiled: Why France's Full Veil Ban does not Violate the European Convention on Human Rights*, 35 Fordham Int'l L.J. 968, 1011 (2012).

44 *Id.*

45 Theresa Perkins, *Unveiling Muslim Women: The Constitutionality of Hijab Restrictions in Turkey, Tunisia, and Kosovo*, 30 B.U. Int'l L.J. 529, 535 (2012).

46 *Id.*

viewed as abusive or oppressive but rather as part of religious and cultural upbringing.[47]

On the other hand, some women wear Islamic dress "as a symbol of community identification and pride in a common heritage or culture."[48] According to their view, the veil could be a sign of confederation and collaboration instead of oppression that is based on misconceptions about Islam.[49] For instance, on university campuses, a group of students puts on fashion shows presenting hijab as modern and trendy attire in an effort to challenge false ideas about Islam.[50] Following September 11, Qama, a young American woman, decided to wear a hijab due to the embarrassment felt by her family and Muslim friends in wearing Islamic clothing.[51] She did so in order to demonstrate that she was not coerced by her relatives to wear the veil and to manifest her Muslim identity.[52] The 2011 revolutions in the Middle East strongly testify that women are not forced to wear Islamic clothing.[53] Many pictures were taken of women wearing Islamic attire.[54] These women were protesting against dictatorial regimes while wearing different styles of dress indicating their identity as Muslims.[55] Obviously, these women were not pressured or coerced to wear such Islamic clothing, nor were they advocating for a new government that would follow strict dress regulations.[56] In other cases, a woman freely chooses to wear a hijab, considering it an integral part of her identity and feeling uncomfortable without it, even if she is aware that others may find it outdated or unfashionable.[57] In addition, some young teenagers also freely opt to wear hijab, even if their female family members do not. This illustrates that there is no pressure or coercion on all female teenagers wearing hijab.[58]

---

47 *Id.*

48 *Id.* at 534.

49 *Id.*

50 University College. Dublin Islamic Soc'y, Hijab Fashion Show 2010, WordPress (Feb. 13, 2010), http://hijabfashionshow.wordpress.com (last visited Aug. 1, 2024).

51 Perkins, *supra* note 45, at 534.

52 *Id.* 534–35.

53 *Id.* at 535.

54 Uzma Mariam Ahmed, Middle East Uprisings: The Feminism Makeover, Wash. Post Blog, (Mar. 28, 2011, 10:45 AM), http://www.washingtonpost.com/blogs/altmuslimah/post/middle-east-uprisings-the-feminism-makeover/2011/03/28/ AFdbwYoB blog.html (last visited Aug. 1, 2024).

55 Perkins, *supra* note 45, at 535.

56 *Id.*

57 *Id.* at 535–36.

58 *Id.* at 536.

In other instances, women choose to voluntarily wear hijabs for religious reasons. According to those women, they are commanded by their religion to wear the hijab.[59] To prove their faithful belief in Islam, they have to fulfill its obligations, which include wearing the hijab; otherwise, they would feel guilty for failing to perform their religious duties.[60] They believe that they have the full right to freely practice their religious duties, one of which is to wear the hijab.[61] Other women choose freely to wear full-face veils or niqabs. They may consider it a means of increasing their commitment to Islamic teachings. In other words, a woman wearing a niqab (montakebah) chooses to adopt the more difficult way of worship in order to fulfill modesty perfectly, believing that her reward will be greater.[62] Most of these women, who willingly wear hijabs or niqabs, believe that their freedom of choice must be respected, considering any state ban or restriction on the wearing of Islamic clothing as a violation of their right to privacy and the right to free exercise of religion.[63] In other words, according to their views, any restrictions imposed on the wearing of Islamic dress are incompatible with their right to embrace Islam, follow their religious rules, and submit to their religious obligations.[64]

2 Women's Islamic Clothing under Egyptian Law

This section primarily focuses on the articles of the Constitution of 1971, which are widely present in influential judicial rulings. Although the Constitution does not explicitly protect the right to free exercise of religion, certain provisions could be interpreted to support a woman's freedom to wear Islamic clothing. This section will examine these provisions, followed by high courts' rulings regarding legal disputes over the wearing of Islamic attire in Egypt.

---

59 Hashmi, *supra* note 15, at 414–15.

60 *Id.*

61 Peter G. Danchin, *Islam in the Secular Nomos of the European Court of Human Rights*, 32 Mich. J. Int'l L. 663, 725 (2011). In some points of view, the Islamic headscarf is considered "a sign of distinction" that "represents respectfulness," and a "woman with the headscarf is a woman who is respected and is treated as a human being and not a sexual object." Hashmi, *supra* note 15.

62 Interview with Huda Ahmad (Aug. 25, 2020) (on file with the author).

63 Case No. 3219/2007 High Administrative Court of Egypt (trans. by author).

64 *Id.*

A *Principles of the Egyptian Constitution Relating to Women's Islamic Clothing*

i Superiority of Shari'a

As referred to in the book, in 1980, Article 2 of the 1971 Egyptian Constitution was changed from "principles of Islamic Shari'a are a source of legislation in Egypt" to "principles of Islamic Shari'a are the main source of legislation in Egypt."[65] Thus, the word "source" has been replaced with "the main source." This amendment was the outcome of a long-term dispute between secularists and Islamists regarding the legitimacy of Islamic Shari'a as the primary source of legislation in Egypt.[66]

In 1985, five years after that amendment, the Supreme Constitutional Court (SCC) clarified for the first time the real meaning of Article 2 of the Constitution by quoting Al- Azhar[67] special legislative commission's report. According to this report, the aim of modifying Article 2 was to "constrain the legislator to have recourse to the binding commands of the Shari'a to the exclusion of any other source in order to discover what (law) he is searching for."[68] However, "if the [legislator] does not find there an explicit ruling, then he [has] to employ the Shari'a resources of innovative reasoning (al-ijtihadiyya) in order to arrive at the proper rules to follow and which do not transgress the foundations and global principles of Shari'a."[69]

---

65 Constitution of the Arab Republic of Egypt, art. 2, Sept. 11, 1971 [hereinafter 1971 Constitution].

66 Luna Droubi, *The Constitutionality of the Niqab Ban in Egypt: A Symbol of Egypt's Struggle for a Legal Identity*, 56 N.Y.L. Sch. L. Rev. 687–88 (2012).

67 Al-Azhar is an independent Islamic institution; it has "exclusive autonomy over its own affairs." It is the most influential center for Islamic education in Egypt and is "responsible for preaching Islam", and the Arabic language in the entire world. Adham Hashish, *The Egyptian Second Republic: The Future of Litigating Islam Before the Supreme Constitutional Court*, 5 Berkeley J. Mid. East & Islamic L. 119, 161–62 (2012).

68 Case No. 20 (19 May 1985) (quoted in Oussama Arabi, *Neo-Shafi'ism or the Islamic Constructive Metaphor in Egypt's High Constitutional Court Policy*, 17 Arab L. Q. 323, 330 (2002)).

69 *Id.* The 2011 Constitutional Declaration was enacted by the Egyptian Supreme Council of the Armed Forces, which assumed office following the 25th Revolution and the overthrow of Mubarak's regime, without making any modifications to Article 2. Droubi, *supra* note 66.

In the 2012 Constitution, which was enacted during the one-year tenure of President Mohammad Morsi and in the 2014 Constitution, Article 2 remained unchanged from the 1971 Constitution. Constitution of the Arab Republic of Egypt, Dec. 26, 2012, art.2 [hereinafter 2012 Constitution]; Constitution of the Arab Republic of Egypt, Jan. 18, 2014, art. 2 [hereinafter 2014 Constitution]. Nevertheless, a new article was included in the 2012 Constitution to define and clarify the meaning of Article 2. Article 219 of

Article 2 of the Egyptian Constitution, after its amendment, could be interpreted to support a woman's freedom to wear Islamic clothing. This argument is based on the primacy of Islamic Shari'a rules over other laws, legislation, regulations, or administrative resolutions in Egypt.[70] In accordance with the correct interpretation of Shari'a, wearing the Islamic headscarf, or hijab, is a religious duty for a Muslim woman.[71] Therefore, a woman's right to wear a hijab is fundamental, and any statutes restricting a woman's free choice to wear a hijab would be deemed unconstitutional.

On the other hand, in accordance with the accurate interpretation of Shari'a, the niqab is optional for a Muslim woman; she has full freedom to choose whether or not to wear it.[72] Therefore, the niqab has been a subject of controversy in Egypt.[73] Several administrative resolutions have been issued to restrict a woman's freedom to wear a niqab.[74] Some women adversely affected by such resolutions have brought a number of lawsuits before specialized courts, whose rulings on the matter of the niqab have been contradictory. This book will investigate these rulings in further detail in the following sections.[75]

ii Protecting the Individual's Personal Freedom

The first phrase of Article 41 of the 1971 Constitution states that "Individual freedom is a natural right and must be safeguarded and inviolable."[76] This

---

the 2012 Constitution stated that "principles of Islamic Shari'a include total arguments of Islamic Shari'a, its fundamental rules and endorsed sources of Ahl Sunna and Jama'a doctrines." 2012 Constitution, *supra* note 69, at art. 219. Nonetheless, in response to widespread demonstrations against President Morsi, the Supreme Council of the Egyptian Armed Forces suspended the 2012 Constitution and established a fifty-member committee to draft a new constitution. Since President Morsi belongs to the Muslim Brotherhood, the 2012 Constitution was amended to include Article 219, which grants Shari'a a more elevated legal status. This article was, however, eliminated in the 2014 Constitution.

70 Article 2 of the Egyptian Constitution stipulates that principles of Islamic Shari'a are the main source of Egyptian legislation. 1971 Constitution, *supra* note 65, art. 2. Therefore, Islamic Shari'a has superiority over any other laws, and any domestic laws that contradict the standards of Shari'a should be deemed unconstitutional.

71 Mahmoud, *supra* note 33, at 18 (trans. by author).

72 *Id.*

73 Droubi, *supra* note 66, at 697.

74 *Id.*

75 The High Administrative Court (HAC) gave women absolute freedom to wear niqabs. However, the Supreme Constitutional Court (SCC) upheld restrictions on the niqab in educational institutions, as mentioned in further detail later in the book.

76 1971 Constitution, *supra* note 65, art. 41. Article 34 of the 2012 Constitution literally states the same phrase. 2012 Constitution, *supra* note 69, art. 34. Similarly, Article 54 of

text could be adopted as an argument to support a woman's freedom to wear Islamic clothing, including a niqab, and proscribe the State from interfering with a woman's freedom to choose her favorite clothing even if she decides to cover her face and wear a niqab.[77] The High Administrative Court (HAC) relied on such an argument to grant a woman the full right to wear a niqab; it declared the unconstitutionality of a statute imposing restrictions on the niqab.[78]

iii Banning Discrimination

Article 40 of the 1971 Constitution states that "[all] citizens are equal before the law. They have equal public rights and duties without discrimination on grounds of race, ethnic origin, language, religion or creed."[79] This article can be understood in light of two contradictory lines of argument.

The first argument advocates imposing restrictions on a woman's Islamic clothing, in particular the niqab, considering it a barrier or an obstacle to a woman that prevents her from properly engaging in daily life.[80] According to this argument, the niqab can be seen as a tool of discrimination against a woman and should therefore be banned by the State.[81] In its sole ruling on this matter, the Supreme Constitutional Court (SCC) relied on this rationale to uphold the constitutionality of an administrative resolution banning female students from wearing the niqab.[82] The SCC found that unveiling "is more protective [for her] virtue (*hiya'*), preserves her psychological health, and keeps her from being stigmatized."[83]

---

the 2014 Constitution states that personal freedom is a natural right that shall be respected and protected by the State. 2014 Constitution, *supra* note 69, art. 54.

77 Case No. 183/1989/ High Administrative Court of Egypt (trans. by author); Case No. 3219/2007, *supra* note 63 (trans. by author).

78 Case No. 183/1989, *supra* note 77 (trans. by author).

79 1971 Constitution, *supra* note 65, art. 40. Similarly, Article 53 of the 2014 Constitution states that citizens shall be equal before the law. They should have equal rights, freedoms and duties without discrimination on grounds of belief, religion, origin, race, sex, color, disability, language, or any other ground of discrimination. 2014 Constitution, *supra* note 69, art. 53. In addition, Article 40 of the 1971 Constitution was replaced by Article 33 of the 2012 Constitution. Under this article, the principle of non-discrimination is defined in a broader context. This article required the State to ensure equality between individuals but did not specify the forms of discrimination that should be eliminated. 2012 Constitution, *supra* note 69, art. 33.

80 Droubi, *supra* note 66, at 697.

81 *Id.*

82 Clark Benner Lombardi, *Islamic Law as a Source of Constitutional Law in Egypt: The Constitutionalization of the Shari'a in a Modern Arab State*, 37 Colum. J. Transnat'l L. 81, 112 (1998).

83 *Id.*

The second argument is based on the prohibition of religious discrimination. According to this argument, restricting a woman's right to wear Islamic clothing could be considered a form of religious discrimination. Therefore, any restriction on the niqab should be prevented, and a woman should have the full right to choose her preferred religious clothing in line with her beliefs without any interference. The High Administrative Court (HAC) heavily relied on this argument to overturn an administrative resolution restricting a female student's freedom to wear a niqab.[84] In addition, it stated that regardless of whether the niqab is mandatory under Shari'a, a woman has the full right to choose to wear it. The HAC affirmed that Article 40 of the Constitution grants a female student the complete freedom to choose her religious attire, whether it is mandatory or optional, hijab or niqab.[85]

iv Freedom of Religion

Article 46 of the 1971 Constitution ensures the right to freedom of belief and protects individuals' freedoms to practice their "religious rites."[86] The High Administrative Court (HAC) issued a decision based on this article, granting a female student the absolute right to wear a niqab at public educational institutions.[87] The HAC stated that the right to free exercise of religion could be derived from this article. In other words, the Court declared that any restriction imposed on the right to free exercise of religion violates the absolute right to freedom of religion.[88]

On the other hand, the SCC found that, according to the 1971 Constitution, freedom of religion or belief is unconditional, while the freedom to practice religious duties can be restricted if it undermines the "protection of the public order," "ethical values," or "rights of others and their freedoms."[89]

B *Decisions of High Courts*

The wearing of the hijab is not controversial in Egypt, since the majority of Egyptian women wear this type of religious clothing; however, the wearing of the niqab has sparked significant debate. Two Egyptian courts have

---

84 Case No. 183/1989, *supra* note 77 (trans. by author).

85 *Id.*

86 1971 Constitution, *supra* note 65, art. 46. Similarly, Article 64 of the 2014 Constitution stipulates that freedom of belief is absolute, but freedom of practicing religious rituals is regulated by law. 2014 Constitution, *supra* note 69, art. 64.

87 Case No. 3219/2007, *supra* note 63 (trans. by author).

88 *Id.*

89 Brown & Lombardi, *supra* note 23, at 458.

addressed the issue of the niqab: the Supreme Constitutional Court (SCC) and the High Administrative Court (HAC). In 1996, the SCC issued its sole ruling on the niqab, whereas the HAC issued three rulings on the niqab in 1989, 2007, and 2010.

i The Supreme Constitutional Court's Decision of 1996

In 1994, the Egyptian Ministry of Education issued a two-part administrative resolution; it entirely banned the wearing of the niqab for elementary school girls, while permitting them to wear the hijab with the permission of their parents.[90] A parent of two veiled girls challenged this administrative order before the Administrative Court of Alexandria, complaining that both of his daughters were expelled from school for wearing niqabs.[91] The plaintiff's argument was based mainly on the violation of Article 2 of the 1971 Constitution, which assures that the principles of Shari'a are the main source of legislation.[92] To support his argument, the plaintiff added that the resolution violated Article 41 of the 1971 Constitution, protecting the personal freedom of individuals, and Article 46, protecting the freedom of religion.[93] In his claim, the plaintiff accused the Minister of Education, the Educational Directorate of Alexandria, and the school manager.[94]

The Administrative Court of Alexandria referred the case to the SCC in order to review the constitutionality of such an administrative order.[95] The SCC deemed the case admissible because the argument about constitutional violations was reasonable.[96]

Concerning the alleged violation of Article 2, the SCC concluded that Shari'a imposes modest clothing on a woman; however, it does not require her to wear a specific style of apparel, such as a hijab or niqab.[97] The Court reasoned that "[t]here is no indicator (dalil) in the Qur'anic texts or in Sunna that requires legally conforming women's clothing."[98] In addition, it declared that Shari'a does not include a reference requiring a woman to wear a niqab so that nothing of a woman's body appears except her eyes.[99]

90 *Id.* at 441–42.
91 *Id.*
92 *Id.* at 442.
93 *Id.*
94 *Id.* at 440.
95 *Id.* at 443.
96 *Id.* at 456–57.
97 *Id.* at 455.
98 *Id.* at 455–56.
99 *Id.*

Therefore, the SCC concluded that the contested decision did not violate Article 2 of the Constitution.[100] Nevertheless, the Court clarified that no source in Shari'a forbids a woman from wearing a niqab.[101] In other words, the Court concluded that regardless of whether a woman wears a niqab or not, she does not violate Shari'a as long as she dresses modestly.[102]

With respect to the alleged violation of Article 41 of the Constitution protecting the personal freedom of individuals, the SCC found that the contested decision did not violate this article. In its reasoning, the Court noted that Article 41 "means that individual freedom (hurriyya shaksiyya) does not bar the legislator … from placing limits on the clothes that some people wear … so that [their clothes] have a distinct identity."[103] The Court added that the legislator could compel students to wear one type of clothing, and as a result, they could be distinguished from others "in such a way that their apparel is uniform, is of one type and is suitable, identifying them and making them known, facilitating the manner of dealing with them."[104]

With regard to the alleged violation of Article 46 protecting the freedom of belief, the SCC differentiated between individuals' freedom of creed and their freedom to practice their religious duties.[105] The Court considered that the right to practice religious duties "represents the manifestation" of the right to freedom of religion.[106] The Court added that the freedom of religion "is unlimited"; however, the freedom to practice religious duties could be restricted "affirming some of the higher interests connected with it – in particular, what connects it with the protection of the public order and ethical values and the defense of the rights of others and their freedoms."[107] Therefore, the Court concluded that the contested decision did not violate Article 46 of the Constitution.[108]

ii Decisions of the High Administrative Court

a *The Case of Ain-Shams University (1989)*

The events of the case began with the issuance of a new regulation by Ain-Shams University that prohibits veiled students from accessing specific areas of the campus.[109] A female student of the Faculty of Literature

---

100 *Id.* at 456.
101 *Id.* at 438.
102 *Id.*
103 *Id.* at 459.
104 *Id.*
105 *Id.* at 457–58.
106 *Id.*
107 *Id.* at 458.
108 *Id.* at 460.
109 Case No. 183/1989, *supra* note 77 (trans. by author).

wearing a niqab brought a case against the university.[110] Her argument was based on the violation of Article 40 of the Constitution banning discrimination on religious grounds[111] and the violation of Article 41 of the Constitution protecting the right to personal freedom of individuals.[112] The university argued that Shari'a does not require a woman to wear a niqab, and therefore the contested decision did not violate its rules. In addition, the university contended that the prohibition of the niqab was justified, as it prevented outsiders or imposters from entering the campus and causing disruptions or harassment to the students.[113]

The HAC ruled in favor of the plaintiff and revoked the contested decision.[114] To reach this conclusion, the HAC employed independent reasoning (ijtihad)[115] to deduce the legal status of the niqab in Islam.[116] As a result, the Court concluded that the niqab is neither mandatory nor prohibited under Shari'a.[117] In contrast to the SCC's ruling,[118] the HAC stated that permitting the niqab to be worn under Shari'a gives a woman absolute freedom to choose whether or not to wear it.[119] Thus, according to the Court, no one or entity has the right to interfere with a woman's religious style of dressing as long as she adheres to the regulations of Shari'a. The Court also noted that the university administration could have achieved discipline on campus by adopting alternative approaches. In other words, the Court noted that the university could have verified the veiled students' identities through female officers or supervisors.[120] In addition, the HAC declared that the contested decision violated Article 41 of the Constitution, protecting the right to personal freedom.[121] It stated that a Muslim woman must have absolute

110 *Id.*

111 1971 Constitution, *supra* note 65, art. 40.

112 *Id.* art. 41.

113 Case No. 183/1989, *supra* note 77 (trans. by author).

114 *Id.*

115 Under Shari'a, the concept of ijtihad gives a judge the power to create logical legal solutions for new legal challenges. In other words, a judge can deduce new legal norms from the reasoning of the main sources of Shari'a, the Qur'an and Sunna. Nevertheless, ijtihad is only allowed when there is no definitive explanation available in credible Shari'a sources. Ali Khan, *Founding Symposium: God, the Person, History, and the Law: Themes from the Work of Judge T. Noonan, JR. Article: Development of Religious Doctrine—Ecumenical Panel: The Reopening of the Islamic Code: The Second Era of Ijtihad*, 1 U. St. Thomas L. J. 341, 344 (2003).

116 Case No. 183/1989, *supra* note 77 (trans. by author).

117 *Id.*

118 Brown & Lombardi, *supra* note 23, at 441–42.

119 Case No. 183/1989, *supra* note 77 (trans. by author).

120 *Id.*

121 1971 Constitution, *supra* note 65, art. 41.

freedom to choose between wearing a hijab or niqab. In other words, as stated by the Court, a woman is free to choose any interpretation of Shari'a in light of her personal tendency and social environment.[122]

b *The Case of the American University in Cairo* (2007)

The events of this case started when the American University in Cairo (AUC) issued an administrative resolution banning the niqab on the university campus for security reasons.[123] A female student wearing niqab was denied access to the library of the university.[124] As a result, she brought a case before the HAC, alleging that the administrative resolution violated Article 41 of the Constitution protecting personal freedom and Article 46 of the Constitution protecting the freedom of religion.[125]

The HAC acknowledged the unconstitutionality of the contested decision and afforded a rationale similar to that of the case of Ain-Shams University. The Court held that since the niqab is permissible under Shari'a, a woman's right to wear it is constitutional.[126] Therefore, administrative resolutions must not restrict constitutional rights or circumscribe a woman's free choice to wear a niqab.[127] In its reasoning, the Court stated that the freedom of religion is protected under the Constitution,[128] indicating that the wearing of the niqab is a manifestation of such freedom. In other words, the Court noted that the right to free exercise of religion is closely connected with a constitutional right (the right to freedom of religion), and therefore it should not be circumscribed by administrative resolutions.[129]

c *The Case of Al-Azhar University* (2010)

Al-Azhar University issued an administrative decision banning female teachers and students from wearing niqabs inside final exam rooms.[130] One of the affected students challenged the constitutionality of this decision by bringing a case before the HAC, alleging that it violated the personal freedom of individuals protected by Article 41 of the Constitution.[131]

---

122 Case No. 183/1989, *supra* note 77 (trans. by author).
123 Case No. 3219/2007, *supra* note 63 (trans. by author).
124 *Id.*
125 1971 Constitution, *supra* note 65, arts. 41,46.
126 Case No. 3219/2007, *supra* note 63 (trans. by author).
127 *Id.*
128 1971 Constitution, *supra* note 65, art. 46.
129 Case No. 3219/2007, *supra* note 63 (trans. by author).
130 Droubi, *supra* note 66, at 697.
131 1971 Constitution, *supra* note 65, art. 41.

The HAC ruled in favor of the plaintiff, affirming that no restrictions could be imposed on the wearing of the niqab.[132] Moreover, the Court declared that a woman is entirely free to choose her preferred attire based on her own preferences and social milieu. In other words, the Court held that a woman's freedom to choose the wearing of the niqab is protected under international human rights standards and the Egyptian Constitution, and therefore the contested decision should not restrict this freedom.[133]

In summary, both the SCC and the HAC concurred that the niqab is permissible under Shari'a; however, they differed on its legality within public educational institutions. The SCC upheld the restriction on a woman's right to wear a niqab in such settings.[134] In contrast, the HAC affirmed a woman's absolute freedom to choose her preferred Islamic attire, including the niqab.[135] The SCC emphasized that covering a woman's face violates her

132 Droubi, *supra* note 66, at 697.

133 *Id.*

134 Brown & Lombardi, *supra* note 23, at 459–60.

135 Case No. 183/1989, *supra* note 77; Case No. 3219/2007, *supra* note 63 (trans. by author). The second section of the 1971 Constitution, from Article 40 to Article 63, was devoted to rights and freedoms that should be afforded to individuals. 1971 Constitution, *supra* note 65, arts. 40–63. Nevertheless, the Constitution did not require the State to protect two fundamental rights that could be relied on as arguments to grant a woman the right to wear religious clothing, whether a hijab or niqab. Such two rights are the right to freedom of choice and the right to free exercise of religion.

Although the issue of wearing religious clothing is a matter of choice, the Egyptian Constitution does not include a direct reference to protecting individuals' freedom of choice. Article 41 of the 1971 Constitution stipulates:

> Individual freedom is a natural right and is safeguarded and inviolable. Save for the case of being caught red-handed, no person may be arrested, inspected, detained or his freedom restricted or prevented from free movement except under an order necessitated by investigations and preservation of the security of the society. Such order shall be given by the competent judge or the public prosecution in accordance with the provisions of the law. The law shall determine the period of custody.

Id. art. 41. This article focuses on protecting civil liberties, such as freedom from searches, arrests, or imprisonment without warrants. James Feuille, *Reforming Egypt's Constitution: Hope for Egyptian Democracy?* 47 Tex. Int'l L.J. 237, 248 (2011). It does not require the State to ensure individuals' freedom of choice on matters of normal private concern. Nevertheless, the HAC deduced the protection of autonomy rights from Article 41 of the Constitution. It expanded the scope of the first phrase of this article to include protection for individuals' freedom to determine their everyday life matters. Case No. 3219/2007, *supra* note 63 (trans. by author); Case No. 183/1989, *supra* note 77 (trans. by author). According to the HAC, a woman should be given a freedom to choose her favorite religious clothing, and any restrictions on such freedom violate Article 41 of the Constitution. *Id.*

rights.[136] Conversely, the HAC decided that covering the face with a niqab is a mere exercise of religious duties.[137] Additionally, the HAC granted students the full right to wear niqabs in light of their personal beliefs, even if those beliefs did not align with the prevailing interpretation of Shari'a.[138]

Nevertheless, it can be argued that the age disparity between the plaintiffs in each case was the primary source of the contention. Since the case considered by the SCC was brought by an elementary-school girl, the Court may have seen that the plaintiff was too young and not mature enough to freely choose the wearing of the niqab.[139] The Court may have concluded that the plaintiff was forced or pressured to wear a niqab. Therefore, the Court upheld the contested decision and permitted the niqab ban in schools.[140] On the other side, the HAC may have concluded that the plaintiffs, who were university students, voluntarily made their decisions to wear the niqab, and that may have led the Court to revoke the contested decisions restricting their freedom to choose the wearing of the niqab.[141]

3 Women's Islamic Clothing under International Law

Since wearing religious clothing is a form of the free manifestation of religion, this section shall discuss women's right to wear Islamic attire, whether the hijab or niqab, in the context of their right to freely manifest their religion.

---

136 Brown & Lombardi, *supra* note 23, at 458.

137 Case No. 3219/2007, *supra* note 63 (trans. by author).

138 The 1971 Constitution does not state or refer to individuals' rights to practice religion. Article 46 of the Constitution requires the State to guarantee personal freedom of belief and protect their rights to practice their religious rites. 1971 Constitution, *supra* note 65, at art. 46. These rites are ceremonies held at certain times and never include the wearing of religious clothing, such as a hijab or niqab. Nevertheless, such defective legislation did not prevent the HAC from affording protection to the right to free exercise of religion. The HAC deduced that right from Article 46 of the Constitution. It broadened the interpretation of Article 46 to protect the right to free exercise of religion. Case No. 3219/2007, *supra* note 63 (trans. by author). Moreover, it stated that the freedom to manifest religion is closely linked with the freedom of belief and revoked any restrictions imposed on a woman's right to fulfill her religious obligation and wear Islamic clothing. *Id.*

139 Droubi, *supra* note 66, at 697.

140 *Id.*

141 *Id.*

A *International Protection of the Right to Free Manifestation of Religion*

Long ago, the United Nations realized the significance of religious freedoms.[142] The U.N. stated in several international instruments that the right to freedom of religion should be respected, protected and promoted, considering this right as one of the main foundations for all human rights initiatives. In this context, President Franklin D. Roosevelt asserted that freedom of religion is one of four fundamental freedoms that should be enshrined in all international human rights instruments.[143]

The UDHR was the first international instrument that called for protection of the right to freedom of religion.[144] Article 18 of the Declaration stipulates that everyone has the right to freedom of religion, and that right consists of two main components: first, one's right to choose or change a religion, and second, his or her right to free manifestation of religion whether by "teaching, practicing, worship," or "observance."[145]

Furthermore, the ICCPR emphasizes one's right to decide or change his or her religion; it requires member states to provide positive procedures that guarantee individuals' capability to enjoy this right.[146] However, the Covenant places restrictions on many rights to protect the public or others' special interests.[147] Every article of the ICCPR begins with a broad statement concerning a specific right, followed by a thorough definition of that right, after which restrictions may be placed if necessary.[148] Concerning the freedom of religion, Article 18 of the Covenant differentiates between the right to freedom of religion and concerns relevant to the exercise of this right.[149] Freedom of religion is absolute, while the free manifestation of religion can be restricted, making it a subject of ongoing controversy.[150]

---

142 Matthew L. Fore, *Shall Weigh Your God and your: Assessing thee Imperialistic Implications of the International Religious Freedom Act in Muslim Countries*, 52 Duke L. J. 423, 440 (2002).

143 *Id.* (quoting Franklin D. Roosevelt, The Annual Message to the Congress (Jan. 6, 1941), in Franklin D. Roosevelt, The Public Papers and Addresses of Franklin D. Roosevelt: Vol. 9, War and Aid to Democracies (1940), at 672).

144 L. Fore, *supra* note 142, at 440–41.

145 G.A. Res. 217 (III) A art. 18, Universal Declaration of Human Rights (Dec. 10, 1948).

146 ICCPR, *supra* note 5, art.18.

147 Roza Pati, *Rights and Their Limits: The Constitution for Europe in International and Comparative Legal Perspective*, 23 Berkeley J. Int'l L. 223, 242–43 (2005).

148 *Id.* at 243.

149 ICCPR, *supra* note 5, art.18.

150 *Id.*

Under Article 18 of the ICCPR,

> 1. Everyone shall have the right to freedom of thought, conscience and religion. This right shall include freedom to have or to adopt a religion or belief of his choice, and freedom, either individually or in community with others and in public or private, to manifest his religion or belief in worship, observance, practice and teaching.
> 2. No one shall be subject to coercion which would impair his freedom to have or to adopt a religion or belief of his choice.
> 3. Freedom to manifest one's religion or beliefs may be subject only to such limitations as are prescribed by law and are necessary to protect public safety, order, health, or morals or the fundamental rights and freedoms of others.
> 4. The States Parties to the present Covenant undertake to have respect for the liberty of parents and, when applicable, legal guardians to ensure the religious and moral education of their children in conformity with their own convictions.[151]

In General Comment 22,[152] the HRC stated that freedom of thought, conscience and religion is "far-reaching and profound."[153] According to the Committee, such freedom includes personal convictions as well as commitments to religion or belief, which require followers of such religion or belief to manifest them whether individually or together in a group. In addition, the Committee clarified that Article 18(1) of the ICCPR protects freedom of conscience and thought, declaring that states should protect such freedom "equally with the freedom of religion and belief."[154] The Committee affirmed that these freedoms must not be subject to derogation "even in time of public emergency" threatening nations.[155]

In addition, the Committee explained that Article 18 is not confined to protecting the followers of traditional religions; rather, it requires member states to protect "theistic, non-theistic and atheistic beliefs," and one's "right not to profess any religion or beliefs."[156] The Committee stressed that

151 *Id.*

152 Human Rights Committee, General Comment 22, art. 18 (48th Sess. 1993). Compilation of General Comments and General Recommendations Adopted by Human Rights Treaty Bodies, U.N. Doc. HRI GEN 1 Rev.1 at 35 (1994).

153 *Id.* para. 1.

154 *Id.*

155 *Id.*

156 *Id.* para. 2.

religious minorities should not be subject to any kind of hostility by followers of predominant religions.[157]

The Committee emphasized that Article 18 differentiates between freedom of thought, conscience, religion, or belief and "freedom to manifest religion or belief," stipulating that no restriction is permitted on freedom of thought and conscience or personal freedoms to adopt or change religion or belief since states should unconditionally protect such freedoms.[158]

Freedom of religious manifestation, according to the Committee, has several kinds such as "worship, observance, practice and teaching."[159] Freedom of worship includes acts of freedom of expression such as rites and ceremonies. Moreover, it includes freedoms related to practicing these acts such as "the building of places of worship, the use of ritual formulae and objects, the display of symbols, and the observance of holidays and days of rest." Freedom of observances or practices of religion or belief has a wider scope than freedom of worship. They include, in addition to ceremonial acts, other customs such as "the observance of dietary regulations, the wearing of a distinctive clothing or head coverings," or the use of a special religious language "customarily spoken" among religious groups.[160] Freedom of teaching includes the freedom to engage in actions pertaining to the main affairs of religious groups, such as preparing seminars or lessons to explain certain concepts of a given religion, or electing teachers, priests or leaders of religious groups. It also includes the distribution and publication of religious materials and writings.[161]

The Committee explained that one's freedom to have or adopt a religion or belief includes his or her freedom to choose a religion or belief as well as to replace or retain his or her religion or belief or even to adopt atheistic views.[162] In addition, the Committee asserted that Article 18(2) requires states to protect individuals from any coercion against their choice of religion or belief, including "the use of threat of physical force or penal sanctions to compel believers or non-believers to adhere to their religious beliefs and congregations, to recant their religion or belief or to convert."[163]

157 *Id.*

158 *Id.* para. 3.

159 *Id.* para. 4.

160 *Id.* When a Muslim woman chooses to wear a hijab, she is adhering to the requirements of her faith. The choice to wear the hijab is motivated by deeply held religious beliefs, making it a significant religious observance and practice.

161 General Comment 22, para.4, *supra* note 152.

162 *Id.* para. 5.

163 *Id.*

Furthermore, the Committee affirmed that, according to Article 18(2), states must eliminate any policies or practices having similar influences, such as acts restricting access to education, employment or medical care to followers of the predominant religion.[164]

With regard to Article 18(4), the Committee emphasized that it permits public schools to adopt some religious subjects, such as the history of religions and ethics, as long as they present them to students impartially.[165] Additionally, the Committee stated that parents, under Article 18(4), are allowed to ensure that their children are given religious education in accordance "with their own convictions."[166] However, the Committee indicated that public education related to religion must be based on non-discriminatory grounds, without any exemptions. The Committee clarified that the purpose of allowing such religious education is to "accommodate the wishes of parents and guardians."[167]

Furthermore, the Committee stated that, consistent with Article 20 of the Covenant, any manifestation of religion must not be connected with war propaganda, and that any religious advocacy deliberately encouraging violence, hostility, or discrimination must be banned.[168]

With respect to Article 18(3), the Committee stated that it allows restrictions on the right to free manifestation of religion as long as such restrictions "are prescribed by law and are necessary to protect public safety, order, health or morals, or the fundamental rights and freedoms of others."[169] This is in contrast to one's freedom to have or adopt a religion or belief, stated in Article 18(1), and freedom of guardians or parents to ensure that religious education provided to their children is in line with their own convictions, enshrined in Article 18(4); such freedoms must not be restricted by any means.[170]

The Committee asserted that states should neutrally apply the limitations stated in Article 18(3) causing no violation of the rights enshrined in the Covenant, in particular, the right to equality and the principle of non-discrimination.[171] According to the Committee, member states should

164 *Id.*
165 *Id.* para. 6.
166 *Id.*
167 *Id.*
168 *Id.* para. 7.
169 *Id.* para. 8.
170 *Id.*
171 ICCPR, *supra* note 5, art. 2.

ensure that restrictions are "directly related and proportionate to the specific need on which they are predicated."[172] In addition, the Committee required states to ensure the non-discriminatory application of such restrictions.[173] Besides, the Committee asserted that persons, who are subject to certain legitimate constraints, such as prisons, should be given the full right to "manifest their religion or belief to the fullest extent compatible with the specific nature of the constraint."[174]

The Committee emphasized that the presence of a certain religion or belief as an official ideology of a state, whether by stating such a religion in "constitutions, statutes, and proclamations of ruling parties" or dealing with that religion "in actual practices," is not considered a violation of Article 18. The Committee declared that such practices do not impair the freedom of religion or belief of those "who do not accept the official ideology or who oppose it."[175] Furthermore, the Committee stressed that states recognizing a certain religion as an official or traditional religion, the religion of the majority of the population, must eliminate any practices based on religious discrimination, such as confining "eligibility for government service" to followers of the predominant religion or distinguishing them with "economic privileges."[176]

Similar to the ICCPR, the CRC permits restrictions on a child's right to free manifestation of religion.[177] It stipulates that a child's right to exercise a religion can be restricted if it violates "public safety, order, health or morals, or the fundamental rights and freedoms of others."[178]

In addition, the CRC includes two potentially contradictory and ambiguous clauses concerning a child's right to education.[179] The first clause allows for a child's education to align with their "cultural identity" and their family's values and traditions.[180] According to the second, a child's education should be in line with international human rights standards and

---

172 General Comment 22, para.8, *supra* note 152.

173 *Id.*

174 *Id.*

175 *Id.* para. 10.

176 *Id.* para. 9.

177 U.N. Convention on the Rts. of the Child, art. 14(3), Nov. 20, 1989, G.A. Res. 44/25, U.N. GAOR 44th Sess., Supp. No. 49, at 167, U.N. Doc. A/44/736 (1989) [hereinafter CRC].

178 *Id.*

179 Perkins, *supra* note 45, at 538–39.

180 CRC, *supra* note 177, art. 29, para. 1(c).

fundamental freedoms.[181] Thus, a child might be exposed to different values, morals, customs and viewpoints.[182] This vague language gives states a vast margin of appreciation. They may not consider both criteria equally, or they may create a strategy that reflects the same balance between both principles.[183]

Although the ICESCR does not stipulate freedom of religion, it ensures the right to education that promotes "understanding, tolerance and friendship among all nations and all racial, ethnic or religious groups."[184] In addition, the Covenant requires member states to respect parents' freedom in teaching children their own religious and moral values.[185]

CEDAW does not state a woman's right to freedom of religion; however, the Convention emphasizes equality between a man and a woman in all rights and freedoms.[186] Article 10 of the Convention stipulates a woman's right to equality with a man in terms of educational opportunities.[187] An argument could be made based on this article to prevent educational institutions from expelling female students for wearing hijabs.

In recognition of the significance of the right to freedom of religion, the United Nations issued a Declaration on the Elimination of All Forms of Intolerance and of Discrimination Based on Religion or Belief.[188] Article 1(3) of the Declaration is identical to Article 18(3) of the ICCPR.[189] This article stipulates that "freedom to manifest one's religion or beliefs may be subject only to such limitations as are prescribed by law and are necessary to protect public safety, order, health or morals or the fundamental rights and freedoms of others."[190]

181 *Id.* para. 1(b).

182 Perkins, *supra* note 45, at 539.

183 *Id.*

184 International Covenant on Economic, Social and Cultural Rights, art. 13(1), *opened for signature* Dec. 16, 1966, G.A. Res. 2200A, at 49, U.N. GAOR, 21st Sess., Supp. No. 16, U.N. Doc. A/6316 (entered into force Mar. 23, 1976).

185 *Id.* para. 3.

186 Convention on the Elimination of All Forms of Discrimination Against Women, G.A. Res. 34/180, at 193, U.N. GAOR, 34th Sess., Supp. No. 46, U.N. Doc. A/34/46 (Dec. 18, 1979).

187 *Id.* art. 10.

188 Declaration on the Elimination of All Forms of Intolerance and of Discrimination Based on Religion or Belief, G.A. Res. 36/55, U.N. GAOR, 36th Sess., Supp. No. 51, U.N. Doc. A/36/684 (Nov. 25, 1981).

189 *Id.* art. 1(3).

190 *Id.*

B Regional Protection of the Right to Free Manifestation of Religion

Under the African Charter on Human and Peoples' Rights, freedom of conscience is protected.[191] In addition, the Charter requires states to ensure individuals' enjoyment of the right to free exercise of religion, stipulating that no one may be subject to laws or measures that restrict such a right.[192]

As for the American Convention on Human Rights, under Article 12, freedom of religion is absolute.[193] However, freedom to manifest one's religion can be limited for the protection of "public safety, order, health, or morals, or the rights or freedoms of others."[194]

With regard to the European Convention on Human Rights, Article 9 requires states to protect the right to freedom of religion and the right to free manifestation of religion.[195] The former right is unconditional, while the latter can be subject only to such restrictions as are "necessary in a democratic society in the interests of public safety, for the protection of public order, health or morals, or for the protection of the rights and freedoms of others."[196]

It is worth mentioning that the conditions necessary to restrict one's right to free manifestation of religion in accordance with Article 12(3) of the ACHR[197] and Article 9(2) of the ECHR[198] are the same as the conditions of Article 18(3) of the ICCPR.[199] They provide the same restrictions with slight phrasing variations.[200]

---

191 African Charter on Human and Peoples' Rights, *opened for signature* June 27, 1981, OAU Doc. CAB/LEG/67/3 rev. 5, 21 I.L.M. 58 (1982), (entered into force Oct. 21, 1986).

192 *Id.*

193 American Convention on Human Rights, art. 12, *opened for signature* Nov. 22, 1969, OEA/ser. K/XVY1.1, Doc. 65, Rev. 1, Corr. 1 O.A.S.T.S., No. 36 (1970) (entered into force July 18, 1978) (hereinafter American Convention).

194 *Id.*

195 European Convention for the Protection of Human Rights and Fundamental Freedoms, art. 9, *opened for signature* Nov. 4, 1950, Europ. T.S. No. 5, 213 U.N.T.S. 221 (entered into force Sept. 3, 1953) [hereinafter European Convention].

196 *Id.*

197 American Convention, *supra* note 193, art. 12.

198 European Convention, *supra* note 195, art. 9.

199 ICCPR, *supra* note 5, art. 18.

200 Article 12(3) of the American Convention on Human Rights stipulates that "freedom to manifest one's religion and beliefs may be subject only to the limitations prescribed by law that are necessary to protect public safety, order, health, or morals, or the rights or freedoms of others." American Convention, *supra* note 193, art. 12(3). Article 9(2) of the European Convention on Human Rights stipulates that "freedom to manifest one's religion or beliefs shall be subject only to such limitations as are prescribed by law and are necessary in a democratic society in the interests of public safety, for the

Regarding the Regional Treaty Bodies, there are no well-known precedents in Africa established by the African Court on Human and Peoples' Rights or the African Commission on Human and Peoples' Rights clarifying a woman's right to wear Islamic clothing[201] Similarly, neither the Inter-American Court of Human Rights nor the Inter-American Commission on Human Rights has adopted any well-known views clarifying their stance on a woman's right to wear Islamic clothing in the public sphere.[202]

Nonetheless, due to a number of significant challenges in Europe decided by the European Commission of Human Rights, the European Court of Human Rights (ECtHR), and the Court of Justice of the European Union (CJEU) concerning restrictions on women's wearing of Islamic clothing, some of these very important challenges will be discussed in the following paragraphs. The hijab-related cases will be examined first, then the niqab cases.

i Restrictions on Students' Hijab

The European legal framework for human rights upholds restrictions on hijab-wearing students. First, the resolutions of the European Commission of Human Rights will be discussed, followed by the cases decided by the European Court of Human Rights.

---

protection of public order, health or morals, or for the protection of the rights and freedoms of others." European Convention, *supra* note 195, art. 9(2).

201 In the case of Endorois v. Kenya, the African Commission on Human and Peoples' Rights relied on the HRC's General Comment 22. It stated that the right to freedom of religion includes protection of "theistic, non-atheistic and atheistic beliefs." Ctr. for Minority Rights Dev. (Kenya), Commc'n No. 276/03, para. 164. Moreover, it stressed that any restrictions imposed on religious practices must be "proportionate to the specific need on which [they are] predicated." *Id.* at para. 172.

202 As for the Inter-American Court of Human Rights, it tackled the case of the Last Temptation of Christ v. Chile. The Last Temptation of Christ (Olmedo Bustos et al. v. Chile), Inter-Am. Ct. H.R. (ser. C) No. 73 (Feb. 5, 2001). To go in-depth, the Chilean government prevented one of its citizens from exhibiting or projecting the film (The Last Temptation of Christ), claiming that it contains outrageous clips for Christians. *Id.* para. 60. The core of the case was mainly based on the right to freedom of expression protected by Article 13 of the Convention. *Id.* para. 103. However, with regard to the violation of the right to freedom of religion protected by Article 12 of the Convention, the Court declared that the right to freedom of religion "is one of the foundations of democratic society." *Id.* para. 79. In addition, the Court declared that since Chile "did not impair or deprive anyone of their right to maintain, change, profess or disseminate their religion or beliefs with total freedom," it did not violate individuals' freedom of religion. *Id.*

a *Resolutions of the European Commission of Human Rights*

1 Karaduman v. Turkey (1993)

The events of Karaduman v. Turkey began when Karaduman, a graduate student of the Faculty of Pharmacy at the University of Ankara, sought to obtain her bachelor's diploma.[203] The university requested a personal photo from her as a required document.[204] However, solely because of her hijab, they refused to accept her personal photo.[205] Student Affairs officials demanded that she submit a personal photo without a head covering.[206] Their argument was based on a circular regulation that required uncovered heads in photographs for academic diplomas. Nevertheless, Karaduman refused to take off her Islamic headscarf in her personal photograph and brought many cases before the Turkish domestic courts, but none of them ruled in her favor. Therefore, she filed a complaint before the European Commission of Human Rights, which declared the application inadmissible because the applicant did not "[satisfy] the exhaustion of domestic remedies requirement and that this part of her application must accordingly be rejected, pursuant to Article 27 para. 3 of the Convention."[207]

Nevertheless, the Commission determined that the wearing of Islamic headscarves in public educational institutions of states like Turkey, whose vast majority are Muslims, would place some kind of pressure on students

203 Karaduman v. Turkey, App. No. 16278/90 (Admissibility Decision). All citations to this judgment are derived from the website of the European Court of Human Rights, which does not include page or paragraph references, available at http://cmiskp.echr.coe.int/tkp197/search.asp?skin=hudoc-fr (last visited Aug. 21, 2024). Turkey was the first country to impose a sweeping prohibition on the wearing of the hijab in public educational institutions and governmental entities, despite the fact that 99 % of its population is Muslim. U.S. Dep't of State, Bureau of European and Eurasian Affairs, Background Note: Turkey, available at http://www.state.gov/r/pa/ei/bgn/3432.htm (last visited Aug. 21, 2024). Secular Turkey started in 1923 with the reign of Ataturk. From that time, Ataturk began to modernize Turkey through social and political reforms called Kemalism. *Id.* This word refers to secularism, nationalism, and western orientation. *Id.* The hijab has been prohibited in Turkish public educational institutions on the grounds that it undermines the principle of absolute secularism. Aliah Abdo, *The Legal Status of Hijab in the United States: A Look at the Sociopolitical Influences on the Legal Right to Wear the Muslim Headscarf*, 5 Hastings Race & Poverty L. J. 441, 453 (2008). In 2000, more than 37 thousand female students were expelled from schools, and more than 24 thousand female teachers were fired for wearing hijabs. *Id.*

204 Karaduman v. Turkey, App. No. 16278/90, *supra* note 203.

205 *Id.* Islam requires a Muslim woman to wear a hijab in public, which includes personal photographs since they may be visible to everyone.

206 Karaduman v. Turkey, App. No. 16278/90, *supra* note 203.

207 *Id.*

"who do not practice that religion or those who adhere to another religion."[208] In addition, it stated that because the Turkish university was a secular institution, it had the full power to refuse to supply or issue any official documents reflecting a religious identity.[209] Therefore, the Commission found that the State's interference did not violate the European Convention on Human Rights.[210]

2 Bulut v. Turkey (1993)

The facts of Bulut v. Turkey[211] are similar to those of Karaduman. After finishing her university studies, Bulut applied for her provisional certificate and submitted a personal photo with an Islamic headscarf.[212] The university refused to accept such a photo and requested that she submit one without a hijab. After the claim was considered by the European Commission, it determined that the application was inadmissible; however, it noted that such interference with the plaintiff's right to free manifestation of religion did not violate Article 9(2) of the ECHR. In addition, the Commission stated that the university had the power to protect its secular nature and public order, which could be disturbed if the disciplinary rules of the university were not respected.[213]

b *Decisions of the European Court of Human Rights*

This study will examine the ECtHR's cases in depth, outlining the necessary conditions required to restrict students' hijabs at educational institutions.

1 Sahin v. Turkey (2005)

Sahin v. Turkey[214] is often recognized as the best-known example of the prohibition of students' hijabs in public educational institutions.[215] The facts of

---

208 *Id.* Article 9 (2) of the European Convention on Human Rights stipulates that the right to free manifestation of religion could be restricted for the protection of the rights and freedoms of others. European Convention, *supra* note 195, art. 9, para. 2.

209 Karaduman v. Turkey, App. No. 16278/90, *supra* note 203.

210 *Id.*

211 Bulut v. Turkey, App. No. 18783/91 (Admissibility Decision). All citations to this decision are from the website of the European Court of Human Rights, which does not include page or paragraph references, available at http://cmiskp.echr.coe.int/tkp197/search.asp?skin=hudoc-fr (last visited Aug. 21, 2024).

212 *Id.*

213 *Id.*

214 Leyla Sahin v. Turkey (Sahin II), No. 44774/98 (Eur. Ct. H.R. Nov. 10, 2005), available at http://cmiskp.echr.coe.int/tkp197/search.asp?skin=hudoc-en (last visited Aug. 21, 2024).

215 The hijab ban in Turkey was not limited to educational institutions; rather, female officials working at governmental entities were prevented from wearing the hijab during work hours. A close review of Mere Kavakci's case reveals the suffering of a member of

the case started when a female student of the Medical School at Istanbul University, named Leyla Sahin, wore a hijab while attending classes at school.[216] Due to a university resolution preventing veiled female students and bearded male students from entering the university, Miss Sahin was suspended from school after she refused to remove her hijab.[217] Sahin entered another university and brought several complaints before Turkish domestic courts to challenge Istanbul University's resolution. After Sahin exhausted all domestic remedies in Turkey, she brought a case before the ECtHR.[218] Miss Sahin claimed that the hijab ban violated Article 9 of the ECHR protecting freedom of religion and the free exercise of religion, and Article 2 of Protocol No. 1 to the Convention protecting the right to education.[219]

---

the Turkish Parliament due to her refusal to remove her hijab. After being elected as a member of the Turkish Parliament in 1999, members of the Secular Ruling Party defied her and refused to allow her to take the oath while wearing her hijab. As a consequence of her refusal to remove her hijab, she was not only dismissed from parliament but also stripped of her Turkish citizenship. In turn, she traveled with her family to Washington, where she urged western governments to interfere and protect the religious freedoms and human rights of Turkish citizens. Faisal Kutty, *Ousted Turkish M.P. Merve Kavakci Calls on Canada to Help Hijab-Wearing Muslim Women*, Wash. Rep. on Middle E. Aff. (Wash., D.C.), Dec. 2000, http://www.wrmea.com/archives/Jan Feb 2001/0101048.html.

Nevertheless, in 2002, the Turkish Justice and Development Party came to power, and henceforth it prioritized repealing the hijab ban in educational institutions. In 2008, the headscarf ban was abolished. The Turkish parliament approved constitutional amendments to lift the hijab ban by voting 411 in favor and 103 against. Thus, the Turkish law was modified to read: "No one at any case shall be prevented from his/her right to education." Selcan Hacaoglu, *Turkish Lawmakers Vote on Head Scarves*, ABC News, Feb. 9, 2008, http://abcnews.go.com/International/wireStory?id=4266357.

216 (Sahin II), No. 44774/98, para.15 (Eur. Ct. H.R. Nov. 10, 2005).

217 *Id.* para. 16. On February 23, 1998, the Vice-Chancellor of the University of Istanbul issued a circular stipulating that

> students whose heads are covered (who wear the Islamic headscarf) and students (including overseas students) with beards must not be admitted to lectures, courses or tutorials. Consequently, the name and number of any student with a beard or wearing the Islamic headscarf must not be added to the lists of registered students. However, students who insist on attending tutorials and entering lecture theatres although their names and numbers are not on the lists must be advised of the position and, should they refuse to leave, their names and numbers must be taken and they must be informed that they are not entitled to attend lectures. If they refuse to leave the lecture theatre, the teacher shall record the incident in a report explaining why it was not possible to give the lecture and shall bring the incident to the attention of the university authorities as a matter of urgency so that disciplinary measures can be taken.

Id.

218 *Id.* para. 1.

219 *Id.* para. 3.

With regard to Article 9, Miss Sahin argued that the headscarf ban in Turkish higher educational institutions was an unjustified interference with her right to free manifestation of religion.[220] The Court responded to this argument in two stages. Initially, the Court determined whether the interference occurred. Secondly, the Court reviewed whether the interference met the necessary conditions of Article 9(2) of the ECHR.[221] These conditions are as follows: (1) to be "prescribed by law," (2) to have a "legitimate aim," and (3) to be "necessary in a democratic society."[222] As a result, the ECtHR Chamber unanimously ruled that the interference did not violate Article 9 of the Convention.[223]

Nevertheless, Miss Sahin challenged the rule before the Grand Chamber of the Court. However, the ECtHR Chamber's decision was upheld with a sweeping majority of sixteen to one.[224] Due to the significance of that ruling, this study will discuss the analysis of the Court in detail as follows:

a *First Condition (in Accordance with the Law)*

According to the Court, in order for the interference to be prescribed by law, it must meet the following three standards: (a) it must have a foundation within domestic law, whether it is stated as permissible in domestic statutes of the concerned state or referred to in the interpretations of domestic supreme courts.[225] (b) The second condition is that the legal basis that permits such interference should "be accessible to the person concerned," and (c) the interference should be "foreseeable" and reasonable in specific circumstances.[226]

With regard to the first standard, the Court found such interference was based on a foundation of domestic law: a resolution issued by the Turkish Supreme Constitutional Court in 1991.[227] In that resolution, the Turkish Supreme Constitutional Court interpreted a statute banning the wearing of the Islamic headscarf in Turkish higher educational institutions; it affirmed the constitutionality of the statute.[228]

---

220 *Id.* para. 70.
221 *Id.* para. 75.
222 *Id.*
223 *Id.* para. 8.
224 *Id.* para. 166.
225 *Id.* paras. 84,98.
226 *Id.* para. 84.
227 *Id.* paras. 89, 92, 98.
228 *Id.*

As for the second standard, the Court found that since the valid source of law, the decision of the Turkish Constitutional Court, was published in an official gazette on July 31, 1991, it was accessible to Miss Sahin.[229]

Regarding the third standard, the Court found that the interference was foreseeable to Miss Sahin since the University of Istanbul issued regulations preventing female students from wearing head scarves before her enrollment at the university.[230] These regulations were issued in 1994, whereas Miss Sahin enrolled at the university in 1997.[231]

b Second Condition (Legitimate Aim)

The Court declared that the interference was justified in order to protect the rights and freedoms of others and preserve the public order of the university.[232] It is important to note that Miss Sahin testified before the Chamber that such an interference was done for permissible reasons, such as upholding the principle of secularism and ensuring neutrality in Turkish universities.[233]

c Third Condition (Necessity in a Democratic Society)

The Court found that the interference was "necessary in a democratic society" and did not violate the second paragraph of Article 9 of the ECHR. The Court reasoned that such interference was based on democratic foundations since it "prevent[ed] certain fundamentalist religious movements from exerting pressure on students."[234] In addition, the Court noted that the interference was aimed at ensuring "peaceful co-existence between students" and protecting "public order and the beliefs of others."[235] Moreover, the Court declared that the interference was necessary to protect the principle of secularism, which is ranked as a fundamental principle of the Turkish State, and promote the principle of gender equality since Muslim female students could be forced or pressured to wear Islamic headscarves.[236]

---

229 *Id.* para. 93.

230 *Id.* paras. 97–98.

231 *Id.*

232 Sahin II, No. 44774/98, para. 99.

233 Leyla Sahin v. Turkey (Sahin I), No. 44774/98, para. 83 (Eur. Ct. H.R. June 29, 2004), available at http://cmiskp.echr.coe.int/tkp197/search.asp?skin=hudoc-en (search by application number) (last visited Aug. 21, 2024).

234 Sahin II, No. 44774/98, para. 111.

235 *Id.*

236 *Id.*

The Court clarified that with respect to the application of the Convention's principles, a margin of appreciation should be afforded to member states of the ECHR.[237] It added that, particularly in cases related to Article 9 of the ECHR, it is necessary to grant states a "margin of appreciation" because the nature of the connection between the state and religion varies widely between countries, and therefore, no consensus for banning or permitting the wearing of religious symbols in public educational institutions has been reached.[238]

The Court noted that it "[did] not lose sight of the fact that there are extremist political movements in Turkey which seek to impose on society as a whole their religious symbols and conception of a society founded on religious precepts."[239] The Court, therefore, affirmed that, in accordance with the Convention's provisions, the State could "take a stance against such political movements."[240] Thus, according to the Court, the interference was based on a "social need" within Turkish society in order to preserve the public order of the whole community and prevent violations against the rights and freedoms of other students who recognize hijab as a religious duty but decide not to wear it.[241]

The Court determined that "there was a reasonable relationship of proportionality between the means employed and the legitimate objectives pursued by the interference."[242] In addition to the margin of appreciation given to the State, the Court afforded more deference to the university's capacity to determine whether to ban or allow the wearing of Islamic headscarves, describing the university as a better place "than an international court to evaluate local needs and conditions."[243] Moreover, the Court praised the regulatory process of the headscarf ban, affirming that it balanced interests and considered them all.[244] It clarified that such a ban did not prevent Muslim students from exercising their religious duties in

237 *Id.* para. 109.

238 *Id.* The Court reasoned that "rules [of wearing Islamic clothing in public universities] will "vary from one country to another according to national traditions and the requirements imposed by the need to protect the rights and freedoms of others and to maintain public order," and therefore, "the choice of the extent and form such regulations should take must inevitably be left up to a point to the State concerned, as it will depend on the specific domestic context." *Id.*

239 *Id.* para. 115.

240 *Id.*

241 *Id.*

242 *Id.* paras. 117–18.

243 *Id.* para. 121.

244 *Id.* para. 159.

accordance with the limits imposed by the university officials that must not be exceeded.[245] Accordingly, the Court found that the interference was justified by legitimate objectives and was necessary in a democratic society, and therefore it decided that the headscarf ban did not violate Article 9(2) of the ECHR.[246]

With respect to the alleged violation of Article 2 of Protocol No. 1 to the ECHR[247] protecting the right to education, the Court clarified that the right to education includes individuals' right to attend educational institutions.[248] In addition, the Court noted that the right to education is significant and fundamental.[249] Nevertheless, it stated that such a right is not absolute and can be limited by states to serve other legitimate objectives, where states are given a margin of appreciation to decide whether to impose restrictions on such a right or not.[250] What is more, the Court affirmed that Article 2 of Protocol No. 1 should be interpreted in the context of other articles of the Convention.[251] As for Miss Sahin's case, the Court reasoned that restrictions imposed on her right to education served the legitimate aim of protecting secularism and neutrality in public educational institutions.[252] Thus, the Court ruled that the Islamic headscarf ban did not violate Article 2 of Protocol No. 1 to the ECHR.[253]

2 Dogru v. France (2008)

In 2008, the ECtHR decided another case involving an eleven-year-old girl who wore an Islamic headscarf while attending secondary school.[254] After

---

245 *Id.* para. 120. The Court reasoned:

> It is quite clear that throughout that decision-making process the university authorities sought to adapt to the evolving situation in a way that would not bar access to the university to students wearing the veil, through continued dialogue with those concerned, while at the same time ensuring that order was maintained and in particular that the requirements imposed by the nature of the course in question were complied with.
>
> *Id.*

246 *Id.* para. 123.

247 Article 2 of the Protocol stipulates that "no person shall be denied the right to education." Protocol No. 1 to the ECHR, opened for signature Mar. 20, 1952, Europ. T.S. No. 9.

248 Sahin II, No. 44774/98, para. 141.

249 *Id.* para. 153.

250 *Id.* para. 145.

251 *Id.* paras. 155, 157.

252 *Id.* para. 158.

253 *Id.* para. 162.

254 Dogru v. France, No. 27058/05 (Eur. Ct. H.R. Dec 4, 2008), available at http://cmiskp.echr.coe.int/tkp197/search.asp?skin=hudoc-en (search by application number) (last visited Aug. 21, 2024).

being prevented from wearing a hijab during physical education classes, Miss Dogru compromised and asked the school officials to allow her to wear a hat instead of her Islamic headscarf.[255] Because the school's officials refused, she was expelled from school.[256] After exhausting all domestic legal remedies in France, she brought a case before the ECtHR.[257] Her argument was based mainly on the violation of her rights enshrined in Article 9 of the ECHR, protecting the right to free manifestation of religion, and Article 2 of Protocol No. 1 to the ECHR, protecting the right to education.[258]

The Court unanimously issued its decision against Miss Dogru, confirming that no violations were committed against her rights, whether the right to free manifestation of religion or the right to education. As for the right to free manifestation of religion, the Court reviewed the conditions stipulated in Article 9(2), which permit interference with this right, and found that all of them were met. Regarding the first condition, that the interference must be prescribed by law, the Court explained that preventing Miss Dogru from wearing an Islamic headscarf during physical education classes was based on non-binding governmental circulars provided to her parents prior to her enrollment.[259] Concerning the second condition, the Court affirmed that

---

In 1989, the controversy over the hijab started in France when three Muslim students were suspended from school for wearing hijabs; they filed complaints in French courts. The French Supreme Administrative Court stated that female students have the right to wear the hijab as long as they do not pressure, provoke, proselytize, propagandize, or disturb school activities. Thus, the Court gave educational institutions the authority to evaluate each hijab-wearing student on an individual basis and determine whether she can continue her education. Stephanie Walterick, *The Prohibition of Muslim Headscarves from French Public Schools and Controversies Surrounding the Hijab in the Western World*, 20 Temp. Int'l & Comp. L. J. 251, 256–57 (2006).

Dogru's case had been decided before the French law of 2004 was enacted. In 2004, due to the promotion of secularism in France, a law was enacted to ban students from wearing religious symbols that conspicuously exhibit religious affiliation, including large Christian crosses, Sikh turbans, Jewish yarmulkes and Islamic headscarves. *Id.* at 251.

Despite the law's broad language, it only applied to Muslims who wore turbans or hijabs; no student was ever expelled for wearing a cross or yarmulke. Although this law appeared neutral, it actually discriminated against religious minorities because it allowed students to wear items that were not religiously required, such as small crosses. Cynthia DeBula Baines, *L'Affaire des Foulards: Discrimination, or the Price of a Secular Public Education System?* 29 Vand. J. Transnat'l L. 303, 304 (1996). Despite the law's broad language, it only applied to Muslims who wore turbans or Islamic headscarves; no student was ever dismissed for wearing a crucifix or yarmulke.

255 Dogru v. France, No.27058/05, para. 13.

256 *Id.* para. 8.

257 *Id.* para. 1.

258 *Id.*

259 *Id.* para. 56.

the interference was based on legitimate aims: "protecting the rights and freedoms of others" as well as "protecting the public order."[260] With regard to the third condition, that the interference be necessary in a democratic society, the Court clarified that the school's argument claiming that all kinds of veils, including the Islamic headscarf, were banned during physical education for health and safety purposes was "not unreasonable."[261]

In addition, the Court noted that "the disciplinary proceedings against the applicant fully satisfied the duty to undertake a balancing exercise of the various interests at stake."[262] The Court clarified that because the ban was limited to physical classes, it could not be regarded "as a ban in the strict sense of the term." The Court noted that, according to the information provided by the State, the school administration requested on seven different occasions that the student remove her Islamic headscarf in physical classes, but she refused. Similarly, the school officials attempted several times to talk or dialogue with the applicant, but she declined each time.[263] Furthermore, the Court found that these events "led to a general atmosphere of tension" and disturbed the public order within the school.[264]

As for the alternative solution suggested by the applicant, to cover her hair with a hat during physical classes, the Court noted that "it is difficult for the Court to judge whether wearing a hat instead would be compatible with sports classes."[265] It clarified that the argument of "whether the pupil expressed a willingness to compromise, as she maintains, or whether – on the contrary – she overstepped the limits of the right to express and manifest her religious beliefs on the school premises, as the Government maintains, and which appears to conflict with the principle of secularism, falls squarely within the margin of appreciation of the State."[266] Furthermore, the Court acknowledged that Dogru's punishment, being expelled from school, was not "disproportionate" because she could have pursued studying at school through "correspondence classes."[267] Thus, the Court ruled that the interference did not violate Article 9(2) of the Convention.[268]

Regarding the alleged violation of Article 2 of Protocol No. 1 to the ECHR,[269] protecting the right to education, the Court noted that the plaintiff

260 *Id.* para. 60.
261 *Id.* para. 73.
262 *Id.* para. 74.
263 *Id.*
264 *Id.*
265 *Id.* para. 75.
266 *Id.*
267 *Id.*
268 *Id.* para. 78.
269 *Id.* para. 79.

did not exhaust domestic remedies in France, as she did not raise this complaint "before any of the national courts dealing with the case."[270] Nevertheless, the Court considered the complaint admissible because it was related to the one examined above, the complaint of a violation of Article 9(2).[271] On reviewing the claim, the Court noted that the right to education is not violated by applying disciplinary measures, including the educational institution's capacity to "temporarily or definitively" suspend any student who violates its "internal rules."[272] According to the Court, disciplinary measures are regarded as an "integral part" of the educational system "whereby a school seeks to achieve the object for which it was established."[273] In addition, the Court stated that there is no need to review the Article 2 complaint because "no separate question arises under its provision" and the "relevant circumstances" are identical to those of Article 9.[274]

ii Restrictions on Teachers' Hijab (Dahlab v. Switzerland, 1998)

The events of Dahlab v. Switzerland[275] started when Mrs. Dahlab, a teacher at a primary school, converted to Islam.[276] In order to fulfill her religious duties, she decided to wear an Islamic headscarf when teaching in classes. After Dahlab returned from maternity leave, school officials prevented her from wearing her Islamic dress while engaged in the performance of her duties as a teacher.[277] Dahlab decided to file a complaint with the ECtHR.[278] Although the Court declared that the complaint was inadmissible,[279] it clarified that the interference satisfied the requirements stated in Article 9(2) of the ECHR. The Court explained that the interference was prescribed by law in Switzerland and was for legitimate aims to protect "rights and freedoms of others, public safety and public order."[280]

In addition, the Court stated that the interference, in light of the margin of appreciation afforded to states, was necessary in a democratic society for three reasons. First, the interference was aimed at protecting "the principle

270 *Id.* para. 80.
271 *Id.* para. 82.
272 *Id.* para. 83.
273 *Id.*
274 *Id.* para. 84.
275 Dahlab v. Switzerland, No. 42393/98 (Eur. Ct. H.R. May 16, 1988), available at http://cmiskp.echr.coe.int/tkp197/search.asp?skin=hudoc-en (search by application number) (last visited Aug. 21, 2024).
276 *Id.* § A.
277 *Id.*
278 *Id.* "The Facts".
279 *Id.* "The Law" § (2).
280 *Id.* "The Law" § (1).

of denominational neutrality in schools." According to the Court, because the applicant was a civil servant who represented the state, she should have respected the principles of secularism and never promoted one faith or belief over others. The Court described the Islamic headscarf as a powerful religious symbol by which the applicant showed her endorsement of Islam.[281]

The second foundation adopted by the Court was the protection of pupils' vulnerabilities in primary schools. The Court found that the wearing of the Islamic "headscarf might have some kind of proselytising effect" on very young children "seeing that it appears to be imposed on women by a precept which is laid down in the Koran."[282]

The third reason was the anti-democratic message provided by the hijab. In other words, the Court declared that it was too difficult to reconcile the Islamic headscarf with the "message of tolerance, respect for others and, above all, equality and non-discrimination that all teachers in a democratic society must convey to their pupils."[283]

iii Employment Discrimination on the Basis of Hijab

If the employment discrimination or violation occurs in the government or public sector, the European Convention on Human Rights and, potentially, the European Court of Human Rights (ECtHR) will be relevant within the European legal framework. On the other hand, when the employer is in the private sector rather than the government, the European Union Council Directive and the Court of Justice of the European Union's (CJEU) jurisdiction apply. The following are some notable decisions of the ECtHR and CJEU in this respect.

a Decision of the European Court of Human Rights (Ebrahimian v. France, 2015)

On November 26, 2015, the European Court of Human Rights ruled that the non-renewal of a public employee's contract for wearing a hijab does not violate the European Convention on Human Rights.[284] In that case, Ebrahimian, a social worker at a public hospital in France, refused to remove her hijab while performing her job duties, and therefore her employment contract was not renewed.[285]

281 *Id.*

282 *Id.*

283 *Id.*

284 Ebrahimian v. France, No. 64846/11, press release issued by the Registrar of the ECHR 370 (2015), available at http://www.dagbladet.no/f/nikab.pdf (last visited Jul. 21, 2024).

285 *Id.*

The ECtHR found that the hospital's decision did not violate Article 9 of the ECHR protecting the right to freedom of thought, conscience and religion.[286] The Court noted that the interference was prescribed by law, Article 1 of the French Constitution. It mentioned several rulings of domestic courts that had reaffirmed secularism and neutrality principles in French public institutions.[287] In addition, the Court stated that the interference with Ebrahimian's rights served the legitimate aim of protecting the rights and freedoms of others.[288]

The Court further noted that the interference was necessary in a democratic society. As stated by the Court:

> [T]he requirement of neutrality of public officials could be regarded as justified in principle: the State, as employer of the applicant in a public hospital, could consider it necessary that she refrain from expressing her religious beliefs in discharging her functions in order to guarantee equality of treatment of patients.[289]

In addition, the Court reasoned that although public officials should enjoy full freedom of conscience, they are prohibited from manifesting their religious beliefs while performing their job duties. According to the Court, that restriction "is derived from the principle of the secular nature of the State, and the principle of the neutrality of public services." Furthermore, the Court stipulated that "national authorities were better placed to assess the proportionality of the disciplinary penalty, which had to be determined with regard to all the circumstances in which a breach of the requirement of neutrality had been found in order to be compatible with Article 9 of the Convention."[290]

The Court determined that the national authorities did not exceed their "margin of appreciation in finding that there was no possibility of reconciling Ebrahimian's religious convictions with the obligation to refrain from manifesting them."[291] In other words, the Court found that domestic courts

286 *Id.* "Decision of the Court."

287 *Id.* Article 1 of the French Constitution stipulates that "France shall be an indivisible, secular, democratic and social Republic. It shall ensure the equality of all citizens before the law, without distinction of origin, race or religion." 1958 CONST. art. 1 (Fr.).

288 Ebrahimian v. France, "Decision of the Court", *supra* note, 284.

289 *Id.*

290 *Id.*

291 *Id.*

did not overstep their bounds by affording greater weight to the State's interest in protecting the principle of secularism than to Ebrahimian's right to freely manifest her religious beliefs, as well as by deciding to prioritize the State's impartiality and neutrality requirements.

b Decisions of the Court of Justice of the European Union

1 *Achbita v. G4S Secure Solutions (2017)*

In Achbita v. G4S Secure Solutions,[292] a multinational security company had a legal dispute with Samira Achbita, a receptionist working at the company's Belgian office. Achbita had previously worked for the company before she started to wear a hijab.[293] She was instructed to remove her hijab because the company's dress code prohibited workers from wearing religious symbols or clothing. She was dismissed for refusing to comply with the regulations.[294] After exhausting all domestic remedies, she decided to file a complaint with the CJEU alleging a violation of the European Union Council Directive prohibiting religious discrimination in the workplace.[295]

The CJEU ruled that Achbita's dismissal did not constitute "direct discrimination" under the Directive since the employer's dress code was neutral and did not target a particular religious faith.[296] In addition, the Court determined that the company's policy of religious neutrality, as evidenced in its restriction on religious attire, did not constitute "indirect discrimination" because it served the company's proclaimed legitimate aim.[297] The Court concluded that the right to maintain a religiously neutral workplace outweighed Achbita's religious claim to wear the hijab, and thus the interference with her rights was proportional and justified.[298]

2 *Bougnaoui v. Micropole (2017)*

In Bougnaoui v. Micropole,[299] Bougnaoui was hired by the French company Micropole as a design engineer.[300] She decided to wear a hijab, and no

292 Case C-157/15, Achbita v. G4S Secure Sols. NV, 2017 wl celex 62015CJ0157 (Mar. 14, 2017).

293 *Id.* paras. 11–13.

294 *Id.*

295 *Id.* para. 17.

296 *Id.* para. 30–32.

297 *Id.* para. 35.

298 *Id.* para. 40.

299 Case C-188/15, Bougnaoui v. Micropole sa, 2017 WL CELEX 62015CJ0188 (Mar. 14, 2017).

300 *Id.* para 13.

objections were raised.[301] She began working for one of the company's clients. The client informed the company that Bougnaoui's hijab caused distress among some employees.[302] Therefore, the company demanded that Bougnaoui remove her hijab, and since she refused, she was fired.[303]

Bougnaoui brought this case to the CJEU. Her primary argument was based on a violation of EU law's prohibition on religious discrimination.[304] However, the company argued that Bougnaoui was warned before the beginning of her internship that she would encounter difficulties due to her hijab, and that she denied having any concerns about the demand for neutrality in customer meetings when questioned during her interview.[305]

The CJEU determined that Bougnaoui was a victim of direct religious discrimination because she was fired in response to a client's complaint about her hijab.[306] The Court reasoned that, despite the fact that Bougnaoui was informed of Micropole's neutrality policy, the policy was not implemented until the client complained.[307] The Court further clarified that EU law allows employers to restrict religious freedoms only if there is a genuine and decisive occupational necessity that is objectively required by the nature of the activity or the environment in which it is performed.[308] However, the Court concluded that this was not the case in this instance because Bougnaoui was not instructed to remove her hijab in order to comply with the company's neutral dress code, but rather to accommodate the client's specific requests, which did not justify such discrimination.[309]

iv Acceptance of the Hijab for Ordinary Citizens in Key Governmental Institutions or "Courts" (Lachiri v. Belgium, 2018)

In Lachiri v. Belgium,[310] Lachiri was a Muslim woman who wore a hijab. She joined other family members as a civil party in a criminal case surrounding her brother's murder.[311] In 2007, the accused was sent to a criminal court on accusations of premeditated attack and wounds that led to her

301 *Id.*
302 *Id.* para. 14.
303 *Id.*
304 *Id.* para. 31.
305 *Id.* para. 14.
306 *Id.* para. 41.
307 *Id.* para. 30.
308 *Id.* para. 39.
309 *Id.* para. 40.
310 Lachiri v. Belgium, App. No. 3413/09 (ECtHR, 18 September 2018). This judgment is only available in French. However, the ECtHR has issued a press release in English. available at https://hudoc.echr.coe.int/eng-press#&gt (last visited, Aug. 20, 2024).
311 *Id.* Principle Facts.

brother's unintentional death.[312] Lachiri and the other civil parties filed an appeal, arguing that the crime should be categorized as murder. On the day of the hearing before the Brussels Court of Appeal, she was informed that she could not enter the courtroom unless she removed her hijab. Lachiri refused to take off her hijab and chose not to attend the hearing.[313] After exhausting all domestic remedies in Belgium, she brought a case before the ECtHR alleging the violation of her right to free exercise of religion enshrined in Article 9(2) of the European Convention on Human Rights.[314]

The ECtHR found that the act of wearing the hijab was inspired and motivated by religious belief.[315] Therefore, the Court determined that there was an interference with Article 9 of the European Convention on Human Rights (ECHR) because Lachiri was prevented from entering the courtroom because she refused to remove her hijab.[316] In addition, the Court found that the interference was prescribed by law since Article 759 of the Belgian Judicial Code necessitates that all courtroom attendees remove their head coverings.[317] Furthermore, the Court concluded that the interference served a legitimate aim. It was also established by the Court that the need to appear bareheaded before the judge or in court was meant to prevent disrespectful conduct towards the judiciary and avoid disruption of court proceedings. Accordingly, the Court reasoned, this aim might be associated with the exception specified in Article 9(2) for the "protection of public order"[318]

Concerning whether the interference was necessary in a democratic society, the Court found that Lachiri did not behave in a manner that was disrespectful or that posed, or was likely to pose, a threat to the orderly proceedings of the hearing to which she was a party.[319] In light of this, the Court determined that the state's interest in preserving its public order was insufficient to restrict the plaintiff's right to free manifestation of religion.[320] In addition, the Court emphasized that in public institutions, such as courts and public schools, neutrality may take precedence over the right to manifest one's faith or beliefs. Nonetheless, the Court reasoned that banning the plaintiff from entering the courtroom could not uphold the principles of secularism and religious neutrality towards beliefs, as the plaintiff is an

312 *Id.*
313 *Id.*
314 *Id.* Complaints, Procedure, and Composition of the Court.
315 *Id.* Decision of the Court, Article 9 (Freedom of Thought, Conscience, and Religion).
316 *Id.* para. 1.
317 *Id.*
318 *Id.*
319 *Id.* para. 2.
320 *Id.*

ordinary Belgian citizen and not a member of the judicial system or a public official exercising official responsibilities.[321] Therefore, the Court decided that the need for limiting Lachiri's ability to exercise her religion in a democratic society was not established and was unjustified. The Court thus ruled that Article 9 of the European Convention was violated.[322]

v Appraisal of the European Courts' Decisions on Hijab

Despite its judgment in Lachiri v. Belgium, the ECtHR has consistently supported hijab restrictions. In Lachiri, the Court did not uphold the ban on the hijab because the plaintiff was merely a private citizen attending as a civil party a criminal trial in which her brother was a victim. Therefore, the Court did not identify any violations of the public order or the principles of secularism, neutrality, or impartiality. In contrast, in all other cases, the Court upheld the prohibition on the hijab, regardless of whether it was worn by students, teachers, or government or public employees. According to the ECtHR, the ban on the hijab is typically justified and necessary in a democratic society. The Court determined that the hijab ban promotes neutrality and secularism standards, as well as gender equality, the freedoms and rights of others, and public order values. However, the Court was unable to articulate substantial and significant reasons for its rulings. Therefore, the Court relied heavily on the margin of appreciation afforded to states and stipulated that domestic authorities "are better placed than an international court to evaluate local needs and conditions."[323] In other words, the Court upheld the ban on the hijab, without examining any supposed benefits or supporting justifications for the restriction in a clear and adequate manner.

In addition, the terms used by the ECtHR were flexible and susceptible to many interpretations. For example, instead of saying that the state's argument is reasonable, the Court described it as "not unreasonable."[324] In addition, the same style was used once again by describing the university's punishment as "not disproportionate"[325] instead of using the word "proportionate." Furthermore, the Court employed the same kind of flexible phrases in declaring that the state did not violate Article 9(2)[326] of the ECHR and refrained from stating that the hijab ban was in line with that article.

---

321 *Id.*

322 *Id.*

323 Sahin II, No. 44774/98, para. 121.

324 Dogru v. France, No. 27058/05, para. 117.

325 *Id.* para. 76.

326 Sahin II, No. 44774/98, para. 123; Dogru v. France, No. 27058/05, para. 78.

Furthermore, the ECtHR violated Islam by claiming that it "appears difficult to reconcile the wearing of an Islamic headscarf with the message of tolerance, respect for others and, above all, equality and non-discrimination."[327] In addition, the Court made assumptions unrelated to the underlying instances. Specifically, it claimed that there were Islamic movements seeking to control the university, and in turn, the state had the right to prevent them from doing so by banning the hijab.[328] To continue fostering incorrect and irrelevant premises, the Court alleged that the hijab creates "a general atmosphere of tension"[329] among university students, and therefore the state had the right to ban the hijab as a pretext for protecting the public order inside the university.

Concerning the CJEU, the study discussed two cases involving hijab-wearing female employees in the private sector. In the Bougnaoui case, the CJEU did not support the prohibition, while in the other scenario, it did. It should be noted, however, that in Bougnaoui, the Court did not uphold the ban on the hijab since its objective was not to comply with a company's neutral dress code policy, but rather to accommodate a client's special requests, which did not justify such a restriction. Despite this, it should be apparent that the Court's explicit and unequivocal direction is to uphold the ban on the hijab in support of the employer's proclaimed policy of religious neutrality and the preservation of a religiously neutral workplace. Nonetheless, the Court's reasoning is not very persuasive.

A court's rationale for upholding a claim limiting an individual's right must very clearly explain and highlight the benefits of such a limitation. That is to say, the European courts should have ruled in favor of Muslim women's freedom to wear hijabs in the workplace and public educational institutions if they lacked evidence to support their reasons against this

---

327 Dahlab v. Switzerland, No. 42393/98, the law. One of the main aspects of Islam is the full submission to Allah out of free will and conviction, as opposed to coercion or seduction. Islam's approach to adherents of other religions is to demonstrate the unwavering Islamic principle of tolerance towards their beliefs. In this respect, the Qur'an says "there is no compulsion in [accepting] religion. The right course has become clear from error." Qur'an, *Surat Al-Baqarah* 2:256. In addition, many Qur'anic texts stipulate that Muslims should treat non-Muslims fairly and with respect. The Qur'an says: "Allah does not forbid you concerning those who do not fight you because of religion and do not expel you from your homes from being righteous towards them and acting justly towards them. Indeed, Allah loves those who act justly." Qur'an, *Surat Al-Mumtahanah* 60:8. "And they give food in spite of their love for it to the poor, the orphan, and the captive, [Saying]: We feed you only for the acceptance of Allah. We wish neither from you reward nor gratitude." Qur'an, *Surat Al-Insan* 76:8–9.

328 Sahin II, No. 44774/98, para. 115.

329 Dogru v. France, No.27058/05, para. 74.

practice. The European courts should not have relied on erroneous assumptions and irrelevant justifications in order to prohibit hijabs in public workplaces and educational institutions. Furthermore, if the ECtHR and CJEU really wished to protect the principle of neutrality, they should have committed to neutrality and never diminished individuals' rights without compelling grounds. Moreover, if the ECtHR aimed at protecting the freedoms of others, it should have protected the freedoms of Muslim women who voluntarily opted to wear the hijab and enabled them to avoid violating their religion at work, universities and schools. Accordingly, the author argues that all arguments supporting restrictions on the hijab are weak and insufficiently convincing; if a woman freely decides to wear a hijab, the state must respect her choice and ensure that she enjoys unrestricted access to all public places.

vi The Ban on Niqab (S. A. S. v. France, 2014)

In July 2014, the ECtHR upheld France's ban on the full-face veil in all public places.[330] At the outset, the French Parliament passed a law, preventing all citizens from concealing their faces in public places.[331] Consequently, a French Muslim female who wore a niqab brought a case against France to challenge such a law, claiming the violation of her right to practice her religious faith.[332] Before discussing the core of the judgment, it must be noted that the applicant confirmed to the Court her free choice to wear a niqab, as none of her family members coerced her to dress in this manner.[333] She added that she did not wear the niqab in public at all times, but she wished to be entitled to wear it when she chose to do so.[334] Moreover, the applicant confirmed to the Court her willingness to reveal her face in cases of security or identification checks.[335] The applicant's main line of argument was based on the violation of Articles 8 and 9 of the European Convention on Human Rights.[336] Article 8 protects the right to privacy, while Article 9 protects the right to free manifestation of religion or belief.

---

330 S.A.S. v. France, No. 43835/11 (Eur. Ct. H.R. July 1, 2014), available at http://hudoc.echr.coe.int/sites/eng/pages/search.aspx?i=001-145466 (last visited Aug. 21, 2024).

331 *Id.* at 14.

332 *Id.* at 3.

333 *Id.* at 11.

334 *Id.* at 12.

335 *Id.* at 13.

336 *Id.* at 3.

The Court found that there was interference with the applicant's right to privacy and to free manifestation of religion, and therefore it began to examine the case in light of the conditions stated in the second paragraph of Articles 8 and 9 of the ECHR.[337] In other words, the Court reviewed whether such interference was prescribed by law, for a legitimate aim, or necessary in a democratic society.

Concerning the first condition, the Court found that the interference was prescribed by law as it was mentioned in Sections 1, 2 and 3 of a domestic law enacted on October 11, 2010.[338]

With regard to the second condition, the State provided several arguments in order to demonstrate that the interference served a legitimate objective. The State argued that the limitation imposed on the wearing of the full-face veil was aimed at protecting the principle of gender equality.[339] However, the Court found that the State "cannot invoke gender equality in order to ban a practice that is defended by women – such as the applicant – in the context of the exercise of [their] rights, unless it were to be understood that individuals could be protected on that basis from the exercise of their own fundamental rights and freedoms."[340] In addition, the State claimed that the interference was aimed at respecting the principle of human dignity; however, the Court found that the respect of human dignity could not "legitimately" be a foundation for banning a full-face veil in all public places.[341] The Court noted that many of those who observe the full-face veil perceive it as strange; however, it clarified that the full-face veil could be a type of "the expression of a cultural identity which contributes to the pluralism that is inherent in democracy". The Court reasoned that the State was not able to demonstrate that women wearing the clothing in question "seek to express a form of contempt against those they encounter or otherwise to offend against the dignity of others."[342]

Nevertheless, concerning the State's argument that the full-face veil is "problematic" because it is irreconcilable with the "fundamental requirements of living together in French society,"[343] the Court found that this argument was valid and could be connected with the "legitimate aim of the

337 *Id.* at 110–11.
338 *Id.* at 112.
339 *Id.* at 119.
340 *Id.*
341 *Id.* at 120.
342 *Id.*
343 *Id.*

protection of the rights and freedoms of others."[344] In other words, the Court clarified that revealing the face plays a significant role in "social interaction" between individuals, and therefore it found that "the barrier raised against others by a veil concealing the face is perceived by the respondent State as breaching the right of others to live in a space of socialisation which makes living together easier."[345]

Regarding the third condition, the Court found that the ban was necessary in a democratic society.[346] The Court noted that the niqab ban might have a negative impact on Muslim women, who wish to wear the full-face veil for certain reasons based on their religious faiths.[347] In addition, the Court stressed that the niqab ban could restrict their autonomy, isolate them, and diminish respect for their private lives, and that they might regard the ban as a "threat to their identity."[348] Besides, the Court acknowledged that a large number of national and international actors in the field of fundamental human rights protection found the full face ban "disproportionate."[349] The Court admitted that the ban "may have upset part of the Muslim community, including some members who are not in favour of the full-face veil being worn."[350] Nevertheless, the Court found that face concealment in public places is opposed to "the ideal of fraternity" and incompatible with the "minimum requirement of civility" necessary for "social interaction" between individuals in a democratic society, and therefore it "falls within the powers of the State to secure the conditions whereby individuals can live together in their diversity."[351] The Court found that the State was entitled to give "particular weight" to the social interaction between individuals and that this interaction could be negatively affected by the concealment of faces in public places.[352] Accordingly, the Court declared that the ban could be merely justified because it sought to ensure the principle of living together.[353]

344 *Id.* at 121.
345 *Id.* at 122.
346 *Id.* at 141.
347 *Id.*
348 *Id.*
349 *Id.* at 147. The Court noted examples of these actors, such as the French National Advisory Commission on Human Rights, the Parliamentary Assembly of the Council of Europe, and the Commissioner for Human Rights of the Council of Europe. *Id.*
350 *Id.* at 148.
351 *Id.* at 141.
352 *Id.*
353 *Id.* 142.

The Court further noted that, although the scope of the ban was broad because it prohibited the full-face veil in all public places, it did not restrict individuals' freedom to wear non-face-covering religious clothing.[354] In other words, the Court acknowledged the fact that the ban primarily affected a Muslim woman who decided to wear the full-face veil for religious reasons; however, it found that the ban was not mainly based on the "religious connotation of the clothing in question but solely on the fact that it conceals the face."[355]

Furthermore, the Court admitted that the ban prevented a woman who wears the full-face veil in public from expressing her beliefs and personality, and therefore it could restrict "the reach of pluralism" in French society. However, the Court found that France, by adopting the ban, sought "to protect a principle of interaction between individuals, which … is essential for the expression not only of pluralism, but also of tolerance and broadmindedness without which there is no democratic society."[356] Therefore, the Court stated that "in matters of general policy, on which opinions within a democratic society may reasonably differ widely, the role of the domestic policy-maker should be given special weight."[357] In other words, the Court declared that "France had a wide margin of appreciation in the present case."[358]

Similarly, in Belcacemi and Oussar v. Belgium[359] and Dakir v. Belgium[360], the ECtHR examined the full-face veil, the niqab, and maintained its restrictive stance. The Court reiterated its decision in S.A.S. v. France and substantially relied on it.[361] In a similar reasoning to S.A.S., the Court declared that the restriction attempted to promote the conditions of social coexistence and the concept of "living together."[362] The Court concluded that the restriction satisfied a legitimate aim since it contributed to the protection of the

354 *Id.* at 151.

355 *Id.*

356 *Id.* at 153.

357 *Id.* at 154.

358 *Id.* at 155.

359 Belcacemi v. Belgium, App. no. 37798/13 (July 11, 2017), http://hudoc.echr.coe.int/eng?i=001-175636.

360 Dakir v. Belgium, App. no. 4619/12, P 68 (July 11, 2017), http://hudoc.echr.coe.int/eng?i=001-175660.

361 John Witte, *Comment: Faith in Strasbourg and Luxembourg? The Fresh Rise of Religious Freedom Litigation in the Pan-European Courts,* 70 Emory Lj 587, 630 (2021)

362 Belcacemi v. Belgium. *supra* note 359, at 51.

rights and freedoms of others and could thus be deemed necessary in a democratic society.[363]

vii Appraisal of the ECtHR's Decisions on Niqab

The ECtHR stated that states, by adopting the niqab ban, sought to protect principles of tolerance, pluralism and broadmindedness within their communities. Nonetheless, it can be argued that these principles may be better protected by another approach allowing minority groups to express their beliefs through wearing the niqab in public places. In addition, instead of providing states with a broad margin of appreciation regarding the niqab ban, it would be better for the Court to protect Muslims' right to privacy and their freedom to manifest religion and give them the opportunity to enjoy the fundamental rights set out in the European Convention on Human Rights. As for the argument claiming that the niqab has a negative effect on the social interactions between individuals within a society and is incompatible with the principle of "living together," the author argues that this argument is hardly convincing. The author affirms that interactions are based on the actual personalities of individuals and have no relation to dress. In addition, if the Court aimed to protect the principle of living together, it must have prohibited numerous clothing styles that may disturb others. However, the ban was primarily intended to restrict the religious practice rights of some minorities. In addition, the author argues that banning the niqab may have a negative effect on the unity of a society. In other words, the minorities, who are completely deprived of their right to choose their preferred religious clothing, may become more isolated and alienated due to their negative feelings towards the society whose choice impairs their right to free exercise of their own beliefs and violates their private lives.

To conclude, the author argues that restrictions on the wearing of the full-face veil, the niqab, in some places, such as airports and banks, may serve a compelling state interest to protect public safety. In addition, restrictions on the niqab in some social places, such as educational institutions or workplaces, could protect the rights and freedoms of others and support social interactions between individuals in these places. However, the complete ban on the niqab in all public places never serves any compelling state interest and discriminates against Muslim women who freely choose to wear such Islamic attire.

---

363 *Id.*

4 Women's Islamic Clothing under American Law

A *An Overview of Muslim Women in the U.S.*

Millions of Muslims live in the United States of America, coming from different parts of the world and with a variety of nationalities and traditions.[364] African Muslims were the first group to arrive in America and were enslaved as early as the discovery of America.[365] They are the largest Muslim population living in the United States.[366] In the eighteenth century, a great number of Arabs arrived in the United States from Iraq, Egypt, Syria, Jordan, and other Arab countries.[367]

Muslim women living in the United States belong to four different Islamic schools of jurisprudence: Shafi'a, Malikia, Hanafia, and Hanabila.[368] Some of them were born and raised as Muslims in the United States; others immigrated to America as Muslims from their homelands, while the rest converted to Islam.[369] Therefore, they have different views on a woman's Islamic dress. Some of them advocate the niqab, whereas others support the wearing of the hijab in its various styles. This controversy is based on a woman's affiliation with a certain Islamic jurisprudential school and her own perception.[370]

Given this diversity, challenges to Muslim women's dress could be brought before courts in light of two legal foundations, Title VII of the Civil Rights Act of 1964 and the Free Exercise Clause of the First Amendment of the Constitution.[371] Title VII of the Civil Rights Act prohibits employment discrimination based on religion,[372] while the Free Exercise Clause prohibits state practices that restrict the free exercise of religious beliefs.[373]

---

364 Ali S. Asani, *Islam Enduring Myths and Changing Realities: "So That You May Know One Another": A Muslim American Reflects on Pluralism and Islam, in Islam: Enduring Myths and Changing Realities*, 588 ANNALS 40, 49 (2003).

365 Abdo, *supra* note 203, at 446.

366 *Id.*

367 Rachel Saloom, *I Know You Are, But What Am I? Arab-American Experiences through the Critical Race Theory Lens*, 27 Hamline J. Pub. L. & Pol'y 55, 59 (2005).

368 Asani, *supra* note 364, at 49.

369 *Id.*

370 Abdo, *supra* note 203, at 446.

371 U.S. Const. amend. I.

372 42 U.S.C. § 2000e-2(a).

373 Emp't Div., Dept. of Human Resources v. Smith, 494 U.S. 872, 877 (1990).

B *Title VII of the Civil Rights Act (EEOC v. Abercrombie & Fitch Stores, Inc. (2015))*

As previously stated in this book, Title VII of the Civil Rights Act outlaws the following practices for an employer:

> (1) to fail or refuse to hire or to discharge any individual, or otherwise to discriminate against any individual … because of such individual's … religion, … or
> (2) to limit, segregate, or classify his employees or applicants for employment in any way which would deprive or tend to deprive any individual of employment opportunities or otherwise adversely affect his status as an employee, because of such individual's … religion. …[374]

In a recent case, EEOC v. Abercrombie & Fitch Stores, Inc., the Supreme Court issued a ruling granting a Muslim woman the right to wear the hijab in the workplace.[375] The facts of that case started when Samantha Elauf was denied a job at Abercrombie & Fitch clothing store due to the hijab she wore in order to fulfill her religious duties.[376] The employer found the hijab incompatible with "Abercrombie's employee dress policy." On Elauf's behalf, the Equal Employment Opportunity Commission (EEOC) filed a lawsuit claiming that such a policy violated Title VII of the Civil Rights Act, under which no person could be denied a job due to his or her religious practice if such practice "could be accommodated without undue hardship."[377]

The U.S. Supreme Court ruled in favor of Elauf. In reviewing the case, the Court stated that the disparate treatment provision of Title VII of the Civil Rights Act prohibits an employer from "fail[ing] … to hire" an applicant "because of" "such individual's … religion."[378] In addition, the Court noted that, under Title VII, the word "religion" includes "all aspects of religious observance and practice, as well as belief, unless an employer demonstrates that he is unable to reasonably accommodate to a religious observance or practice without undue hardship on the conduct of the employer's business."[379] Therefore, the Court found that, under that law, employers are required to

374 42 U.S.C. § 2000e-2(a).

375 EEOC v. Abercrombie & Fitch Stores, Inc., 135 S. Ct. 2030 (2015).

376 *Id.*

377 *Id.*

378 42 U.S.C. § 2000e-2(a).

379 *Id.* § 2000e(j).

make suitable accommodations for religious practices, such as the wearing of the hijab, that do not impose "undue hardship" on them.[380]

In addition, the Court stated that an employer could be found liable, under Title VII, only if an employee shows that his or her "need for an accommodation was a motivating factor in the employer's decision."[381] Therefore, the Court rejected the employer's main line of argument claiming that the applicant could not demonstrate disparate treatment discrimination without first proving that "an employer has actual knowledge of the applicant's need for an accommodation."[382] In other words, the Court explained that Title VII "does not impose a knowledge requirement ... as some anti-discrimination statutes do."[383] For instance, the Court noted that, under the Americans with Disabilities Act of 1990, discrimination includes "an employer's failure to make reasonable accommodations to the known physical or mental limitations of an applicant."[384] However, the Court found that Title VII does not include such a limitation because it forbids "certain motives, regardless of the state of the actor's knowledge."[385]

According to the Court, "[m]otive and knowledge are separate concepts."[386] Therefore, "[a]n employer who has actual knowledge of the need for an accommodation does not violate Title VII by refusing to hire an applicant if avoiding that accommodation is not his motive."[387] On the other hand, an employer "who acts with the motive of avoiding accommodation" could be found liable under Title VII "even if he has no more than an unsubstantiated suspicion that accommodation would be needed."[388]

In contrast, prior to the Supreme Court's decision in Abercrombie, lower courts in the U.S. upheld discrimination against a Muslim female employee wearing a hijab. The case of Wiley v. Pless Security, Inc.,[389] illustrates such discrimination. In that case, a Muslim woman working as a security guard at the Georgia Department of Revenue G.D.R. decided to wear a hijab.[390] Her supervisors demoted her to another position, claiming that her hijab disturbed people in the G.D.R., but she refused and decided to resign.[391]

380 Abercrombie & Fitch, 135 S. Ct. 2030.
381 *Id.*
382 *Id.*
383 *Id.* at 2032–33.
384 *Id.* at 2033.
385 Abercrombie & Fitch, 135 S. Ct. at 2032–33.
386 *Id.* at 2033.
387 *Id.*
388 *Id.*
389 Wiley v. Pless Security, Inc., 2006 U.S. Dist. LEXIX 50894 (N.D. Ga. July 12, 2006).
390 *Id.* at 1.
391 *Id.*

The United States District Court for the Northern District of Georgia ruled in favor of the G.D.R.[392] The Court reasoned that the plaintiff resigned without proving any violations of her rights, as "the potential adverse employment action never occurred because the plaintiff quit first."[393] In addition, the Court noted that the plaintiff's supervisors tried "to accommodate [her] religious practice by transferring her to another location" and therefore concluded that there was no "direct evidence of discrimination" against the plaintiff.[394]

Another case involving hijab-based employment discrimination is Webb v. the City of Philadelphia.[395] The events of the case started when a female police officer converted to Islam and sought to wear a hijab.[396] Therefore, she submitted a memorandum to her supervisors requesting to wear an Islamic head covering, but they refused.[397] Shortly thereafter, she decided to wear a hijab at work and refused to remove it.[398] She was punished with disciplinary charges for refusing to take off her hijab; she was suspended for thirteen days.[399] Therefore, she filed a lawsuit claiming that she was subjected to religiously-based employment discrimination.[400]

The United States District Court for the Eastern District of Pennsylvania ruled against the claimant, holding that the State had a compelling interest in preventing her from wearing a hijab with her work uniform.[401] In its reasoning, the Court noted that the State could have faced "undue hardship" if it had accommodated the plaintiff by allowing her to wear a hijab when performing her duties as a police officer.[402] The Court found that a law preventing police officers from wearing religious symbols "promote[s] the need for uniformity," and "enhances cohesiveness, cooperation and the esprit de corps of the police force."[403] Furthermore, the Court found that "prohibiting religious symbols and attires helps to prevent any divisiveness on the basis of religion both within the force itself and when it encounters the diverse population of Philadelphia."[404]

---

392 *Id.* at 3.
393 *Id.* at 2–3.
394 *Id.* at 2.
395 Webb v. City of Phila., 2007 U.S. Dist. LEXIX 46872 (3d Cir. April 7, 2009).
396 *Id.* at 2–3.
397 *Id.*
398 *Id.* at 3.
399 *Id.* at 4.
400 Id. at 5.
401 *Id.* at 21.
402 *Id.* at 13.
403 *Id.* at 11–12.
404 *Id.* at 12.

The Court distinguished this case from Fraternal Order of Police v. City of Newark,[405] in which the U.S. Court of Appeals for the Third Circuit allowed the claimants, who were police officers, to wear beards for religious considerations.[406] In that case, the State prevented police officers from wearing beards for religious reasons, while providing an exception for others to wear beards for medical causes.[407] The State argued that allowing officers "to wear beards for religious reasons would undermine the force's morale and esprit de corps."[408] However, the Court found that the State provided "no legitimate explanation as to why the presence of officers who wear beards for medical reasons does not have this effect, but the presence of officers who wear beards for religious reasons would."[409] In other words, the Court did not "understand why religious exemptions threaten important city interests but medical exemptions do not."[410] Therefore, the Court decided that the State's argument was invalid because if "religious exemptions threaten important city interests," medical exceptions would do the same.[411] On the other hand, in Webb,[412] the Court found that the law banned the wearing of religious symbols "under all circumstances" and did not provide a medical or secular exception.[413] Therefore, the Court declared that the State "established compelling non-discriminatory reasons" for enacting such a law.[414]

C *The Free Exercise Clause*

The First Amendment of the United States Constitution states that "Congress shall make no law respecting an establishment of religion, or

405 170 F.3d 359 (3d Cir. 1999).

406 *Id.* at 367.

407 *Id.* at 366.

408 *Id.*

409 *Id.* at 366–67.

410 *Id.* at 367.

411 *Id.*

412 Webb v. City of Phila., No 07-3081, 2007 U.S. Dist. LEXIX 46872.

413 *Id.* at 13.

414 *Id.* It could be argued that less restrictive means could be found to meet a state's interest without impeding the right to free exercise of religion of Muslim women wearing hijabs. Abdo, *supra* note 203, at 481. A firefighting and paramedic company gave administrative leave to one of its female employees because of her Islamic headscarf, alleging that restrictions on the hijab were made for safety concerns. *Id.* The woman turned to the Council on American-Islamic Relations (CAIR), a Muslim civil rights group that negotiated a compromise between the company's interests and the woman's right to free exercise of religion. *Id.* The company's officials, after their negotiations with CAIR, permitted the employee to work on the condition that she wears a white or blue headscarf, but in the event of a fire, she should replace her headscarf with a fire-retardant hood or helmet. *Id*

prohibiting the free exercise thereof; or abridging the freedom of speech, or of the press; or the right of the people peaceably to assemble, and to petition the Government of grievances."[415]

Regarding religion, this Amendment contains two clauses: the Establishment Clause and the Free Exercise Clause. The first prevents the State from "establishing or endorsing an official or de facto state religion."[416] On the other hand, the Free Exercise Clause prevents the State's interference in individuals' religious beliefs. In Employment Division, Department of Human Resources v. Smith, the Supreme Court clarified the scope of the Free Exercise Clause. The Court declared that the government "may not compel affirmation of religious belief, punish the expression of religious doctrines it believes to be false, impose special disabilities on the basis of religious views or religious status, or lend its power to one or the other side in controversies over religious dogma."[417]

Because the U.S. Supreme Court did not rule on the wearing of the hijab or niqab in light of the Free Exercise Clause, this study shall clarify the Court's standards on the right to free exercise of religion in general. The study will subsequently discuss how lower courts applied these standards to the hijab and niqab.

D *Supreme Court Cases on the Right to Free Exercise of Religion*

i Braunfeld v. Brown (1961)

The facts of Braunfeld v. Brown[418] started when Jewish merchants sought to challenge the Sunday closing law forcing merchants to close their stores on Sunday.[419] They wanted to close their business on Saturday, the Sabbatarian day of their faith, instead of Sunday, in order to avoid losing clients for two days a week rather than one day.[420]

The Supreme Court held that a Sunday closing law did not violate the First Amendment of the Constitution because it did not compel Jewish merchants to open their stores and work on Saturday, the Sabbatarian day of their faith, and therefore it did not substantially burden their right to free exercise of religion.[421] The Court stated that "the statute at bar does not

415 U.S. Const. amend. I.
416 Abdo, *supra* note 203, at 450.
417 Emp't Div. v. Smith, 494 U.S. 872, 877 (1990).
418 Braunfeld v. Brown, 366 U.S. 599 (1961).
419 *Id.* at 601.
420 *Id.* at 601–02.
421 *Id.* at 609–10.

make unlawful any religious practices of appellants; [it] simply regulates a secular activity and, as applied to appellants, operates so as to make the practice of their religious beliefs more expensive."[422] According to the Court, if the State regulates a conduct by adopting a "general law within its power, the purpose and effect of which is to advance the State's secular goals, the statute is valid despite its indirect burden on religious observance unless the State may accomplish its purpose by means which do not impose such a burden."[423]

The Court avoided violating the Establishment Clause of the First Amendment of the Constitution, which prohibits favoritism toward any religious group.[424] The Court held that allowing Jewish merchants to open their stores on Sunday constituted preferential treatment over their competitors because a small number of merchants who are legally able to serve a large number of potential clients may receive greater benefits than a large number of merchants serving the same number of potential clients.[425]

ii Sherbert v. Verner (1963)

Sherbert was denied unemployment benefits due to her usual absence on Saturdays, the day she attended religious services.[426] The Supreme Court ruled in favor of Sherbert establishing three basic standards for reviewing cases involving religious exercise.[427] The first was that the Court examined whether the State's regulation burdened Sherbert's free exercise of religion.[428] The second standard was based on the availability of the first one. In that instance, the Court had to transfer the burden of proof to the State to demonstrate that it had a compelling interest in maintaining this regulation.[429] Moreover, the Court established a third standard requiring the State "to demonstrate that no alternative forms of regulation would [accomplish its interests] without infringing First Amendment rights."[430]

In addition, the Court noted that this case is different from Braunfeld,[431] in which Jewish merchants were not allowed to open their businesses on

422 *Id.* at 605.
423 *Id.* at 607.
424 U.S. Const. amend. I.
425 Braunfeld v. Brown, 366 U.S. 599, 608–09 (1961).
426 Sherbert v. Verner, 374 U.S. 398–99 (1963).
427 *Id.* at 408–10.
428 *Id.* at 403.
429 *Id.* at 406–07.
430 *Id.*
431 Braunfeld v. Brown, 366 U.S. 599 (1961).

Sunday in order not to have an advantage over their competitors.[432] This is a contradictory view becauste the employee would be preferred in Sherbert, where the applicant refused to work on Saturdays while her coworkers did, and the Court treated them all equally regarding unemployment benefits.[433] In contrast, in Braunfeld, Jewish merchants were forced to choose between two equally unpleasant alternatives: the loss of economic interest (to close their store two days per week) or the violation of their right to free exercise of religion (to work and not worship on Saturdays).[434]

iii Wisconsin v. Yoder (1972)

In Wisconsin v. Yoder,[435] Amish parents refused to send their children to a Wisconsin school, claiming that the school's mandatory attendance policy violated their free exercise of religion.[436] The Court ruled in favor of the claimants, holding that the policy violated the Free Exercise Clause.[437] In its reasoning, the Court emphasized the sincerity of the religious belief.[438] Then, the Court sought to balance the State's interest in education against the claimants' right to practice religion and the parents' interest with respect to "the religious upbringing of their children."[439]

The Court noted that the State's interest in education is not completely free from a "balancing process" when it burdens fundamental rights and interests, such as the right to free exercise of religion enshrined in the Free Exercise Clause of the First Amendment and the "traditional interest of parents" concerning the religious background of their children.[440] It is worth mentioning that the Court adopted a new standard stipulating that the state interest must be of "sufficient magnitude to override the interest claiming protection under the Free Exercise Clause."[441] In other words, the Court

---

432 Sherbert v. Verner, 374 U.S. 398, 408–09 (1963).

433 Rodney J. Blackman, *Showing the Fly the Way Out of the Fly-Bottle: Making Sense of the First Amendment Religion Clauses*, 42 Kan. L. Rev. 285, 376–77 (1994).

434 *Id.*

435 Wisconsin v. Yoder, 406 U.S. 205 (1972).

436 *Id.* at 207.

437 *Id.* at 234.

438 *Id.* at 211.

439 *Id.* at 214.

440 *Id.*

441 *Id.* In Spence v. Bailey, a high school student refused to attend the R.O.T.C. (Reserve Officers' Training Corps) program because his religion was based on conscientious objection to war. 465 F.2d 797–98 (6th Cir. 1972). State law requires that every student choose between attending one year of physical education and training at R.O.T.C. Because Spence's high school did not have a gym for male students, in order to graduate,

reasoned that "only those interests of the highest order and those not otherwise served can overbalance legitimate claims to the free exercise of religion."[442]

iv Widmar v. Vincent (1981)

In Widmar v. Vincent,[443] the Court applied the principle of equal protection and required the State to treat religious expression similarly to other forms of expression.[444] The Court stressed that religious speech must be provided protection equal to other forms of speech if there is no appropriate reason for different treatment, and therefore allowed religious groups to use a university's properties for worship since other groups used them for other purposes.[445]

---

he had no choice but to attend R.O.T.C. *Id.* The United States Court of Appeals for the Sixth Circuit found that the State's compelling interest did not override Spence's right to free exercise of religion and therefore held that the mandatory R.O.T.C program unconstitutionally burdened Spence's right enshrined in the Free Exercise Clause. *Id.* at 800. In its reasoning, the Court considered Wisconsin v. Yoder as a precedent, quoting its holding that "only those interests of the highest order and those not otherwise served can overbalance legitimate claims to the free exercise of religion." *Id.* (quoting Wisconsin v. Yoder, 406 U.S. 205, 215 (1972)). In addition, the Court noted that the regulation was obviously comparable to that in Sherbert because it forced "the conscientious objector either to engage in military training contrary to his religious beliefs, or to give up his public education." *Id.* at 799. According to the Court, the regulation was held unconstitutional in Sherbert because it compelled the applicant either to behave contrary to his religion "by accepting employment on Saturday" or to be denied "unemployment compensation." *Id.*

In Moody v. Cronin, parents of public-school students complained against mandatory attendance for coeducational gym classes because their children's religion prohibited them from being exposed to members of the opposite gender if they wore immodest clothes. 484 F. Supp. 270, 272 (C.D. Ill. 1979). The United States District Court for the Central District of Illinois ruled in favor of the parents, preventing the school from suspending children who refused to attend the mandatory coeducational physical classes. *Id.* at 277. In its reasoning, the Court applied the standard of least restrictive means, finding that the children's right to free exercise of religion outweighed the state's interest in demanding that the children attend the coeducational gym lessons. *Id.* In addition, the Court considered Yoder as a precedent, quoting its holding that "a state's interest in universal education, however [the Court highly ranks it], is not totally free from a balancing process when it impinges on fundamental rights and interests, such as those specifically protected by the Free Exercise Clause of the First Amendment." *Id.* at 276 (quoting Wisconsin v. Yoder, 406 U.S. 205, 214 (1972)).

442 *Id.*

443 Widmar v. Vincent, 454 U.S. 263 (1981).

444 *Id.* at 276–77.

445 *Id.*

In its reasoning, the Court declared that the state's interest could not be regarded "as sufficiently compelling to justify content-based discrimination against respondents' religious speech."[446] In addition, the Court decided that "the University seeks to enforce a content-based exclusion of religious speech" and, therefore, it violated "the fundamental principle that a state regulation of speech should be content-neutral."[447]

v Thomas v. Review Board of the Indiana Employment Security Division (1981)

In Thomas v. Review Board of the Indiana Employment Security Division,[448] Thomas was an Indian person who terminated his work due to his religious beliefs. The State refused to grant him unemployment benefits.[449] The U.S. Supreme Court ruled in favor of the plaintiff, applying a new standard, the

---

446 *Id.* at 276.

447 *Id.* at 277. In Davis v. Page, parents of students who were members of the "Apostolic Lutheran faith" objected to a public school's audio-visual equipment use and compulsory attendance of music and health classes, claiming that such activities were "religiously offensive." 385 F. Supp. 395, 397 (D.N.H. 1974). Their argument was based on the violation of their children's rights enshrined in the First Amendment and their fundamental right to control the moral and religious upbringing of their children. *Id.* The United States District Court for the District of New Hampshire decided in favor of the school after conducting a balancing test. In its reasoning, the Court noted that the "system of education could not survive if parents were allowed to dictate the courses and modes of study." *Id.* at 406. In addition, the Court declared that "[w]here it is found that the abridgment of plaintiffs' constitutional guarantees are the result of secular educational activity and that the only available alternative would be to preclude the children from virtually all school courses and programs, the state's interests in treating all students equally prevails." *Id.*

In Grove v. Mead School District, the plaintiffs, as parents of a child at a public school, sought to eradicate the religiously objectionable curriculum, claiming that it burdened their child's right enshrined in the Free Exercise Clause of the First Amendment. 753 F.2d 1528, 1531 (9th Cir.1985). However, the school, on its own initiative, permitted the child to be excluded from that curriculum and allowed him to leave the class during that session. *Id.* The United States Court of Appeals for the Ninth Circuit determined that no burden on the child's right to free exercise of religion could exist because the school voluntarily allowed the child not to study a religiously objectionable curriculum, and therefore the Court did not engage in First Amendment analysis. *Id.* at 1533–34. In addition, the Court reasoned that the removal of the curriculum would have an effect on public education, which would be left "in shreds" by the elimination of "everything that is objectionable to any of the religious bodies existing in the United States or inconsistent with any of their doctrine." *Id.* at 1533.

448 Thomas v. Review Bd. of Ind. Emp't Sec. Div., 450 U.S. 707 (1981).

449 *Id.* at 709.

least restrictive means, to justify its ruling.[450] The Court reviewed whether the State applied the least restrictive means to prevent the Indian man from practicing his religion.[451] To determine the issue, the Court reviewed this case in light of four tests, as follows:

(1) Whether or not there was a religious conviction.[452]

(2) Whether the State's regulation burdened the individual's religious beliefs in practice.[453]

(3) Whether the regulation served the State's compelling interests.[454]

(4) Whether less restrictive means were available to achieve the State's compelling interests.[455]

Notably, the Court placed the burden of proof concerning the first and second tests on the claimant. In other words, the claimant was required to prove the sincerity of his religious beliefs and the burden caused by the regulation.[456] On the other hand, the Court required the State to prove the third and fourth suppositions. The State had to demonstrate that it could not accomplish its interests without burdening the individual's religious beliefs. In addition,"the state may justify an inroad on religious liberty by showing that it is the least restrictive means of achieving some compelling state interest."[457]

Thus, the U.S. Supreme Court established in Sherbert, where "the employee was dismissed by the employer's action,"[458] the principle of an alternative form of regulation.[459] On the other hand, in Thomas, where the work was terminated without the employer's intervention, the Court applied the principle of the least restrictive means to limit the State's authority to enact a regulation restricting the right to free exercise of religion.[460] The Court found that "the termination [, in both cases,] flowed from the fact that the employment, once acceptable, became religiously objectionable because of changed conditions."[461]

---

450 *Id.* at 718.

451 *Id.*

452 *Id.* at 713–14.

453 *Id.* at 717–18.

454 *Id.* at 718.

455 *Id.*

456 *Id.*

457 *Id.*

458 Thomas, 450 U.S. at 718.

459 Sherbert, 374 U.S. at 406–07.

460 Thomas, 450 U.S. at 718.

461 *Id.*

vi Bowen v. Roy (1986)

In Bowen v. Roy,[462] the claimants alleged that according to their religious beliefs, their "spiritual purity" was violated by the use of technology, including the use of social security numbers, because it may "rob the spirit of man."[463] They sought to obtain government food stamps and welfare benefits for their children without providing their social security numbers.[464] The Court ruled against the individuals, holding that the procedure was not incompatible with the Free Exercise Clause.[465]

The Court distinguished the state's regulation in this case that "indirectly" required "a choice between securing a governmental benefit and adherence to religious beliefs" from other state regulations that criminalize "religiously inspired activity" or obviously compel "conduct that some find objectionable for religious reasons."[466] The Court noted that the nature of the burden in this case, the indirect governmental burden on religious freedom, is relevant to the burden of Sherbert, where the Court applied the standard of an alternative form of regulation, and the burden of Thomas, where the standard of the least restrictive means was applicable.[467] Nevertheless, the Bowen Court refused to consider Thomas and Sherbert as legal precedents because it found that the requirement of submitting a social security number is neutral and clearly "promotes a legitimate and important public interest."[468] On the other hand, in Sherbert and Thomas, the State's requirement was viewed "as a protection against unequal treatment rather than a grant of favored treatment for the members of the religious sect," and therefore the State was obliged to demonstrate a compelling reason for that requirement.[469]

---

462 Bowen v. Roy, 476 U.S. 693 (1986).

463 *Id.* at 696–97.

464 *Id.*

465 *Id.* at 712.

466 *Id.* at 706.

467 Bowen, 476 U.S. at 706–07.

468 *Id.* at 708.

469 *Id.* The Bowen Court noted that, in Sherbert and Thomas, the "statutory conditions" provided that an employee would not be eligible for unemployment benefits if he or she left work without a good cause. It asserted that the good cause criterion established a "mechanism for individualized exemptions," and that "if a state creates such a mechanism, its refusal to extend an exemption to an instance of religious hardship suggests a discriminatory intent." Therefore, the Court in Thomas and Sherbert considered that a "religiously motivated resignation without good cause tends to exhibit hostility, not neutrality, towards religion." *Id.*

vii O'Lone v. Estate of Shabazz (1987)

In O'Lone v. Estate of Shabazz,[470] Muslim inmates of New Jersey's Leesburg State Prison were prevented from performing their mandatory religious ceremony, Friday Prayer (Jumu'ah), "a weekly congregational service regularly held in the main prison building and in a separate facility known as the Farm."[471] They sought to challenge that procedure.[472] Their argument was based on the grounds of equality with followers of other religions; the prison policy allowed Christian inmates to perform prayer on Sunday and Jewish inmates to attend services on Saturday.[473] The Court ruled against the Muslim inmates, preventing them from practicing their prayer on Friday.[474] It declared that the prison's officials were not required to prove the absence of a less restrictive alternative, the standard of Thomas utilized by the Court in many cases.[475]

The Court reasoned that Muslim service on Friday has security risks that need proper safety procedures determined only by the prison's administration.[476] In other words, according to the Court, "evidence showed that the return of prisoners during the day resulted in security risks and administrative burdens that prison officials found unacceptable."[477] The Court held that the prison's policy was not discriminatory because Friday, unlike Saturday and Sunday, is a work day where prisoners have to work eight hours.[478]

In his dissent, Justice Brennan, joined by Justice Marshall, Justice Blackmun and Justice Stevens, noted that the prison's administration was capable of providing the proper safety for the religious ceremony, Friday prayer, since it was not "presumptively dangerous."[479] He added that the State should "demonstrate that the restrictions they have imposed are necessary to further an important government interest, and that these restrictions are no greater than necessary to achieve prison objectives."[480] Regarding the eight-hour work on Friday, Justice Brennan asserted that the prison's administration was capable of arranging work schedules by which Jewish inmates

470 O'Lone v. Estate of Shabazz, 482 U.S. 342 (1987).

471 *Id.* at 344–45.

472 *Id.*

473 *Id.*

474 *Id.* at 345.

475 *Id.* at 350.

476 *Id.* at 346.

477 *Id.*

478 *Id.* at 351–52.

479 *Id.* at 354 (Brennan, J., dissenting).

480 *Id.*

could attend services on Saturday, Christian inmates could attend services on Sunday, and Muslim inmates could attend services on Friday.[481]

In contrast to O'Lone's majority decision, in a recent case, Holt v. Hobbs,[482] the Supreme Court strongly protected a Muslim inmate's right to free exercise of religion. In that case, the Court did not apply the Free Exercise Clause; however, the Court applied the Religious Land Use and Institutionalized Persons Act (RLUIPA), which was enacted by Congress in 2000, to the facts of the case.[483] This Act provided "a very broad protection for [prisoners'] religious liberty."[484] Under the Act, if a prison's policy substantially burdens a prisoner's right to free exercise of religion, the prison must prove that such a policy is necessary to attain a compelling state interest.[485]

The facts of Holt started when an Arkansas prison inmate, Holt, in line with his religious beliefs, filed a lawsuit to protect his right to keep his beard uncut.[486] The Arkansas prison rooming policy prohibited beards for inmates, with the exception of quarter-inch beards for medical reasons.[487] Holt requested permission to wear a half-inch beard, consistent with his religious beliefs, but the prison denied his request.[488]

The Supreme Court ruled in favor of Holt.[489] The Court clarified that the "substantial burden" of the RLUIPA test "asks whether the government has substantially burdened religious exercise ..., not whether the RLUIPA claimant is able to engage in other forms of religious exercise."[490] The State argued that the burden on Holt's right to free exercise of religion was "slight" because he would be credited by his religion "for attempting to follow his religious beliefs, even if that attempt proved to be unsuccessful."[491] However, the Court refuted that argument, stipulating that RLUIPA "applies to an exercise of religion regardless of whether it is compelled."[492] In addition, the State argued that Holt's beliefs differed from mainstream Islamic beliefs

481 *Id.* at 365 (Brennan, J., dissenting).
482 Holt v. Hobbs, 135 S. Ct. 853 (2015).
483 42 U.S.C. § 2000cc (2012).
484 Burwell v. Hobby Lobby Stores, Inc., 134 S. Ct. 2751, 2760 (2014).
485 42 U.S.C. § 2000cc.
486 Holt v. Hobbs, 135 S. Ct. at 861.
487 *Id.* at 860.
488 *Id.* at 860–61.
489 *Id.* at 867.
490 *Id.* at 862.
491 *Id.*
492 *Id.*

because only a small percentage of Muslims believe that men should wear beards. The Court rejected that argument, clarifying that "the protection of RLUIPA, no less than the guarantee of the Free Exercise Clause, is not limited to beliefs which are shared by all of the members of a religious sect."[493]

viii Employment Division v. Smith (1990)

Employment Division v. Smith[494] is another interesting case in which two persons, an Indian and a white man, were driven away from their work in a private drug rehabilitation organization because they "ingested peyote, a hallucinogenic drug," for "sacramental" reasons at a religious ceremony "of their Native American Church."[495] As a result, the State denied them unemployment compensation due to their bad behavior.[496]

The majority of the Court ruled against the plaintiffs and refused to consider as legal precedents earlier cases such as Sherbert and Thomas, in which the Supreme Court decided that the State could not "condition the availability of unemployment insurance on an individual's willingness to forgo conduct required by his religion."[497] The Court compared Thomas and Sherbert, stating that their employments were terminated due to causes, which were not violations of criminal codes.[498] In contrast, in this case, the claimants were fired from employment for their bad behavior of violating the criminal code by having drugs, which is a serious crime in the United States.[499] Additionally, the Smith Court noted that the regulation was valid because "the State is free to regulate a physical conduct," while in other Sabbatarian cases, the Court held that states' regulations burdened individuals' religious beliefs without regulating a specific physical conduct, and therefore found the regulations unconstitutional.[500]

In her concurrence, Justice O'Conner rejected the majority's reasoning but agreed with the result. According to her view, the Free Exercise Clause does not differentiate between religious beliefs and religious conducts.[501] She affirmed that "conduct motivated by sincere religious belief, like the

---

493 *Id.* at 862–63.
494 Emp't Div. v. Smith, 494 U.S. 872 (1990).
495 *Id.* at 874.
496 *Id.*
497 *Id.* at 876. Here the law was neutral and generally applicable, thus not triggering strict scrutiny, but rational basis review.
498 *Id.*
499 *Id.*
500 *Id.* at 878–79.
501 *Id.* at 893 (O'Connor, J., concurring in the judgment).

belief itself, must be at least presumptively protected by the Free Exercise Clause." Therefore, a law that prohibits religious conduct conflicts with the Free Exercise Clause of the First Amendment of the Constitution.[502] Nevertheless, Justice O'Conner agreed with the majority's result, opining that the State satisfied the test because it had a compelling interest in preventing its citizens from possessing drugs, and that "granting a selective exemption" for peyote would strongly impair such an interest.[503]

On the other hand, in his dissent, Justice Blackmun stated that the State's interest in prohibiting the religious use of peyote was not "sufficiently compelling to outweigh" individuals' right to the free exercise of religion."[504] This is because peyote has never harmed anyone before,[505] and it is permissible in some American states since, unlike heroin and marijuana, it contains a small portion of illegal substances.[506] In contrast to Justice O'Conner's concurrence, Justice Blackmun stated that allowing an exemption for the religious-based use of peyote does not necessarily obligate the State to grant similar exemptions to other religious groups. This is because "the unusual circumstances that make the religious use of peyote compatible with the State's interests in health and safety" need not be applicable to other religious claims.[507] Therefore, he opined that the State's regulation should have permitted the use of peyote narrowly at religious ceremonies.[508]

ix Church of Lukumi Babalu Aye v. City of Hialeah (1993)

In Church of Lukumi Babalu Aye v. City of Hialeah,[509] the Supreme Court struck down a city ordinance prohibiting animal sacrifice of the "Santeria religion" but allowing similar secular practices.[510] The Court noted that the Free Exercise Clause requires the State to ensure "religious tolerance," so that legislators could not "devise mechanisms, overt or disguised, designed to persecute or oppress a religion or its practices."[511] In addition, the Court declared that the law must be neutral, holding that the ordinance violated

502 *Id.*
503 *Id.* at 905 (O'Connor, J., concurring in the judgment).
504 *Id.* at 921 (Blackmun, J., dissenting).
505 *Id.* at 911–12.
506 *Id.* at 916.
507 *Id.* at 917–18.
508 *Id.* at 921.
509 Church of Lukumi Babalu Aye v. City of Hialeah, 508 U.S. 520 (1993).
510 *Id.* at 547.
511 *Id.*

the Free Exercise Clause of the First Amendment because it was intended to target Santeria.[512]

In its reasoning, the Court declared that "[a] law burdening religious practice that is not neutral or not of general application must undergo the most rigorous of scrutiny."[513] In other words, the Court stated that "to satisfy the commands of the First Amendment, a law restrictive of religious practice must advance interests of the highest order and must be narrowly tailored in pursuit of those interests."[514]

E *Lower Court Cases on Women's Islamic Dress*

This study will discuss some lower courts' decisions on the wearing of Islamic dress, whether the hijab or niqab, and clarify the restrictions imposed on such a religious duty.

i Restrictions on Students

There are no rules issued by any court in the U.S. concerning students' Islamic headscarves in educational institutions; however, in Isaacs v. Board of Education, the United States District Court for the District of Maryland issued a rule on the wearing of a cultural head-wrap.[515]

The facts of the case started when an eighth-grade student, Shermia Isaacs, wore a multicolored head-wrap at a Maryland school to celebrate her African-American and Jamaican heritage.[516] Once the school's officials noticed her appearance, they asked her to take off her head covering, claiming that it violated the "no-hats" policy of the school.[517] Isaacs and her family tried to persuade the school's officials to allow her to attend classes with her head-wrap, but they were determined to deny that request. After attending the entire educational year without covering her head, Isaacs brought a lawsuit seeking to prove that the school's "no-hat" policy violated her constitutional right to freedom of speech.[518]

In reviewing the case, the Court noted that the wearing of ethnic clothing neither relates to the right to free exercise of religion nor to the right to security of person guaranteed by the 14th Amendment of the

512 *Id.* at 546.
513 *Id.*
514 *Id.*
515 Isaacs v. Bd. of Education, 40 F. Supp. 2d 335 (D. Md. 1999).
516 *Id.* at 336.
517 *Id.*
518 *Id.*

Constitution.[519] However, the Court's decision was based on the right to freedom of expression enshrined in the First Amendment, applicable to the states via the Fourteenth Amendment of the U.S. Constitution.[520]

The test applied by the Court was to determine whether "intent to convey a particularized message was present," and if so, whether "in the surrounding circumstances the likelihood was great that the message would be understood by those who viewed it."[521] The Court found that the student's message, that she celebrates her African-American and Jamaican heritage by wearing the head-wrap, would never be understood by others, and therefore the student had no need to wear it.[522] Thus, the Court considered that the State's legitimate interest in adopting the "no hats" policy outweighed the applicant's interest in wearing the ethnic headscarf.[523] The Court noted that a head-wrap would possibly cause "a conflict in the hallways, obscure the teacher's view, obscure students' view of the blackboard, allow students to hide contraband, and foster a less respectful climate for learning."[524]

ii Restrictions on Teachers

In Cooper v. Eugene School District, the Supreme Court of Oregon revoked a teacher's certificate for wearing a turban based on a statute prohibiting instructors from wearing religious attire.[525] Under the statute, "no teacher in any public school shall wear any religious dress while engaged in the performance of duties as a teacher."[526] The statute also stated the teacher's teaching certificate would be revoked if he or she violated the law.[527]

The Court clarified that the validity of such a law could "be justified by a determination that the religious dress necessarily contravenes the wearer's role or function at the time and place beyond any realistic means of accommodation."[528] In addition, the Court stated that the State's interest in enacting a law banning teachers from wearing religious dress is compelling because the purpose of such a law is to preserve state neutrality and "avoid the appearance of sectarian influence, favoritism, or official approval in the public school."[529] Therefore, the Court ruled that the statute did not violate

---

519 *Id.* at 339.
520 *Id.*
521 *Id.* at 336 (citing Spence v. Washington, 418 U.S. 405, 409 (1974)).
522 *Id.* at 336–37.
523 *Id.* at 336.
524 *Id.* at 340.
525 Cooper v. Eugene Sch. Dist. No. 4J, 723 P.2d 298, 308 (Or. 1986).
526 Or. Rev. Stat. § 342.650 (2006).
527 *Id.* at 655.
528 *Id.* at 307.
529 *Id.* at 313.

the guarantee of religious freedom stated in Oregon's Constitution and the U.S. Constitution.[530]

In Pennsylvania, there was a statute prohibiting public school teachers, while performing their professional duties, from wearing a dress, a mark, an insignia, or an emblem that indicates their adherence to a certain religion.[531] In addition, under the statute, any violations lead to a one-year suspension of work, which can be extended to five years in cases of recurrence.[532] Concerning the applications of this statute, the study will discuss the following two cases brought by two female teachers wearing hijabs:

In U.S. v. Board of Education,[533] the Third Circuit for the District of Philadelphia rejected a challenge brought by a female teacher who was fired for wearing a hijab.[534] The Court held that the statute carries a compelling state interest because its aim is to maintain the secular nature of public schools, and therefore it did not violate the guarantee of religious freedoms enshrined in the U.S. Constitution.[535]

In EEOC v. Reads,[536] the U.S. District Court for the Eastern District of Pennsylvania held that a colorful headscarf did not violate Pennsylvania's law since it was not clearly recognized as a religious dress.[537] The Court declared that the purpose of the statute is to prevent teachers from dressing in a way that could "be understood by their students as an endorsement of religion" and the prohibited garb should "indicate the wearer's religious affiliation."[538] In addition, the Court ruled that "[a]ttire which is either facially neutral or sufficiently ambiguous that it will not be perceived as religious does not pose this threat," and therefore it is not banned under the Statute.[539]

iii Hijab at Airports

The study shall discuss the case of Kaukab v. Harris[540] decided by the U.S. District Court for the Northern District of Illinois. On November 7, 2001, a girl wearing an Islamic headscarf, Samar Kaukab, was coming back to her

530 *Id.*

531 24 Pa. Stat. Ann. § 111–112 (2006).

532 *Id.*

533 Bd. of Educ. for the Sch. Dist. of Phila., 911 F.2d, 882.

534 *Id.*

535 *Id.* at 890.

536 759 F. Supp. 1150 (E.D. Pa).

537 *Id.* at 1153.

538 *Id.* at 1160.

539 *Id.*

540 Kaukab v. Harris, 2003 U.S. Dist. LEXIX 13710 (N.C. Ill. Aug. 6, 2003).

home in Columbus, Ohio, after finishing her work in Chicago.[541] Kaukab was subjected, alone with a group of passengers, to invasive searches.[542] After being thoroughly searched with the hand-held metal detector on her legs and crotch area, she was asked to remove her Islamic headscarf, but she refused to do so in public or in front of men.[543] After a very long discussion with the airport security men, a female guard took her to a private room and searched her in a very invasive manner.[544] She removed the hijab, the sweater, and most of Kaukab's clothes so that Kaukab's underwear was revealed.[545] The female guard patted her underwear and brassiere searching her completely in an uncivilized way.[546] Kaukab brought a claim for violating her right to free exercise of religion enshrined in the First Amendment, the right to be free from arbitrary searches enshrined in the Fourth Amendment, and the right to equal protection enshrined in the Fourteenth Amendment of the U.S. Constitution.[547]

The Court denied Kaukab's request due to the lengthy delay between the incident and the filing of the complaint.[548] In addition, it noted that there was no "need to declare the rights of the parties for any future purpose."[549] The Court added that the "Aviation and Transportation Security Act of 2001" gives the "Transportation Security Administration" the power, in all airports, to control passenger screening.[550]

iv Niqab Ban in Driver's License Photos (Freeman v. State of Florida, 2001)

In February 2001, a woman named Sultana Freeman got her driver's license while wearing a niqab in the license photo.[551] After September 11, 2001, the Florida Department of Highway Safety and Motor Vehicles required Freeman to exchange her previous photo with an unveiled one.[552] She refused

541 *Id.* at 8.

542 *Id.*

543 *Id.* at 9–10.

544 *Id.* at 10.

545 *Id.* at 11–13.

546 *Id.*

547 *Id.* at 1–2.

548 *Id.* at 31.

549 *Id.*

550 *Id.*

551 Freeman v. Dep't of Highway Safety & Motor Vehicles, 924 So. 2d 48, 51 (Fla. Dist. Ct. App. 2006).

552 *Id.* at 52.

and her license was revoked.[553] The Court held that the State's compelling interest in protecting the public from criminal activities and security threats outweighed the plaintiff's "right to have her picture taken with her veil." In addition, the Court found that the plaintiff failed to prove that the requirement of a full-face photo for a driver's license "substantially burdened her free exercise of religion."[554]

The Court of Appeal for the Fifth District of Florida relied on "experts on the Islamic faith who testified about the necessity of wearing a veil under the Islamic faith."[555] They testified that Islamic law allows exceptions to veiling practices as a result of necessity, which includes "medical necessity, identification for burial purposes, [and] identification for purposes of receiving bequests or inheritance."[556] They added that the state of necessity could be applied if a photo was required for identification purposes, and that necessity could therefore outweigh the requirement to wear a veil or become an exception to such an obligation. They referred to Saudi Arabia's law, under which a woman is required to have a full-face photo for identification documents such as passports.[557] The Court adopted this view and held that because Freeman's "religion (Islam) does not forbid all photographs," the photo requirement "merely inconvenienced" her right to free exercise of religion.[558] The Court added that "the state faces a heavy dual burden of demonstrating a compelling interest and that the regulation [requiring a driver's license with a full-face photo] is the least restrictive means to meet that interest."[559] Nevertheless, in contrast to this case, other American courts, in similar cases, have ruled in favor of non-Muslim plaintiffs and allowed them to obtain their driver's licenses without being photographed.

In Quaring v. Peterson,[560] a woman named Quaring refused to have her photo taken for her driver's license because she was a member of the Christian Pentecostal Church, believing that the Second Commandment bans photographing God's creations.[561] The United States Court of Appeals for the Eighth Circuit issued a ruling that was entirely different from the Freeman decision. The Court determined that "by requiring Quaring to comply

553 *Id.*
554 *Id.* at 56.
555 *Id.* at 52.
556 *Id.*
557 *Id.*
558 *Id.* at 57.
559 *Id.* at 56.
560 Quaring v. Peterson, 728 F.2d 1121 (8th Cir. 1984).
561 *Id.* at 1123.

with the photograph requirement, the state places an unmistakable burden upon her exercise of her religious beliefs."[562] The Court ruled in favor of the plaintiff; however, it noted that Quaring's beliefs differed from the mainstream Christian beliefs because she adopted them based on her own interpretation of certain Bible passages.[563] The Court clarified that "the burden on Quaring is indistinguishable from the burden placed upon a Sabbatarian by the State in Sherbert v. Verner."[564] In Sherbert, the Supreme Court held that the "denial of benefits on the Sabbatarian's exercise of her religion" forced the plaintiff to choose between "following the precepts of her religion and forfeiting benefits, on the one hand, and abandoning one of the precepts of her religion [not working on Saturdays] in order to accept work, on the other hand."[565] In the same way, Quaring's Court reasoned that the photo requirement put the plaintiff "to the choice of following an important precept of her religion or forgoing the important privilege of driving a car."[566]

Another case is Bureau of Motor Vehicles v. Pentecostal House of Prayer,[567] in which members of the Pentecostal Church believed that the Second Commandment in the Bible prohibits photographing creatures.[568] The Supreme Court of Indiana agreed that "the state has a strong interest in insuring driver competency."[569] However, the Court applied the alternative form of regulation standard, introduced by the Supreme Court in Shebert,[570] to reason that since "other alternatives available to the [state] would satisfy the purpose" of the photo requirement, the State's interest disproportionately burdened the plaintiff's right to free exercise of religion.[571] In addition, the Court applied the Supreme Court's standard of Yoder[572] clarifying that

---

562 *Id.* at 1124–25.

563 *Id.*

564 *Id.* In Sherbert v. Verner, the Supreme Court established the alternative form of regulation standard and held that the State violated the plaintiff's right to the free exercise of religion by depriving her of unemployment benefits due to her refusal to work on Saturdays, the Sabbath of her faith. Shebert v. Verner, 374 U.S. 398, 402 (1963).

565 *Id.* at 404.

566 Quaring v. Peterson, 728 F.2d 1121, 1124–25 (8th Cir. 1984).

567 Bureau of Motor Vehicles v. Pentecostal House of Prayer, Inc., 380 n.e.2d. 1225 (Ind. 1978).

568 *Id.* at 1126.

569 *Id.* at 1129.

570 Shebert v. Verner, 374 U.S. 398 (1963).

571 380 N.E.2d. 1225, 1129 (Ind. 1978).

572 Wisconsin v. Yoder, 406 U.S. 205 (1972). In this case, the U.S. Supreme Court ruled in favor of the claimants and held that the school's mandatory attendance violated the

"when the right to free exercise of religion comes in conflict with state or federal legislation, such right may be overbalanced only by those governmental interests of the highest order and those not otherwise served."[573]

F *Appraisal*

Concerning the hijab in the workplace, consideration should be given to the U.S. Supreme Court's ruling in EEOC v. Abercrombie & Fitch, in which the Court put an end to the lengthy debate on employment discrimination on the basis of the hijab.[574] The Court found that denying a Muslim woman employment because of her hijab constitutes religious discrimination.[575] The Court emphasized that a job-seeking woman is not obliged to make a special request for religious accommodation in order to be provided with the option to wear a hijab.[576] Nonetheless, this ruling only applies to private sector professions; no decisions have been issued yet by the Supreme Court concerning the ban on hijab in public sector jobs. Thus, it remains unclear whether the Court permits the wearing of the hijab in public employment or views it as incompatible with the norms of state neutrality and secularism.

It is evident that the Supreme Court accords the right to free exercise of religion guaranteed by the First Amendment of the U.S. Constitution great deference. The Court confirms that the State must have a compelling interest in order to restrict that right.[577] In addition, the Court established standards to strike a balance between the State's compelling interest and an individual's right to free exercise of religion under the First Amendment. In Sherbert, the Court established the standard of "alternative forms of regulation."[578] The Court stipulated that the State must show that "no alternative forms of regulation" would achieve its interest "without infringing First Amendment right."[579] However, in Thomas, the Court established the standard of "least restrictive means". The Court affirmed that the State should

First Amendment of the Constitution. *Id.* at 234. The Court adopted a new standard stipulating that the State's interest must be of "sufficient magnitude to override the interest claiming protection under the Free Exercise Clause." *Id.* at 214.

573 380 N.E.2d. 1225, 1127 (Ind. 1978).

574 Abercrombie & Fitch, 135 S. Ct. 2030.

575 *Id.*

576 *Id.*

577 Sherbert v. Verner, 374 U.S. 398, 406 (1963); Thomas v. Review Bd. of Ind. Emp't Sec. Div., 450 U.S. 707, 718 (1981).

578 Sherbert v. Verner, 374 U.S. at 406–07.

579 *Id.*

demonstrate that no "less restrictive means" could accomplish its interests without burdening the First Amendment's right.[580] In Yoder, the Court stipulated that the State's interest "must be of sufficient magnitude" to outweigh individuals' right to free exercise of religion.[581] Furthermore, the Court stated that religious practices should be treated as neutrally as other secular practices. For instance, in Widmar, the Supreme Court emphasized that religious expression should necessarily be accorded the same protection as other forms of speech, confirming that "state regulation of speech should be content-neutral."[582] Similarly, in Babalu Aye, the Court stated that strict scrutiny should be applied if the State intends to have a negative impact on religious practices.[583] In that case, the Court stated that the Free Exercise Clause requires the State to ensure "religious tolerance," so that it could not create instruments to oppress a religion or its practices.[584]

In contrast to these decisions, in other cases, the Court held that the State's interests could prevail over an individual's First Amendment right to free exercise of religion. For instance, in Braunfeld, the Court held that the Sunday closing law does not compel Jewish merchants to open their stores on Saturday, and therefore, the law does not create a burden on the right to free exercise of religion.[585] However, due to the Court's decision, Jewish merchants were compelled to choose between financial losses if they closed their establishments two days a week and a burden on their right to free exercise of religion if they worked instead of worshipping on Saturdays.[586] Similarly, in Bowen, the Court held that a requirement for submitting social security numbers serves an "important public interest" and does not violate the Free Exercise Clause.[587] In addition, in Smith, the Court confirmed that the State's compelling interest in regulating physical conduct and banning bad behaviors such as peyote use outweighed an individual's right to free exercise of religion.[588]

Furthermore, regarding Muslims' right to free exercise of religion, in the O'Lone case, the Supreme Court upheld clear discrimination against Muslim prisoners, the ban on Muslim inmates, who wanted to perform their

580 Thomas v. Review Bd. of Ind. Emp't Sec. Div., 450 U.S. 707, 718 (1981).
581 Wisconsin v. Yoder, 406 U.S. at 214.
582 Widmar v. Vincent, 454 U.S. 263, at 277.
583 Babalu Aye, 508 U.S. 520, 457 (1993).
584 *Id.*
585 Braunfeld v. Brown, 366 U.S. 599, 609–10 (1961).
586 *Id.*
587 Bowen v. Roy, 476 U.S. 693, 708 (1986).
588 Emp't Div. v. Smith, 494 U.S. 872, 878–79 (1990).

mandatory religious ceremony, Friday Prayer.[589] However, the prison administration permitted Jewish and Christian prisoners to perform prayers on Saturdays and Sundays.[590] The Court found that the Islamic prayer posed potential security dangers, and therefore it could be banned by the State.[591] Instead of compelling the prison administration to provide proper security for the Islamic event, the Court focused on the risks that might occur during the Muslim prayer.[592] The Court's decision was entirely biased against Muslim detainees, confirming that the State is not required to prove the absence of less restrictive alternatives than banning the Friday prayer.[593] In contrast to this decision, in Holt v. Hobbs, the Supreme Court upheld a Muslim prisoner's right to wear a beard on the prison campus.[594] In that case, the Supreme Court did not apply the Free Exercise Clause to the facts of the case. The Court applied RLUIPA, finding that the prison administration substantially burdened a Muslim prisoner's religious exercise by banning him from keeping his beard uncut.[595] In spite of this, the Supreme Court has not yet issued a ruling on a Muslim woman's right to wear head coverings on prison campuses.

Moreover, lower courts in the United States have not adequately protected Muslims' right to free religious manifestation. In educational institutions, lower courts upheld laws prohibiting teachers from wearing religiously motivated clothing while performing their duties. For instance, the Supreme Court of Oregon held that the state's interest in enacting a law banning a teacher from wearing a turban is compelling because the purpose of such a law is to promote the principle of neutrality and avoid prejudice in favor of a certain religion in public schools.[596] In addition, the Third Circuit Court for the District of Philadelphia found that laws banning teachers from wearing hijabs while performing their job duties did not violate the religious freedoms enshrined in the Constitution. The Court reasoned that such laws serve a compelling state interest because they aim to foster the secular nature of public schools.[597] Regarding students, there are no decisions on female students' right to wear hijabs; however, the U.S.

---

589 482 U.S. 342, 345 (1987).

590 *Id.*

591 *Id.* at 346.

592 *Id.*

593 *Id.* at 350.

594 Holt v. Hobbs, 135 S. Ct. at 862.

595 *Id.*

596 Cooper v. Eugene Sch. Dist. No. 4J, 723 P.2d 298, 313.

597 Bd. of Educ. for the Sch. Dist. of Phila., 911 F.2d, 882, 890 (3d Cir. 1990).

District Court for the District of Maryland prevented a female student from wearing an ethnic headscarf, ruling that the state's interest in adopting the "no hats" policy outweighed the student's interest in wearing a cultural head-wrap.[598] Furthermore, Muslim women are always subject to invasive inspections and searches at airports and seaports. This is manifested in Kaukab v. Harris, in which the U.S. District Court for the Northern District of Illinois ruled against a Muslim woman wearing a hijab.[599] After she suffered severe violations at the Chicago airport, including having a hand-held metal detector put on her legs and crotch area and being inspected in an uncivilized manner, she was not given a satisfactory verdict.[600] Accordingly, the author argues that the U.S. Constitution's Free Exercise Clause does not currently afford Muslim women wearing hijabs sufficient protection. American courts have not yet applied this provision fairly to protect Muslim women's right to wear the hijab in public without interference from the state.

Concerning the niqab, in Freeman v. State of Florida, the Court of Appeal for the Fifth District of Florida held that the State has a compelling interest in banning the niqab in driver's license photos.[601] The Court declared that the state's compelling interest in protecting the public from criminal activities and security risks outweighed the plaintiff's right to comply with her faith requirements and have her picture taken with her niqab.[602] On the other hand, other American courts found that the requirement of a full-face photo places an undue burden on non-Muslims' right to free exercise of religion. For instance, the U.S. Court of Appeals for the Eighth Circuit declared that such a requirement gives the plaintiff "the choice of following an important precept of her religion or forgoing the important privilege of driving a car."[603] Thus, the Court determined that the full-face photo requirement imposed an "unmistakable burden" on the plaintiff's right enshrined in the First Amendment of the Constitution, and therefore she was able to have a driver's license without a photograph.[604] Similarly, the Supreme Court of Indiana allowed the plaintiff to have a driver's license without a photo

598 Isaacs, 40 F. Supp. 2d at 336.

599 Kaukab v. Harris, 2003 U.S. Dist. LEXIX 13710.

600 *Id.* at 10–31.

601 Freeman v. Dep't of Highway Safety and Motor Vehicles, 924 So. 2d 48, 56 (Fla. Dist. Ct. App. 2006).

602 *Id.*

603 Quaring v. Peterson, 728 F.2d 1121, 1124–25 (8th Cir. 1984).

604 *Id.*

requirement.[605] The Court applied the Supreme Court's standard of Sherbert, the alternative form of regulation. The Court declared the State could protect its public safety in alternative ways instead of burdening the plaintiff's right to free exercise of religion.[606] In addition, the Court applied the Supreme Court's standard of Yoder, clarifying that the right to free exercise of religion could be "overbalanced only by those governmental interests of the highest order and those not otherwise served."[607] The author endorses and confirms that the Freeman Court's argument is entirely valid. In other words, the author upholds that the niqab could be restricted in identification photos for safety reasons. However, he argues that American courts should apply the requirement of a full-face photo uniformly to Muslims and non-Muslims in accordance with the principles of equality and impartiality.

5 Concluding Analysis of Women's Right to Wear Islamic Clothing

This chapter has explained that a Muslim woman wears religious dress for two major reasons. The first reason is being compelled to wear Islamic dress, whether a hijab or niqab, by her husband, family or society. Once this occurs, it is an observable infringement of women's rights and an obvious violation of gender equality and human dignity. In such a scenario, the state has to intervene to protect a woman's autonomy rights from being violated, prevent interference in her personal affairs, and ensure that she enjoys the full right to choose her favorite dress.

The second reason is when a Muslim woman decides freely, for religious or cultural identity motivations, to wear Islamic attire. In this case, she is given the choice of whether to wear a hijab or to fully cover her face and wear a niqab, a sitar or a borq'. If a Muslim woman decides freely to wear a hijab, a state must respect, protect and promote her freedom of choice. Therefore, a Muslim woman should enjoy the right to wear a hijab in all public places, such as educational institutions, workplaces, airports or any other place without any restrictions. The right to free manifestation of religion by the wearing of the hijab should be afforded greater weight than states' interest in protecting the principle of secularism and neutrality and should be given precedence over the requirements of impartiality and

605 Bureau of Motor Vehicles v. Pentecostal House of Prayer, Inc., 380 N.E.2d. 1225 (Ind. 1978).

606 Quaring v. Peterson, 728 F.2d at 1129.

607 *Id.* at 1127.

neutrality. The argument that the hijab impairs the rights and freedoms of others is hardly persuasive because states should protect the right to free exercise of religion of those women who choose freely to wear the hijab and promote their right to fulfill the religious obligations imposed upon them. Hijab should not be seen as an optional or symbolic duty; rather, it is a religious obligation that should be respected by states. States should prevent others from undermining or infringing on women's right to free exercise of religion by wearing hijabs. States must ensure that the rights of the majority group are brought to a standstill when they violate the rights of minorities. Furthermore, states should promote the right to free exercise of religion by spreading awareness among others to respect women who freely choose to fulfill their religious obligations and wear the hijab.

With regard to the niqab, a full-face veil, if it is chosen willingly by a Muslim woman, states should respect her right to freedom of choice. The broad banning of the niqab will never serve the compelling interests of states; however, permitting the niqab spreads awareness among others to respect the rights of minorities, which could protect their religious values and promote principles of tolerance, pluralism and broad-mindedness in society. Nevertheless, it could be argued that restrictions on the niqab may actually serve a compelling state interest to protect public safety. Therefore, states may restrict the wearing of the niqab for security reasons, in particular, at airports, banks, etc. In addition, the wearing of the niqab might impair the rights and freedoms of others in some places, such as educational institutions or workplaces. Therefore, restrictions on the niqab in these places might be permissible in order for states to support the social interaction between individuals.

This chapter has discussed several types of discrimination that Muslim women have suffered in both America and Europe. Discrimination against women is more blatant in Europe, and European courts accept it. Throughout that discussion, this chapter clarified that the ECtHR unfortunately upheld clear discrimination against Muslim women. Therefore, it may be claimed that the ECtHR is the European Court for upholding discrimination against Muslim women in light of its numerous and consistent judgments that support discrimination against Muslim women. A detailed examination of the decisions of European courts regarding the clothing freedom of Muslim women reveals that the vast majority of them were issued against such freedom. The ECtHR upheld hijab bans in schools and universities, whether worn by teachers or students. Both the ECtHR and the CJEU have ruled that hijab restrictions may be enforced in European workplaces. Furthermore, bans on the niqab in all European public spaces have been maintained. The ECtHR upheld recent bans on the niqab in France and Belgium.

Comparing the U.S. and European legal approaches to women's freedom to wear Islamic clothing, it is evident that the main judicial stream of the U.S. courts is not as bad as that of the European. The U.S. Supreme Court ruled that denying a Muslim woman the right to wear a hijab violates Title VII of the Civil Rights Act. This decision pertains to employment in the private sector; however, the Supreme Court has not yet addressed the hijab in public sector employment. In addition, courts in the U.S. have not applied the Free Exercise Clause in the U.S. Constitution to appropriately protect and promote a Muslim woman's right to choose her favorite religious dress. Despite some inadequacies in U.S. protection, it is obvious that Muslim women in the U.S. enjoy more legal protection and freedom to choose their religious attire than their European counterparts, where discrimination against them is upheld.

Overall Conclusions

Based on the author's comparative analysis of international law, U.S. law, Shari'a and Egyptian law in relation to a Muslim woman's rights to abortion, work equality, and wearing religious clothing, including the hijab and niqab, the following conclusions were drawn:

First, as for a woman's right to abortion, it is a debatable right disputed by the four above-mentioned laws. In international law, abortion is permitted for justifiable reasons, and there is no differentiation between early and late abortions; that is, abortion is treated uniformly throughout the whole pregnancy duration. The author concludes that both pro-life arguments considering the fetus as a distinct human being and other arguments giving a pregnant woman an absolute right to abortion are not well-established under international law. Regarding U.S. law, despite its decision in Dobbs v. Jackson, the U.S. Supreme Court has long distinguished, for many decades, between early and late abortions, i.e., before and after fetal viability. In other words, early abortion was permitted and regarded as a constitutional right, whereas late abortion was largely unprotected. The same time limit approach applies similarly to Shari'a because the Hadith of Prophet Mohammad, referred to in the book, divides abortion duration between early and late with a fine line of 120 days of pregnancy. In Egyptian law, abortion is entirely banned from the very beginning of pregnancy, except for life-threatening pregnancies.

The author clarifies that a woman's right to work equality is protected by both international and U.S. law. To support this claim, the author shed light on several international human rights instruments emphasizing employment equality. In addition, some specialized international instruments issued by the ILO ban employment discrimination based on gender. Furthermore, several cases decided by the ECJ strongly protect a female worker's right to employment equality. In U.S. law, Title VII of the Civil Rights Act clearly bans any kind of gender-based discrimination. This is asserted by the Supreme Court in cases of disparate treatment or impact employment discrimination. Concerning Shari'a, it is emphasized throughout the book that no religious texts ban women from holding high state positions. In addition, all arguments adopted by some Muslim scholars banning women from this right have been refuted. As for Egyptian law, women's right to employment equality has been violated by human-made rules and misconceptions of the Islamic jurisprudence adopted in Egypt years ago.

 | DOI:10.1163/9789004729506_006

To shed light on a Muslim woman's right to wear religious clothing, the author clearly shows that, under Shari'a, the headscarf, or hijab, is obligatory, whereas the full-face veil, or niqab, is optional. In addition, the purpose of the hijab is to protect women from temptation and sexual harassment by dressing modestly. In Europe, numerous judgments have upheld restrictions on a woman's freedom to wear Islamic clothing, whether in educational institutions or workplaces, holding that the hijab violates the rights and freedoms of others as well as principles of state neutrality and secularism. Furthermore, the ban on Muslim religious clothing by the ECtHR has gone beyond the hijab to include the niqab in all public places. In contrast, in the United States of America, a woman wearing a hijab is given a better position than in Europe. The U.S. Supreme Court ruled that the hijab does not impose undue hardship on employers, who must accommodate this religious duty.

A quick examination of the above-mentioned interpretations of the issues under consideration reveals that international and American laws differ. Abortion is permitted with no time limit but with reasonable justification under international law. In contrast, over many decades, according to the Supreme Court's framework established by Roe and Casey, abortion was allowed during pre-viability without restrictions under U.S. law, whereas it was banned after viability unless a woman's life or health was threatened by pregnancy. Concerning a woman's right to employment equality, international and U.S. law agree that women must be treated equally to men and that any direct or indirect gender-based discrimination should be eliminated in workplaces. Nevertheless, the author argues that a Muslim woman might be subject to employment discrimination based on her religious beliefs. In 2015, the ECtHR upheld employment discrimination against a Muslim woman wearing a hijab. In Ebrahimian v. France, the Court upheld the non-renewal of a veiled woman's working contract in a public hospital, reasoning that the hijab might be incompatible with the principles of state neutrality and secularism in French public institutions. In addition, in the 2017 case Achbita v. G4S Secure Solutions, the CJEU upheld the ban on the hijab in the private sector, reasoning that it contravenes the principle of a religiously neutral workplace. In contrast, the U.S. Supreme Court recently issued a unique verdict holding that the hijab does not cause undue hardship on a private sector employer and that the employer must allow it or violate Title VII of the Civil Rights Act. However, this ruling is confined to private sector jobs. The Supreme Court's view on the wearing of the hijab by public employees is still unclear. Meanwhile, some lower courts have denied public employees the right to wear a hijab. The United States District Court for the Eastern District of Pennsylvania ruled that the State has a compelling interest in preventing a woman from wearing a hijab with her work uniform. According to the Court, the State could face undue hardship if it accommodated a woman by allowing her to wear a hijab when performing her duties as a police officer. No Supreme Court ruling on the hijab in light of the Free Exercise Clause has been issued yet. The wearing of the hijab in educational institutions, whether by students or teachers, has not been considered yet by the Supreme Court. However, some lower courts in the U.S. have banned female teachers' hijabs and students' cultural headwraps inside educational institutions. It is clear that there is an ongoing conflict in Western countries with Muslim minorities between two major values: freedom of religious exercise on the one hand and secularism, state neutrality, the rights and freedoms of others, as well as the principle of living together on the other hand.

To discuss how Shari'a addresses these issues, it becomes clear that both abortion and a woman's right to work are perfectly well-organized. Although Shari'a is not fully in line with international law, it provides a suitable and ideal framework for women's rights. With regard to abortion, the interesting philosophy of Prophet Mohammad creates a just balance between a woman's right to choose an abortion on the one hand, and the fetus's right to life on the other hand. Shari'a distinguishes between abortions during the first 120 days of pregnancy and those performed afterward. Shari'a confirms that a pregnant woman is fully entitled to have an abortion in the early stages of pregnancy based on justifiable reasons such as rape or fetal abnormalities; however, in the late stages, Shari'a tightens restrictions on a woman's right to abortion and confines it to cases in which a pregnant woman's life or health is endangered by pregnancy. In contrast, international human rights standards support a woman's right to abortion, disregard the fetus's right to life and treat abortions before and after viability equally. Therefore, the author argues that Shari'a can help mediate the gap between American and international abortion regulations. While Shari'a, like international law, permits abortion for reasonable causes in the early period of pregnancy, it distinguishes between early and late abortions, similar to the precedents set by the U.S. Supreme Court over many decades.

With regard to gender equality in employment, Shari'a presents a framework that is comparable to international and American law. Shari'a does not ban a woman from holding significant positions within the state, whether as a leader, president, judge, or any other highly exalted role. However, a Muslim woman is required to balance her family and professional obligations. In addition, a woman is not allowed to perform physically demanding professions that contravene her feminine physiological nature. Similarly, international law and American law provide robust protection of a woman's right to work and safeguard her from any kind of direct or indirect discrimination, as well as pregnancy-based discrimination. However, it could be argued that, under such laws, the relationship between a man and a woman is based on competitiveness and rivalry. In contrast, Islamic Shari'a upholds complementary equality between spouses with special consideration for the physiological nature of each partner. In other words, the physiological nature of a wife often involves pregnancy and childbirth, and therefore she has a moral responsibility towards her husband and children who need her care and custody. However, a husband is financially responsible for his wife and children. The author argues that Shari'a gives more support and promotion to a woman by providing her with the right to work and earn an income, while, at the same time, a man is obliged to pay for marital and family-related obligations.

The imposition of the hijab as a religious duty should not be interpreted as a form of discrimination against Muslim women; rather, it is intended to promote modesty by limiting sexual harassment and temptation. In addition, many Muslim women wear hijabs voluntarily as a sign of identity, respect, attractiveness and beauty. However, a Muslim woman should not be forced to wear a hijab by her husband, family or government. As long as a Muslim woman is free to wear a hijab, it should not be considered a violation of the principle of gender equality. A Muslim woman should be given the choice to wear a hijab based on her own willingness. Any pressure imposed on her to wear a hijab against her will, whether from her husband, father or a Muslim community, would be discriminatory on the basis of her gender. In contrast, if a woman freely chooses to wear a hijab, no one should have the right to violate her freedom by compelling her to remove it; otherwise, this would constitute discrimination based on religion. On the other hand, concerning the niqab, if a Muslim woman voluntarily chooses to wear it, states may restrict her freedom for compelling interests such as protecting the public safety. However, states must not widen restrictions on the niqab. In other words, the niqab could be limited or regulated by governments for legitimate reasons, such as crime prevention, security, and identity purposes, but it should not be outlawed in general.

With regard to Egyptian law, despite some rulings of high courts that protected the principle of gender equality based on the proper interpretation of Shari'a, it is clear that Egypt still lacks gender equality. The Egyptian legislator did not follow Shari'a regarding abortion; rather, it composed an entirely different framework in which abortion is prohibited regardless of fetal viability, with one exception for life-threatening pregnancies. If a woman needs an abortion for urgent reasons such as rape or fetal deformity, she has to seek an unsafe abortion by an illegal physician to evade the government's restrictions. As for a woman's right to equality in employment, although several courts' rulings and recent resolutions promoting gender equality in judicial posts have helped elevate Egyptian women's status, Egypt still has a long way to go until women enjoy full equality in the workplace. Egyptian women have been suffering from clear discrimination in employment as well as male superiority in high positions. It could be argued that, although Islamic Shari'a texts perfectly protected women's rights, the context of Shari'a's application in Egypt obviously discriminated against women. This is not the proper application of Shari'a; rather, it is a misunderstanding of Islamic rules, social norms, and cultural stereotypes that dominated Egypt decades and centuries ago.

A close review of the whole book reveals that Shari'a is more consistent with international law than Egyptian law on women's issues and rights. Furthermore, it can be argued that the proper core interpretations of Shari'a are applied in the U.S. instead of Egypt. This can be seen at several points. To start with abortion, the division into early and late stages of pregnancy adopted by Prophet Mohammad over 1500 years ago was similarly applied in Roe v. Wade. However, it is not yet applied in Egypt, even in cases of rape or fetal deformity. As for women's employment equality, things are going along the same lines. In Egypt, there are several cases in which women have been discriminated against based on their gender, whereas in the U.S., things are entirely different. On the other hand, it can be argued that all kinds of discrimination on the basis of the hijab in the U.S., whether in workplaces, schools, universities or other public places, are because of a Muslim woman's choice of being religiously constrained and modest.

To conclude, the author argues that discrimination against Muslim women in Western countries – in both Europe and America – is religion-based discrimination due to the women's commitment to their religious duties. In contrast, discrimination against women in Muslim and MENA-region countries is not related to Islam; rather, it is gender-based discrimination caused by governing regimes adopting misinterpretations of Islamic Shari'a texts in order to justify and legitimize their abusive behaviors. These discriminatory practices, however, are incompatible with Shari'a's fundamental principles and values, which contain a complete set of rules and standards respecting, protecting, fulfilling, honoring, and promoting women's rights.

Index

www.ingramcontent.com/pod-product-compliance
Lightning Source LLC
Chambersburg PA
CBHW051358240926
51852CB00001B/55

9789004729353